Queer
Migration
Politics

FEMINIST MEDIA STUDIES

Edited by Carol Stabile

Queer Migration Politics

Activist Rhetoric and Coalitional Possibilities

KARMA R. CHÁVEZ

UNIVERSITY OF ILLINOIS PRESS

Urbana, Chicago, and Springfield

Thanks to Taylor and Francis for permission to reprint the revised
portions of chapters 1 and 4 that appeared as Karma R. Chávez,
"Border (in)Securities: Normative and Differential Belonging
in LGBTQ and Immigrant Rights Discourse," *Communication
and Critical/Cultural Studies* 7, no. 2 (2010): 136–55;
and Karma R. Chávez, "Counter-Public Enclaves
and Understanding the Function of Rhetoric in Social Movement
Coalition Building," *Communication Quarterly* 59, no. 1 (2011): 1–18.

Library of Congress Cataloging-in-Publication Data
Chávez, Karma R.
Queer migration politics : activist rhetoric
and coalitional possibilities / Karma Chávez.
pages   cm. — (Feminist media studies series)
Includes bibliographical references and index.
ISBN 978-0-252-03810-5 (hardcover : alk. paper) —
ISBN 978-0-252-07958-0 (pbk. : alk. paper) —
ISBN 978-0-252-09537-5 (e-book)
1. United States—Emigration and immigration—Government policy.
2. United States—Emigration and immigration—Social aspects.
3. Immigrants—Civil rights—United States.
4. Gays—Civil rights—United States.
I. Title.
JV6483.C456   2013
325.73086'64—dc23   2013015224

Contents

Acknowledgments

This is a book about coalitional moments, several of which have resulted in its completion. I want to begin by acknowledging my family of origin, including my paternal grandparents, the late Ruth Sánchez Chávez and Arthur Chávez, and my maternal grandparents, Virginia and the late Elmer Sinsel. My grandpa Elmer died just weeks after I finished my doctoral dissertation, and he always encouraged me to achieve at the highest levels educationally. He'd be very pleased with this book. My parents, Kathy Sinsel-Chávez and Armand Chávez, have been great support, as have my siblings, Jacob, Ruben, Katrina, and Sara, as well as many aunts, uncles, and cousins.

I received much early support at Hastings College, especially from Jessica Henry, John Perlich, and Judy Sandeen. I landed at the University of Alabama at the most opportune time in the early 2000s, and I am very thankful for my Bama mentors, especially Dexter Gordon, Marsha Houston, and Jerry Rosiek. In particular, Jerry and Dexter opened my intellectual eyes in ways for which I will always be truly grateful. Becky Atkinson, Lana Estess, Shanara Reid-Brinkley, Nance Riffe, and my other graduate colleagues there helped me to appreciate thinking deeply and complexly.

The concrete foundations for this project emerged during my time at Arizona State University. In addition to my appreciation for various forms of financial and logistical help from the Hugh Downs School of Human Communication and the ASU Graduate and Professional Student Association, I would like to acknowledge friends and colleagues there who provided, and continue to provide, all kinds of support, including Dan Brouwer, Olga Idriss Davis, Sarah Amira De la Garza, Belle Edson, C.A. Griffith, Jennifer Linde, Lucas Messer, H.L.T. Quan, and many others.

I am very grateful to my colleagues at the University of Wisconsin–Madison. The Center for Humanities awarded me with the First Book Award in 2011, and that experience took the book to the next level. Thank you to Heather DuBois Bourenane, Steve Kantrowitz, and others at the center for organizing the seminar and to Lou Roberts for helping me prepare my application. Many thanks to those who read the manuscript and offered incredible feedback: Rob Asen, Cindy I-Fen Cheng, A. Finn Enke, Steve Kantrowitz, María Lugones, and Eithne Luibhéid. My colleagues in the Department of Communication Arts have been immensely supportive, especially those in my area of Rhetoric, Politics, and Culture: Rob Asen, Rob Howard, Jenell Johnson, Steve Lucas, Sara McKinnon, and Sue Zaeske. Shout out also to the Doctor Bitches, whose weekly happy-hour gripe sessions have been a welcome reprieve from the junior faculty grind: Shawnika J. Hull, Sara McKinnon, Leah Mirakhor, and Catalina Toma.

I received terrific feedback and suggestions on portions of this work at lectures given in the following places: University of Iowa, University of Pittsburgh, Southern Illinois University–Carbondale, University of New Mexico, Arizona State University, Tucson Book Festival, Drake University, Governors State University, University of Chicago, University of Wisconsin–Madison, Hastings College, University of Texas–El Paso, University of Manchester, University of North Carolina, the National Communication Association, and the Western States Communication Association. While it is hard to remember every person who offered insight, a few stand out: Angela Aguayo, Barb Biesecker, Dan Brouwer, Craig Gingrich-Philbrook, Sara Guyer, Kent Ono, Christa Olson, Lou Roberts, Humaira Saeed, Ellen Samuels, Jackie Stacey, Nathan Stormer, and a bunch of fierce undergraduates at Drake University. Thanks to all of those named and unnamed who offered me their ears and their thoughts at those lectures.

In addition to those mentioned above, over the past five years numerous people have helped my professional and intellectual growth, some directly connected to this project and others indirectly. The following people have supported and helped to foster my growth in the field generally and/or have been great fellow travelers: Mary Beltrán, Sirma Bilge, Bernadette Calafell, Paige Erickson, Lisa Flores, Karen Foss, Cindy Griffin, Michelle Holling, Ginny McDermott, Shane Moreman, Ulises Moreno, Chuck Morris, Erin Rand, Jan Schuetz, Stacey Sowards, Wendy Weinhold, and Naida Zukic. People directly connected to my thinking on this project include Claudia Anguiano, Amy Brandzel, Aimee Carrillo Rowe, Jara Carrington, Brittany Chávez, Mary Jane Collier, Jigna Desai, Shiv Ganesh, Rachel Levitt, and Ken Lythgoe. Thanks to Natalie Martínez for reintroducing me to Lugones's work. Further, I owe many debts to Eithne Luibhéid for her tireless mentorship in queer migration studies and beyond. Additionally, Giorgia Aiello, Joan Faber McAlister, and Kimberlee Pérez have been incredible friends to me, and without a conversation in spring of 2012 with Kimberlee and Rae Langes, I don't think the book would have come together. I am also grateful to my fellow Against Equality members, Ryan Conrad, Deena Loeffler, Yasmin Nair, and Alexandra Silverstone, who have enhanced my intellectual capacity exponentially. I owe special recognition to Deena for the proofreading!

This book would not be possible without the work of the people I write about in it—both those I know and those I don't. I am so thankful for everyone whose work I feature here, and I want to especially acknowledge the people in Tucson who initiated my thinking about immigration, radical politics, and possibility. I send deep love and gratitude to Cathy Busha and Kat Rodriguez. Many thanks also to Kent Burbank, Lupe Castillo, Margo Cowan, Geovanna De La Ree, Nancy Gallen, Isabel Garcia, Michelle Golden, Oscar Jimenez, Luis Judiz, Alexis Mazón, Jon Miles, Elisa Riesgo, and Kendall Roark. People whom I've encountered more recently, and for whom I am grateful include Rozalinda Borcilă, Yasmin Nair, and Julio Salgado.

My editor, Larin McLaughlin, has been a dream to work with, and I am most appreciative of her, her assistant Dawn Durante; the expert anonymous reviewers who read my book; my copyeditor, Jill R. Hughes; project manager, Tad Ringo; and the University of Illinois Press staff.

Finally, this book would not be possible without three incredible beings: two cats—Chloe, and the late (Ho)Mo—and my fantastic partner, Sara McKinnon. Not only has she read every word and offered feedback, but Sara also has been there through my temper tantrums, self-doubt, and writing mania. It is a complete understatement to say that I could not possibly imagine doing any of this without her. Thanks, baby.

It takes a community to produce a book, and I am so very lucky to have mine. But of course, all mistakes are my own.

Abbreviations

ALP	Audre Lorde Project
CDH	Coalición de Derechos Humanos
DACA	Consideration of Deferred Action for Childhood Arrivals Process
DADT	Don't Ask, Don't Tell
DHS	Department of Homeland Security
DOMA	Defense of Marriage Act
DREAM Act	Development, Relief, and Education for Alien Minors Act
HAVOQ	Horizontal Alliance of Very (or Vaguely or Voraciously) Organized Queers
HRC	Human Rights Campaign
ICE	Immigration and Customs Enforcement
LGBTSTGNC	Lesbian, Gay, Bisexual, Two-Spirit, Trans, Gender-Non-Conforming
LPR	Legal Permanent Resident
NGLTF	National Gay and Lesbian Task Force
NPIC	Nonprofit Industrial Complex
QEJ	Queers for Economic Justice
UAFA	Uniting American Families Act
USCIS	United States Citizenship and Immigration Services

Queer
Migration
Politics

Introduction

rior to 1990 gays and lesbians were legally excluded from migrating to the United States. The Immigration Act of 1990 effectively ended what was known as "homosexual exclusion."[1] President George H. W. Bush signed the act in the context of an already crucial time for gay, lesbian, and queer people in the United States. AIDS continued to ravage gay, immigrant, poor, and non-white communities with little government intervention. Rather than helping, the federal government chose actions like banning migration of HIV-positive people to the United States and debating the viability of quarantining those with HIV/AIDS in camps. The devastation of communities, coupled with the horrific governmental response, prompted a new brand of "queer" activism. Groups like ACT UP (AIDS Coalition to Unleash Power) and Queer Nation developed to change the national conversation and save lives. Such groups put what would soon be recognized as an LGBT community in the US public sphere.[2] These activists reflected earlier approaches of gay liberationists and radical lesbian feminists in the late 1960s and early 1970s. They used in-your-face and anti-normative political tactics to engage in acts of civil disobedience such as "die-ins," where large groups of people would simultaneously fall "dead" in the middle of a public space to call attention to queer lives and deaths. They demanded meetings with politicians, scientists, and pharmaceutical representatives to insist on directing attention and resources to AIDS and on creating access to health care for all. Although still making demands upon the state, such activists emphasized local and national solutions and reenvisioned questions of identity, belonging, and life. Their activism raged against the conservative politics that championed individualism and narrow definitions of family and that became dominant in the United States during the 1980s and early 1990s.

A new professionalization of mainstream gay and lesbian organizing concurrently grew. National nonprofit organizations in existence since 1980 or earlier, including the National Gay and Lesbian Task Force (NGLTF) and the Human Rights Campaign (HRC), as well as the Lambda Legal Defense and Education Fund (LLDEF), rose to greater significance in defining a national gay and lesbian political agenda focused on rights and inclusion.[3] As Urvashi Vaid explains in her book *Virtual Equality*, leaders in such organizations saw new possibilities for accessing national political power in Washington, DC, especially with the 1992 national election of Bill Clinton, given his seeming friendliness to gay and lesbian causes. For example, almost immediately after his election, Clinton announced that he supported the right of gays and lesbians to serve openly in the military.[4] Many gay and lesbian rights advocates imagined Clinton's presidency as an opportunity to advance rights in previously unimagined ways, and their agenda was largely separate from that of many of the queer- and AIDS-oriented groups mentioned above. Instead, these organizations constructed an inclusionary agenda designed to bring lesbians and gays into existing laws and structures. This meant focusing on obtaining marriage and military rights, passing hate crime laws, and supporting employment nondiscrimination provisions.

From within this inclusionary gay and lesbian approach, and after the end of "homosexual exclusion," in 1993 the LLDEF and the International Lesbian and Gay Association convened in New York City to create the Lesbian and Gay Immigration Rights Task Force (LGIRTF, known as Immigration Equality since 2004). The LGIRTF sought to challenge discriminatory immigration laws in the areas of (1) gay and lesbian US citizens' and legal permanent residents' (LPR) ability to sponsor foreign partners; (2) political asylum for gays and lesbians; and (3) migration rights for those with HIV/AIDS.[5] The LGIRTF, in conjunction with other groups, perhaps most notably the Coalition to Lift the Bar, helped get the ban on HIV-positive migrants removed in 2010 after many years of struggle, which was a significant victory. Working along with other organizations and lawyers, the group was also instrumental in moving the US government to consider sexual orientation and sexual identity as legitimate categories for which one could plead for political asylum.[6] According to its early website, a key component of the LGIRTF's work involved "collecting personal stories from couples" in order to educate the lesbian and gay community and the "straight" immigration activist and advocacy community on these issues, particularly the plight of binational same-sex couples; this crystallized as the primary focus of the LGIRTF's work shortly after the group's creation. Meanwhile, despite confidence that Clinton would be a friend to gays and lesbians, his two primary gestures toward this constituency were signing into law the "Don't Ask, Don't Tell" (DADT) military policy in 1993 and the Defense of Marriage Act (DOMA) in 1996. DOMA defined "marriage" as only between an opposite-sex husband and wife, and "spouse" as only a husband or wife of the opposite sex within the administrative bureaus and agencies of the United States, including the Immigration and Naturalization Service (now US Citizenship and Immigration Services, or USCIS). Although Clinton saw DOMA as better than its alternative (i.e., a constitutional amendment banning same-sex marriage), the law effectively codified that which only informally existed: the impossibility for gay and lesbian US citizens and LPRs to sponsor their partners for immigration purposes, even if they qualified on all other grounds and/or were legally married in another country. Groups like the LGIRTF saw this explicit exclusion as a most pressing issue because roughly three-fourths of legal immigration to the United States happens through family reunification.[7]

Through the mid-1990s and early 2000s, many queer activists pursued an agenda of justice and transformation as mainstream gay and lesbian organizers continued focusing on rights and inclusion. The mainstream movement rallied around what came to be called "marriage equality" as its defining issue. Similarly, even as many advocates and activists concerned with gay and lesbian immigrant rights pursued a broader immigration justice agenda, the LGIRTF turned significant attention toward discriminatory immigration laws' impact on same-sex binational couples, campaigning around the notion that love is borderless.[8] On Valentine's Day 2000, Representative Jerry Nadler (D-NY) introduced the Permanent Partners Immigration Act (PPIA, which in 2005 would be renamed the Uniting American Families Act, UAFA). As in all subsequent years, the PPIA died in committee. The act sought to add the words "permanent partner(s)" and "permanent partnership" to the words "spouse(s)," "husband and wife," and "marriage" any time they are mentioned in the document that guides much immigration law—the Immigration and Nationality Act of 1952— thereby granting sponsorship rights to eligible US citizens and LPRs in same-sex binational couples. Even as the legislation continues to fail, collecting and sharing stories of deserving couples divided by discriminatory immigration laws is the primary rhetorical strategy that Immigration Equality and other organizations and advocates use to seek inclusion in immigration law. To date, the best-known intersection among gay and lesbian rights and immigration rights has pertained to binational same-sex couples.[9] In *Queer Migration Politics* I examine instances where migration politics and queer politics meet in ways that challenge this type of inclusionary strategy and shift the political focus to other sites of activism.

Queer Interventions

This type of inclusionary strategy and narrowly normative vision of politics reflected in advocacy for the rights of binational same-sex couples is precisely what prompts queer activists and theorists to respond to and critique contemporary mainstream gay and lesbian politics. One such recent critique appears in a monograph by José Esteban Muñoz, *Cruising Utopia*, which proposes an approach to the future that purposely challenges the pragmatic and presentist politics of the mainstream LGBT movement.[10] Pursuing a politics of "educated hope," Muñoz advocates rethinking queerness as "always on the horizon" and as "a temporal arrangement in which the past is a field of possibility in which subjects can act in the present in the service of a new futurity."[11] To see queerness as such, Muñoz invites readers to consider the potentiality of concrete utopias as found in quotidian moments and in the aesthetic realm of art and performance. In preferring potentiality to possibility, Muñoz muses, "Unlike a possibility, a thing that simply might happen, a potentiality is a certain mode of nonbeing that is eminent, a thing that is present but not actually existing in the present tense."[12] In this way the present has potentiality in it for imagining transformation, but this differs widely from the present pragmatism that Muñoz suggests dominates contemporary LGBT politics and, as my opening alludes to, LGBT immigration politics as well.

Muñoz's proposals and contemplations are alluring, and he is perfectly aware that it is easy to critique utopia as idealistic and disconnected from people's material realities. His work is one important part in a turn toward utopia among those interested in the intersections between queer critiques and neoliberal capitalism, including a special issue of *GLQ*, "Queer Studies and the Crisis of Capitalism," published in 2012.[13] In the introduction to that issue, co-editors Jordana Rosenberg and Amy Villarejo note that queer theorists are reencountering utopia within Marxist traditions "not simply as an unimaginable future but as a diagnostic methodology that zeros in on the uneven action of capitalism, the spatial differentiation of global production, and the prolonged, overlapping, and recursive temporal pulses of social contradiction itself."[14] Similarly, scholars such as Kevin Floyd have highlighted the political necessity of the dialectic between utopia and negation to aid in imagining otherwise. I certainly champion these efforts to utilize utopia in productive ways. But as Floyd notes in his review of Muñoz's book, "Aesthetic critique becomes the inevitable substitute for an activist critique hardly imaginable beyond the terms of the immediately practical. To this extent, at least, the book's implication is consistent with one of the most familiar themes from Marxian cultural analysis: art has a capacity to perform (or at least intimate) what politics too rarely can."[15]

Floyd's critique highlights the perennial problem for utopia in relation to the political. I maintain that a turn to utopia, even concrete or critical utopia, as an alternative for *politics* may risk turning too far from lived and everyday reality, which is why Muñoz and his theoretical inspiration, Ernst Bloch, stick to the discrete realm of the aesthetic.[16] Concrete utopias serve important functions for political imagination, but realms such as political organizing and activism are less suited for a focus on the utopian, given that these realms reflect more starkly the necessary entrenchment that Martin Heidegger referred to as "being-in-the-world." The Latina feminist philosopher and community activist María Lugones aptly articulates such a critique when she writes:

> I won't think what I won't practice. This is also a commitment against utopianism, which seems to me what keeps one out of despair when one cannot act, at all. I have tended, instead, to find activity in the movements of the hand of someone rendered frozen by acts of extreme violation. The commitment is to live differently in the present, think and act against the grain of oppression. I write from the belief that it is only from that ground that the next possibility can be entertained socially, at the edge of realism. My perspective is in the midst of people mindful to the tensions, desires, closures, cracks, and openings that make up the social.[17]

Here, Lugones identifies resources for hope and possibility grounded in small movements and actions, even motility—the sorts of things often considered non-agentic. Such a politics can be called presentist, demanding focus on what is literally before us in the social realm, the constraints, and the resources that necessarily emerge from being in the world in order to envision what is possible next. Community activist Saul Alinsky also emphasized this presentist focus, noting in his book *Rules for Radicals,* "The basic requirement for the understanding of the politics of change is to recognize the world as it is. We must work with it on its terms if we are to change it to the kind of world we would like it to be."[18] Alinsky's comments may invite normative, even conservative politics that are similar to those of the LGBT movement that Muñoz challenges; however, viewed in another way, Alinsky reflects the realities and difficulties of carrying out the daily micro-practices of principled political work like community organizing. Both Alinsky and Lugones thus differ from Muñoz in their realms of emphasis and in the value they find in the present, as well as their perspective on the present. They also highlight the fact that in the realm of activism and movement, a singular narrative that encompasses all such work is insufficient to reflect the texture and complexity of that activism.

Like Lugones and Alinsky, I differ from Muñoz in my realm of emphasis and approach to the present, even as I find significant value in the imaginations that his work enables. As Lauren Berlant remarks, the present is "a thing that is sensed and under constant revision, a temporal genre whose conventions emerge from the personal and public filtering of the situations and events that are happening in an extended now whose very parameters (when did 'the present' begin?) are always there for debate."[19] While there is no doubt that the predominant form of LGBT politics that is visible in the US public sphere is profoundly normative and inclusionary in aim, if the present emerges from the "filtering of the situations and events" that simultaneously exist, then constructing the present of LGBT politics as wholly normative and pragmatic is incredibly limited. Queer and transgender (hereafter, trans) activists in this present moment labor and write outside of, in response to, and against the grain of the normative, inclusionary LGBT movement. Certainly some of this work demonstrates normative investments too, but much of it cannot be encapsulated by the caricature of the mainstream movement. The present thus offers more hope and vision than Muñoz suggests. Utopia enables us to see and experience *potentialities,* often ephemeral, that offer imaginations of something otherwise. The turn to futurity through utopia is equally limited in the *possibilities* it enables for activist politics.

To locate an alternative to both inclusionary approaches and utopian approaches,[20] and to focus attention on a complementary present, I return to LGBT immigration politics—more specifically, queer migration politics.[21] I define "queer migration politics" as activism that seeks to challenge normative, inclusionary perspectives at the intersection of queer rights and justice and immigration rights and justice. Queer migration politics may reflect a queer approach to migration politics. It may refer to politics by and for queer migrants. It may also include collaborations or connections among activists who predominantly identify as queer or with queer politics and those who primarily identify as or advocate on behalf of migrants. My understanding of queerness resonates with Muñoz's in the sense that queerness not only refers to a kind of critique and to non- or anti-normative genders and sexualities, but it also implies what is possible for making lives livable. I also directly draw from the thinking of women of color feminists and queers as my theoretical apparatus, which situates queer as an explicitly intermeshed horizon and condition, a product and process of "theory in the flesh."[22] Therefore, in this study "queerness" is a coalitional term, a term that always implies an intermeshed understanding of identity, subjectivity, power, and politics located on the dirt and concrete where people live, work, and play. By understanding queer as orienting us not toward the "not yet" but rather toward coalition, we find a vital alternative to both inclusionary and utopian politics.

Drawing on queer women of color feminism, in *Queer Migration Politics* I argue that coalition enables a different understanding of activists' rhetorical invention as they discover and innovate responses—creative and sometimes mundane—to predominant rhetorical imaginaries. This is in order to build more livable worlds in relation to other people whose lives, interests, and material conditions might be very different from their own. Women of color feminists have long advocated for the necessity of coalitional politics to address oppression and power at its roots and to utilize difference as a resource rather than a hurdle to be overcome. Lugones maintains that coalition "is always the horizon that rearranges both our possibilities and the conditions of those possibilities."[23] This definition suggests a clear parallel to Muñoz's definition of queerness as *on* the horizon. For Lugones, and in this book, coalition, as the horizon itself, is not hoped for or imagined. Instead, coalition is a present vision and practice that is oriented toward others and a shared commitment to social and political change.

Understanding Coalition

In order to engage the concept of coalition more fully, it is helpful to address its many meanings. Etymologically, the word "coalition" denotes various and separate parts coming together. Some of the earliest usages of "coalition" indicate organic or spiritual "growing together." Political meanings associated with the term emerged along with organic and spiritual meanings and have become common. Politically, "coalition" refers to unions, fusions, and combinations designated for certain kinds of action.[24] Often coalitions are understood as temporary and goal-oriented, and not requiring "permanent incorporation into one body."[25] Late twentieth-century theorizing by feminists, especially women of color, queers, lesbians, and poor and working-class women, has largely taken up these temporal definitions of coalition. Lisa Albrecht and Rose M. Brewer explain, for example, that a coalition is a group that comes together around a particular issue to accomplish a specific goal.[26] Even though the terms often are used interchangeably, the enduring relationships that may form from engaging in coalition are, in Albrecht and Brewer's writing, described as alliances.

Lugones departs from this temporary view of coalition, stating that in thinking about resistance to intermeshing oppressions, coalition, as stated above, is the horizon of possibility. If, in one sense of the word, a horizon refers to a "dividing line between two regions of being,"[27] then a horizon is the space where two seemingly different things merge and remain separate. It is also the space where the distinction between entities blends and blurs. Coalition connotes tension and precariousness in this sense, but it is not necessarily temporary. It describes the space in which we can engage, but because coalescing cannot be taken for granted, it requires constant work if it is to endure. Following Lugones, for me, coalition provides more flexible theoretical utility in that it can describe an enduring alliance at the same time that it can help explicate a juncture that happens to be brief. Moreover, I recognize that even as coalition is an alternative to both utopian and inclusionary politics, coalitional politics sometimes encapsulate or draw upon both. That activists may use discourses that "discipline liberatory impulses and turn them into conservative political projects," Andrea Smith notes, is a necessary danger that does not preclude the possibility of new rearticulations, changing identities, and future political relationships.[28]

Feminists have proposed the most comprehensive body of theory pertaining to coalition and alliance. Aimee Carrillo Rowe maintains that feminists have offered few concrete examples of how to create coalitions, nor of what enables and constrains them.[29] As Nella Van Dyke and Holly J. McCammon explain in their prescient collection, *Strategic Alliances,* even as most social movement activity is inherently coalitional, movement scholars often approach social movements as discrete or singular, denying the work of coalitions and alliances.[30] Like these scholars, I am interested in rectifying these knowledge gaps by examining coalition in a sustained way. My approach differs in that what I analyze is sometimes not *a coalition,* as in an avowed relationship, but instead a space of convening that points toward coalitional possibility.

I explore queer migration politics in the early twenty-first-century United States through the analytic of the *coalitional moment.* A coalitional moment occurs when political issues coincide or merge in the public sphere in ways that create space to reenvision and potentially reconstruct rhetorical imaginaries. In common usage the word "moment" implies both temporality and temporariness. An early definition in the *Oxford English Dictionary* suggests that a moment is "a period of time (not necessarily brief) marked by a particular quality of experience or by a memorable event." Another definition indicates a moment as "a particular stage in a course of events or in the development of something; a turning point; a historical juncture."[31] I use the idea of "moment" in line with these definitions. A moment happens in time but may extend beyond a brief instant. Moments expose a queer temporality.[32] Moments taken in this way reveal that time's passage and the meaning assigned to time need not reflect normative assumptions. Moreover, as the language in the second definition reflects, a moment also has a spatial dimension as a "turning point" or a "juncture." A moment thus possesses both temporal and spatial qualities, and the specific nature of the spatial dimension to a moment implies a coming together or connection whereby there is a possibility for change. Putting "coalition" together with "moment" names the particular sort of moment and possibility it prompts. In this way both a coalition and a moment engender temporal and spatial dimensions and refer to the possibility—fleeting or enduring—of a coming together, or a juncture, for some sort of change. Analysis of coalitional moments provides opportunity to witness activists' creative rhetorical crafting, which sometimes points in the directions of inclusion and utopia but also shows how activists inventively draw resources toward building alternative rhetorical imaginaries and possibilities for livable lives.

Queer migration politics is an ideal area of study in which to learn about coalition through the exploration of coalitional moments. First, the primary subject of queer migration politics, the queer migrant, is an inherently coalitional subject, one whose identities and relationships to power mandate managing multiplicity.[33] The presence of a dynamic identity and subjectivity starkly reveals the necessity of coalitional thinking to account for the complexity of people's lived experiences. Additionally, political space and connections already exist for queer migration politics. Since 2006, with the increase in immigration justice and rights activism in the United States, there has been an explosion of queer migration activist grassroots work, political and media discourse, rhetorical production, and interaction. We can also gain insight about coalitional possibility from queer migration politics given the unlikely alliance suggested by linking LGBTQ politics with immigration politics. More precisely, as separate enterprises LGBTQ activists and immigration activists have engaged in contradictory, even oppositional politics of normalization. LGBTQ activists, for example, have often argued for rights based on their US citizenship, which migrants do not possess, and immigration activists have regularly requested rights because of their strong family and moral values, which LGBTQ people are said to culturally violate. Both movements have also been critiqued for engaging politics in ways that could hurt the other movement. LGBTQ movements have been criticized for engaging in racist and classist politics. Immigration advocates have been accused of positioning LGBTQ issues as separate from immigration rights and justice.[34]

Even as it may seem that LGBTQ politics and migration politics are opposed, queers and migrants have been attacked through shared logics of scapegoating, threat, and deviance. As Smith also argues, the seeming opposition between groups does not preclude the possibility for commonality. Furthermore, queers, migrants, and queer migrants are often positioned in relation to the US nation-state as strangers who exist largely outside national imaginaries of belonging and as subjects who cannot formally access the state as citizens.[35] Although certainly other groups also have been positioned outside of imaginaries and formal structures of belonging—other groups with which queer migrants overlap and intersect—the position of queers/migrants in this way is undeniable. Thus, I further argue that understanding coalition at the intersections of queer migration politics provides important insight into dominant imaginaries of belonging within the US nation-state, how activists understand the boundaries of belonging, and how they subsequently respond and create new possibilities. With a better understanding of the interventions I seek to make in this book, in the next section I locate my work in some key intellectual conversations.

Locating *Queer Migration Politics* in Scholarship

The study of queer migration politics is necessarily located in the emerging field of queer migration studies, which extends the important work done by feminist scholars on gender and migration. For a long time migration studies scholarship in the United States focused largely on male migrants on the assumption that mostly men traveled across international borders looking for work or fleeing political persecution. However, scholars such as Oliva Espín, Mary Romero, Pierrette Hondagneu-Sotelo, and Lynn Fujiwara began shifting the landscape by focusing on women's experiences with migration and living in the United States as laborers, mothers, and community builders.[36] Additionally, emerging scholarship began investigating women's experiences as refugees and asylum seekers and emphasizing the unique challenges women face in negotiating the US immigration system.[37]

As such scholarship grew, it became increasingly clear that, with rare exception, even within feminist scholarship, women were often assumed to be biologically female and all immigrants were assumed to be heterosexual. In an essay demanding more accountability, Eithne Luibhéid argues that sexuality "structures every aspect of immigrant experiences," but immigration scholarship virtually ignores connections among immigration, sexuality, and heteronormativity. As a result of work by Luibhéid and other scholars in the late 1990s and early 2000s, such as Martin Manalansan IV, Lionel Cantú Jr., and Gayatri Gopinath, interdisciplinary research increasingly investigates the identities and experiences of queer migrants,[38] as well as the ways in which immigration laws and policies are constituted through sexuality and gender identity norms alongside those of race, class, gender, nation, and health.[39] Luibhéid's work systematically highlights the many ways that sexuality and appropriate gender performances are integral to immigration policies, procedures, and their implementation. For instance, the Page Act and subsequent Chinese Exclusion Act of the late nineteenth century were implemented to protect the US nation from "undesirables," which meant the supposedly sexually depraved Chinese, especially Chinese women, who were nearly all thought to be prostitutes.[40] Furthermore, beginning in 1917, US federal immigration officials sought to keep homosexuals, other sexual perverts, and gender nonconformers from migrating to the country through the ambiguous designation of "constitutional psychopathic inferiority."

Not only are sexuality and gender systematically central to immigration laws, but as Emma Pérez also suggests, it is no coincidence that "the classifications of homosexual and heterosexual appeared at the same time that the United States began aggressively policing the borders between the United States and Mexico."[41] Because of historically interwoven policing of race and sexuality under the "sciences" of eugenics and sexology, borders between deviance and purity also needed to be patrolled.[42] In this way the US-Mexico border had to be protected to ensure white purity at the same time that nonheterosexuality had to be pathologized to guarantee sexual and marital purity. The protection of this international border is an extension of the protection of other kinds of borders between white and nonwhite, heterosexual and nonheterosexual. Whiteness and heterosexuality coupled with middle-class gender norms have always had an interdependent relationship. The preservation of whiteness literally depends on heterosexuality and appropriate gender norms, creating an interwoven relationship between the "nation-as-white" and the "nation-as-heterosexual" that leads to policing of all kinds of borders.[43] These borders are precisely the ones that are symbolically and physically violated by queers, migrants, and queer migrants. The policing and regulation of borders is perhaps most stark for trans migrants. Scholars in what might be called "trans migration studies" have been integral in illuminating these intersections and relevant systems of power, revealing that binary gender is an immense disciplinary mechanism within the context of migration.[44] Gender that does not conform to cisgender expectations—whether through embodied performance or on various, sometimes conflicting, identification documents—becomes a means to exclude as well as restrict and regulate mobility.[45] Furthermore, as Aren Z. Aizura reveals, for trans people who encounter the US immigration system, there is an assumption that one's social, embodied, and administrative gender (i.e., as listed on identification documents) should be consistent, which places gender-variant people in a very difficult situation since violations of gendered borders can lead to restrictions with regard to national borders.[46]

Although the intersections among migration, sexuality, and gender variance continue to become more apparent to scholars and activists, few scholars have examined how migration politics and activism are connected to queer politics and activism.[47] The notable exceptions have contributed greatly to my thinking. For instance, Dean Spade's discussion of "critical trans politics" builds upon women of color feminism and critical race theory to map a movement agenda that rethinks the role of legal intervention for trans politics. Linking immigration punishment as a primary source of trans subjection in relation to other intersectional systems of power, Spade articulates a transformative trans politics that refuses to reify logics of citizenship as the most efficacious mode of activism.[48] Jasbir K. Puar explores the use of gay, lesbian, and queer politics in the service of nationalist and imperialist projects in order to foster xenophobia. Building on Lisa Duggan's discussion of homonormativity,[49] Puar coins the term "homonationalism" to describe such uses of particular gay identities in the post-9/11 era in the United States.[50] Homonationalism is akin to what Jin Haritaworn, Tamsila Tauqir, and Esra Erdem name "gay imperialism,"[51] or the way that some white gay activists in Europe rely upon orientalist discourses about Muslims in order to promote gay rights, silencing the work of Muslim queers in the process. Working through somewhat similar logics, Adi Kuntsman looks at the complicity of queerness with problematic nationalist formations in Israel among queer Russian immigrants.[52] Kuntsman shows how certain queer migrants' desires for belonging reinforce both racist exclusion of others and orientalist positioning of Palestinians. In a slightly different vein, Fatima El-Tayeb examines how European of color activists creatively respond to supposed European racelessness, an ideology that positions Europeans of color as always foreign. She calls this process "queering of ethnicity,"[53] suggesting that the politics used to challenge both overt and covert racism and xenophobia are queer. Each of these works points to exciting directions for thinking about queer migration politics.

Additionally, Monisha Das Gupta's writing on South Asian immigrant queer organizations reveals how such groups "create transnational identities, spaces, and politics to subvert the relationship between sexuality-based rights and citizenship, which in the United States is increasingly defined through consumer entitlements."[54] These activists do not take up the "consumeristic turn" that has largely created access to citizenship for a certain type of lesbian and gay citizen. Das Gupta's work is important in part because she shows how queer migrants assert themselves through logics outside of citizenship, orienting their politics toward queer and transphobic thinking in their diasporic communities at the "intersection with U.S. ideologies that put immigrants and queers outside the national imaginary."[55] Many other scholars take up questions of migrant and queer belonging within the language of citizenship, arguing that citizenship manifests in numerous forms outside of its legal designation, as social citizenship, cultural citizenship, consumer citizenship, and sexual citizenship, among others.[56]

In this book I extend this aspect of Das Gupta's work and depart from those who theorize belonging primarily through the language of citizenship. I also take a cue from Amy L. Brandzel, who invites us to approach citizenship with a "healthy skepticism."[57] Most people imagine citizenship as an equalizer as more of them become included within its purview. This ideal may be as powerful as it is sentimentalizing given the tension between citizenship's perpetual exclusions and its alluring promises. Citizenship is a "double discourse" that simultaneously mobilizes people and acts of resistance and erases some of those same people, dissident actions, and colonial pasts and presents. Citizenship is also normative, serving both socializing and regulating functions while it "presupposes universality and therefore exacerbates and negates difference."[58] To talk about resistant acts, even within a particular nation-state, as acts of citizenship unnecessarily reproduces it as a problematic double discourse.

Furthermore, to talk about all modes of belonging through the language and logic of citizenship functions to reify the status of modern nation-states that endow legal citizenship and through which most other modes of citizenship are articulated, even if only because of the use of the same term. In relation to the United States, a settler colonialist state, speaking about queer migration activism only through the language of citizenship could also operate in an uneasy alliance with discourses of the elimination and replacement of native people. Simply speaking in terms of belonging as opposed to citizenship does not mitigate the fact that what Scott Lauria Morgensen calls "non-Native" queer politics are produced in relation to native queer politics and through settler colonialism.[59] Still, to entrench all projects of belonging in the language of citizenship does little to ally with decolonial projects. Moreover, as others have shown and as I will affirm throughout this book, many of the characteristics aligned with US citizenship of all kinds tend to reinscribe norms of urbanity, whiteness, heterosexuality, maleness, ability, and middle-classness.[60] Finally, using the language of citizenship to talk about belonging actively works against a project that centers analyzing the rhetoric of those who seek to imagine their ability to belong in a host of communities and spaces, their relationship to nation-states, and their relationships to other people in new ways. In refusing to analyze activist rhetoric through the lens of citizenship, and in declining to use the language of citizenship, I am not negating the significant material rights and privileges bestowed through legal citizenship. I also do not deny that citizenship remains powerful as a discourse in these many forms mentioned above, nor do I contend that some of the activists I write about do not appeal to citizenship.

Despite my departure from the language of citizenship, the nation-state, particularly the United States, remains an important preoccupation in this book. Since the mid-twentieth century, scholars have theorized the nation, nation-state, and nationalism, as well as, more recently, how these concepts matter in globalization.[61] I take as a premise that the nation-state's demise is not imminent even as it matters differently within contexts of global-local tensions and within what some have regarded as "postnational" times.[62] Nation-states remain a primary site through which claims to rights, recognition, and justice are made.[63] Furthermore, collections of people with strong senses of national identity and clear beliefs about who belongs within a particular nation remain as present as ever. National contexts, then, continue as important sites for understanding how people imagine ways of belonging, and nations further remain primary loci for activist challenges to those imaginaries and the material realities they compel. This point is exemplified in *Queer Migration Politics* as the activists who are discussed in each chapter respond to the exigency of what they perceive as unjust laws in the United States and, at least in part, make their pleas to the laws of the land. This impetus and pragmatic character of their activism, however, does not comprise the whole, or even the most significant, aspect of what these activists presently do. Instead it will become clear that the role of the nation-state is noteworthy in igniting activism and does not dictate the ultimate confines or boundaries for that activism.

With a well-defined understanding of the theoretical discussions I am joining, I want to briefly comment on the methodological approach I take to enter those conversations. Although peripheral to my work, there is a large body of social scientific scholarship that addresses the intersections of sexuality, migration, and health in relation to advocacy, campaigns, and prevention.[64] Most accounts of queer migrant identity and organizing are either ethnographic or literary analyses of texts such as art, performance, television, or film.[65] An examination of activist rhetoric in the public sphere and an understanding of the role played by rhetoric in activists' constructions of queer migration politics are missing. This book fills that gap, and in my rhetorical criticism I attend to how activists craft arguments, deploy persuasive strategies, and enact political belonging in ways that work on, with, or against what I call rhetorical imaginaries. Rhetoric is a primary vehicle through which discourses of what contemporary scholars recognize as neoliberalism constitute queers, migrants, and queer migrants as marginal subjects of nation-states in related ways. Thus I take a rhetorical approach to texts, which means highlighting sources of invention, argument construction, persuasive tactics, and message strategies in, or in relation to, the public sphere. More specifically, I offer rhetorical analysis of social movement rhetoric, internal activist strategizing, and media commentary drawn from textual as well as ethnographic sources. Rhetorical analysis of these texts illuminates the logics—what Lugones describes as the connections among meanings—whereby powerful imaginaries are created, sustained, and challenged.[66]

Rhetorical analysis of texts has primarily focused on public culture. The public emphasis with regard to social protest, activism, and movement has almost entirely emphasized "rhetoric of the streets."[67] This book also attends to public rhetoric, especially in chapters 1–3. It is crucial to understand coalitional moments and possibility through public rhetoric because publicity creates not only visibility and accessibility but also accountability. Politicians are often charged with spouting "mere rhetoric" when they make one claim in public and act differently behind closed doors. I maintain that in the contexts analyzed here, which have a variety of coalitional aims, the public declarations of solidarity, alliance, and political desire create expectations for activists to be accountable. For this reason, continuing with an emphasis on public rhetoric is necessary.

However, unlike traditional rhetorical analysis, I also believe that what occurs behind the scenes, especially in what might be described as "counter-public enclaves,"[68] can be equally as important for understanding coalitional possibilities. For this reason the last chapter is primarily an analysis of data gathered through fieldwork and behind the scenes. Spending extensive time like I did with Wingspan and Coalición de Derechos Humanos (Human Rights Coalition, CDH) conducting field research would not have been feasible to do with all of the activists and activist collectives located in disparate parts of the United States that I write about here. Rhetorical analysis of Wingspan's and CDH's internal discussions and rhetorical sense-making, alongside their public rhetoric, provides a useful and illuminative case study for how coalitional moments might lead to coalitional politics and for the kinds of labor that make coalitional moments possible in the first place. Thus, although the contexts of the coalitional politics in chapter 4 differ from the contexts in the other chapters in many ways, the chapter serves as an instructive case study to think about the relationships between rhetoric, movement, and coalition. More concretely, chapter 4 helps to elucidate the physical and intellectual labors that are required to publicly declare solidarity and tend toward coalition.

In addition to entering scholarly discussions, my hope is for this book to be part of activist and political conversations, which are, of course, not entirely separate spheres. This is important to me because I am an activist as well as a scholar. I am also a queer (cisgender), US citizen Chicana whose communities and networks are affected by the things I write about. The seeds and thinking for this book emerged when I lived in Arizona during the early and mid-2000s. When Arizona adopted State Bill (SB) 1070, the "show your papers" law, in 2010, the dire state of affairs for migrants and people of color in Arizona appeared on the rest of the nation's radar. For those of us who live(d) in Arizona, we recognized SB 1070—or "BS 1070," as some of my friends call it—as the latest in a host of xenophobic and racist governmental actions. For example, Section 287(g) of the Immigration and Nationality Act authorizes local law enforcement officers to perform federal immigration functions. Several law enforcement agencies participate, most notoriously the Maricopa County Sheriff's office, led by Sheriff Joe Arpaio.[69] Perhaps especially in Arizona, migrants confront a legal complex comprised of local police, Border Patrol checkpoints, the visible existence of Immigration and Customs Enforcement (ICE) officials, and the presence of several detention facilities and numerous immigration courts. The threats are exacerbated with the expansion of militarization through provisions like ICE's "Secure Communities," or "S-comm," which expands the partnership between federal immigration and local law enforcement officials through an extensive information-sharing program.[70] Such actions are even more possible among a citizenry that largely continues to accept it. Tacit acceptance and active promotion of racism and xenophobia tell only part of the story in Arizona. I had the good fortune of meeting activists who are at the center of overtly challenging these actions and ideologies as migrant rights and justice activists. I also met activists who played more of a supporting role in these battles, like many of the LGBTQ activists I got to know. What I learned from these activists changed my perspectives, and you will be introduced to some of those people and their thinking in this book in chapters 1 and 4. Arizona makes an occasional appearance elsewhere too. If this book has an Arizona bias, there is a good reason for it based on my personal experiences. There is no doubt that Haitians living in New York, Cambodians living in Boston, or Chinese living in San Francisco experience immigration enforcement, laws, and daily negotiations very differently than those largely Latin@ migrant populations in Arizona.[71] But I might add that as activists in Arizona regularly say, "As goes Arizona, so goes the nation." If this prediction is correct—and there is a lot of reason to believe it is, considering the onslaught of Arizona "copycat" bills in other state legislatures—then lessons to be learned from Arizona will be instructive beyond its borders.

This book features more than the geographical and political state of Arizona, and it is not centered on any single ethnic or national group. I write about activist rhetoric produced by a variety of people from around the United States. Some of these activists are people I have also come to know personally through collaboration and support in a variety of capacities. Other activists I do not know outside of their public work. In addition to Tucson, New York, Chicago, and the San Francisco Bay Area are the primary locales of the activists featured in this book. There are many reasons why these kinds of activism often emerge from and solidify within urban centers, given the density and diversity of culture and ideas that cities provide. With queer politics in particular, as scholars such as Kath Weston have shown, the great migrations from rural to urban places that many queer people make have long made cities like San Francisco and New York epicenters for queer thinking and activism.[72] I am aware of this urban bias, and while I make no effort to rectify it here, there is certainly much to be added to this conversation about activism in suburban and rural settings, as the prescient work of scholars like Eli Clare, Mary L. Gray, and Karen Tongson suggests.[73] Despite the urban focus, I selected the activist rhetoric in this book for very particular reasons that will become evident. The rhetoric of these queer migration activists and the coalitional moments they create has something to teach us about coalition, intermeshing oppressions, and alternatives to utopian and inclusionary approaches to politics. Further, the activists I write about here offer glimpses into the kinds of organizing that people are presently doing on the ground. Each vision, strategy, and tactic adopted by activists reflects moments that are worth our attention, even as they sometimes fail in their stated objectives or reach only small, often internal, audiences. As Judith Halberstam has noted, however, even failure may be full of queer possibility.[74] I do not mean to glorify activism or activists, place them in some sort of heroic narrative, or suggest that they are not people with flaws and inconsistencies. It is also possible that some of the people I write about would not characterize themselves as activists, even though from my perspective this is the most apt word to describe their labor. The people I write about in this book are doing important work that is worth our attention, and their work provides others who are interested in questions of belonging, activist resistance, and coalition with new ways of thinking about politics *right now.*

Chapter Previews

The rest of *Queer Migration Politics* unfolds in four chapters, with the first two chapters focusing primarily on the creation of political visions and the second two concerning the use of particular tactical strategies.[75] Although there is some overlap since vision and tactical strategy are intertwined, this delineation fairly characterizes the shape of the book. In the first chapter I explore the rhetoric of manifestos emerging from the energy and exigency of immigration rights and justice protests in 2006. I analyze three manifestos linking queer politics with migration politics written and distributed in 2006 and 2007, and another, which builds upon two of those manifestos, published in 2011. The manifestos represent coalitional moments in that they supply visions for queer, migrant, and queer migrant activism, rights, and justice that point toward coalition. The visions of coalition differ widely from the inclusionary perspective, and yet the visions are offered in concrete and possible terms. In contrast to the normative and the utopian, the authors of these manifestos develop and advance a different political vision, what I call a *differential vision* of queer migration coalitional politics. A differential vision reflects an impure political orientation, whereby activists seek relationships to others who may take different approaches but who resist hegemonic power systems.

Staying with the creation of political vision, in chapter 2 I explore the writing of Indian immigrant and queer migration activist Yasmin Nair. Nair's rhetoric offers unique coalitional moments premised in opposition and confrontation. She directly opposes the political orientation and conditions of belonging set forth by the mainstream LGBT immigration rights community since those conditions leave most migrants out. Nair's vision thus opposes the limited agenda of inclusionary politics that include only "good" people. Some have described her politics as utopian. I argue that the positions she takes engender what I call the rhetoric of *radical interactionality*, a form of rhetorical confrontation that starts critique from the roots of a problem and then shows how power and oppression interact to produce subjects, institutions, and ideologies to enable and constrain political response.

Moving into a sustained examination of coalitional tactical strategies, in chapter 3 I begin with the coalitional moments reflected in migrant youth activism that use coming out as a strategy for demanding migrant belonging. Appropriation of the LGBTQ rights strategy offers a unique way for understanding how coalitional rhetorics can both gesture to inclusionary and utopian politics and offer an alternative to both. I begin this chapter by exploring activism for the DREAM (Development, Relief, and Education for Alien Minors) Act, which would provide a pathway to citizenship for select undocumented youth. Such activism has been both highly utopian in its deployment of the "DREAM" metaphor and simultaneously normative in the type of inclusion the DREAM Act seeks and to whom it would provide inclusion. DREAM activism has also spurred other uses of the coming out strategy, including the development of "undocuqueer" activism and counter-DREAM activism, both of which turn toward coalition beyond the initial appropriation.

Moving from coalitional moments to coalitional politics, in chapter 4 I offer an extended look at two Tucson-based organizations, Wingspan and CDH, groups that have an avowed coalition to jointly fight oppression. The groups have constructed a coalition that refuses the master's tool of divide and conquer by actively taking up the many forms of difference in the service of coalition.[76] Sometimes venturing into both normative and utopian realms with their tactical strategies, the activism of Wingspan and CDH starkly reveals the fraught nature of coalition. This coalition provides insight into the specific kind of strategies that local groups can utilize to foster unlikely political coalitions and educate communities in order to shift local, state, and national ways of thinking, even as these strategies are imperfect and sometimes fail.

In the conclusion I return to the question of coalition as an alternative to normative and utopian approaches, and I offer some final thoughts about the importance of queer migration politics as a lens for thinking about politics. I further remark on the status of a rhetorical perspective for intervening in constructions of national rhetorical imaginaries that can both open and limit the possibilities for political orientations, modes of belonging, and tactical strategies.

CHAPTER 1

The Differential Visions
of Queer Migration Manifestos

For a brief moment in 2009, Shirley Tan and Jay Mercado, a binational lesbian couple living in California, became household names.[1] The couple fought for Tan's right to stay in the United States after she was denied political asylum and, apparently unbeknownst to the couple, placed in deportation proceedings. Tan, a native of the Philippines, and Mercado, a US citizen, eventually learned that Tan was to be deported. They had been together for twenty-three years and parented twin boys when Immigration and Customs Enforcement arrived at their home in late January 2009 and took Tan, a self-described housewife, into custody. After receiving a temporary reprieve through a private bill introduced by Senator Dianne Feinstein (D-CA) and Representative Jackie Speier (D-CA), Tan delivered testimony before the Senate Judiciary Committee on June 3, 2009, urging senators to support the Uniting American Families Act. In her testimony Tan pled on account of her "American family," her "two beautiful children," and the fact that the couple's heterosexual neighbors saw them as their familial "role models."[2] Undoubtedly, this was a sad story, and the gendered nature of the couple's relationship (a housewife and a breadwinner), their successful children, and their suburban, middle-class lifestyle led LGBT and immigration rights organizations as well as the mainstream media to broadcast the story as another example of the country's broken immigration system, the problems of marriage inequality, and the value of all "American" families.[3]

While this extensive focus on a binational same-sex couple was a first for the mainstream media, Tan's testimony built upon the predominant strategy of storytelling used to link LGBT and immigration issues since the 1990s. Before the situation with Tan and Mercado, this strategy had resulted in the 2006 publication of a widely distributed report titled "Family, Unvalued: Discrimination, Denial, and the Fate of Binational Same-Sex Couples under U.S. Law," produced by Human Rights Watch and Immigration Equality.[4] Published amid the intensity of the 2006 immigration rights and justice marches, as well as the onslaught of state legislation and ballot measures designed to narrowly define marriage, the nearly two-hundred-page document represents the first extensive report linking LGBT struggles with immigration. Several large LGBT and immigration rights organizations financially supported its preparation, including the National Gay and Lesbian Task Force, the Lambda Legal Defense and Education Fund, Amnesty International, and UCLA Law School's Williams Institute.[5] Moreover, the report is published on the websites of prominent immigration sites, such as the American Immigration Lawyers Association and Asylum.org, and prominent LGBT groups, including the Human Rights Campaign. In line with Immigration Equality's long-standing rhetorical strategy, "Family, Unvalued" argues that the central concern that LGBT rights proponents should have with immigration pertains to the ability of legal residents and US citizens to legally sponsor their partners for immigration. Secondary concerns include the rights of LGBT asylum seekers to be able to receive refuge in the United States and the importance of ending the now-defunct ban on the migration of HIV-positive people. The report's virtual silence on the plight of undocumented migrants, the rights of migrants not partnered with US citizens, and its overwhelming emphasis on binational couples implies that immigration should be a concern for LGBT people because US LGBT *citizens'* rights are violated under current immigration law.[6] It offers little reason for migrants or migration activists to support LGBT rights. And not surprisingly, it attempts to ameliorate the threat that LGBT people and their migrant partners pose to the nation by relying upon normalizing frames.[7]

To be sure, "Family, Unvalued" is a strategic document that was designed to promote a normative vision of LGBT and immigration politics in order to appeal to powerful people like federal lawmakers and influential supporters of LGBT and immigration rights. And as a result, with its entirely inclusionary aims, it offers the narrowest terrain for coalition building between LGBT and immigration activists.[8] Although this report was widely distributed and received immense support, it was not the only document produced by the exigency created in the political milieu of the mid-2000s. In fact, as mentioned in my introduction, three organizationally produced manifestos linking queer politics and migration politics were also written and distributed in 2006 and 2007, and another, inspired by two of those manifestos was published in 2011.[9] As manifestos—statements that dramatically emphasize the necessity of the "now,"[10] these documents reflect unique coalitional moments emerging from the energy and exigency of the 2006 immigration rights and justice protests.

Because migrant issues were in the public, those who feared they could be left out of any serious debates forcefully entered the scene to set their own terms for migrant justice. Manifestos are an ideal genre to create such a rupture. As the manifesto from the Audre Lorde Project (ALP) puts it, "We have prioritized our work with undocumented folks, low wage workers, and trans and gender nonconforming immigrants of color because we know these are some of the most vulnerable community members in this time and that a true immigrant rights movement will not be successful unless it is these very community members that are leading the way." And as the Queers for Economic Justice (QEJ) manifesto proclaims, "Both movements are depriving themselves of the power and strategic insights that LGBTQ immigrants can provide. We, lesbian, gay, bisexual, transgender, queer, and gender-nonconforming people and allies, stand in solidarity with the immigrant rights movement. With this statement, we call for genuinely progressive immigration reform that helps LGBTQ immigrants." These manifestos put forth visions for queer, migrant, and queer migrant activism, rights, and justice that point toward coalition in ways that are unthinkable from the inclusionary perspective. They also do so in concrete and possible terms.

These manifestos also develop and advance a different political vision from that found in documents such as "Family, Unvalued." I call it a *differential vision* of queer migration coalitional politics, an idea that extends Chela Sandoval's notion of differential consciousness and Aimee Carrillo Rowe's concept of differential belonging.[11] I begin this chapter with a discussion of the manifestos I analyze, both the organizational and political contexts of them, as well as their qualification as manifestos. I then analyze the differential vision of queer migration coalitional politics in the manifestos, arguing that these manifestos provide a political vision by conjoining a political orientation with a mode of political belonging that shifts among and between liberal/inclusionary, progressive, radical, and utopian political perspectives on the left side of the political spectrum in a way that points to coalition.[12] I end with some concluding thoughts about the coalitional possibilities that emerge from the moments these manifestos reflect and create.

Manifestos

As a genre, manifestos "evolved from sovereign proclamations of the 1600s into a form of radical protest of the 1960s."[13] Although they might be categorized as a traditionally masculine rhetorical form, feminists and queers have utilized this form, with those advocating women's rights appropriating it at least since the French Revolution. Moreover, texts from the nascent queer movement in the early 1990s, including the anonymously published "Queers Read This" and the Lesbian Avengers' "Dyke Manifestos," are good examples of queer uses of the genre. As Janet Lyon comments, "Manifestoes chronicle the exclusions and deferrals experienced by those outside the 'legitimate' bourgeois spheres of public exchange; the manifesto marks the gap between democratic ideals and modern political practice. At the same time, however, the manifesto promulgates the very discourses it critiques: it makes itself intelligible to the dominant order through a logic that presumes the efficacy of modern democratic ideals."[14] The manifestos under investigation here conform to this paradox because they each emerge from political conditions produced by state and federal government, and at least in part the redress they seek is through these bodies as well. At the same time, the writers and producers of these texts uphold and advocate positions that are well outside the predominant public discourse surrounding the issues of LGBT immigration politics.

Just after the largest immigrant rights and justice march took place, in April 2006, the New York–based ALP, which calls itself a Lesbian, Gay, Bisexual, Two Spirit, Trans and Gender Non-Conforming (LGBTSTGNC) People of Color center for community organizing, produced its manifesto, "For All the Ways They Say We Are, No One Is Illegal" (short title: "No One Is Illegal"). This text, written by LGBTSTGNC immigrants of color, received wide circulation, including being mentioned in numerous blogs and news sites; academic outlets like S&F Online's special issue on "A New Queer Agenda"; in Juan Battle and Sandra L. Barnes's edited book, Black Sexualities; and by organizations such as the Colorado Immigrant Rights Coalition. The second manifesto comes from QEJ, a New York–based radical organization led largely by people of color that seeks economic justice within the context of gender and sex liberation. It published "Queers and Immigration: A Vision Statement" in early 2007 after an extended collaboration among a team of national queer/gay writers, who are both migrant and nonmigrant, including Debanuj Das Gupta, Adam Francoeur, and Yasmin Nair. Organizations like the NGLTF as well as numerous blogs and academic Listservs distributed the statement, and more than fifty organizations, such as the ALP, Chicago LGBTQ Immigrant Alliance, American Friends Service Committee, and Love Sees No Borders, signed onto the statement.[15]

Specifically in response to measures put on the 2006 Arizona general election ballot that targeted LGBTQ rights (Proposition 107) and migrant rights (Propositions 100, 102, 103, 300),[16] Tucson-based organizations Wingspan and Coalición de Derechos Humanos joined together to produce pre- and postelection statements, which together comprise what I refer to as their manifesto linking queer rights and justice with migrant rights and justice: "Joint Statement: Stand Against Racism and Homophobia" and "Joint Statement: Continued Stand Against Racism and Homophobia."[17] Activists distributed these documents locally over Tucson-based Listservs and posted them on organizational and personal websites. CDH and Wingspan largely consist of constituencies that are either LGBTQ and citizen or migrant/migrant ally and non-LGBTQ. The two-part manifesto was collaboratively written by a large group of LGBTQ and immigration activists in both organizations. At the time, I was a liaison between the two groups as part of my dissertation research, and I was also on the team that wrote and edited the documents.

The fourth manifesto is a work in progress, first made public in 2011, and has been the centerpiece of a national speaking tour by the San Francisco Chapter of Pride at Work, or HAVOQ (Horizontal Alliance of Very [or Vaguely or Voraciously] Organized Queers). "Undoing Borders: A Queer Manifesto" circulates in the form of an activist zine that can be freely accessed and printed from the group's website. It resulted from collective efforts by the Migrant Justice Working Group, which has "been working in a variety of ways to resist the violence created by that [US-Mexico] border here in the Bay and in the borderlands." Throughout 2011 the group gave presentations all over the United States and Canada, and it continues to revise the document by posting questions and soliciting feedback on its website. "Undoing Borders" is directly inspired by both the QEJ and the ALP manifestos, and its authors identify as queer people who organize together in the Bay Area.

Many manifestos are designated as such "retroactively to identify a text's foundational status."[18] With the exception of "Undoing Borders," which calls itself a manifesto, I refer to the other statements as manifestos because of their emergence at such a crucial period and the way they laid a foundation for the explosion of queer migration political discourse after 2006. Moreover, these texts conform to many of the characteristics of manifestos, even though they do so in innovative ways. For example, political manifestos typically refuse dialogue and are often resolutely oppositional and one-sided. While discourse in the public sphere is often imagined to either enter into or invite exchange, manifestos interrupt and declare, even though they may, and often do, function as invitations to people compelled by what they declare. Patricia Cormack further explains that manifestos are usually visceral and excessive in form, style, and content and that they "simultaneously describe and directly *practice* radical social change." This point is an important one, because even as manifestos may seem to be utopian, their very existence is a present political action, a performative gesture that engages and alters the conditions of the public sphere. As Cormack writes, manifestos "occupy a space where practical actions and utopian dreams coincide."[19] The manifesto, as Laura Winkiel puts it, "seizes the present moment in order to intervene in history."[20]

It is counterproductive to construct limiting taxonomies that would delineate the rhetorical form, especially given that political conditions are constantly changing. Yet political manifestos frequently offer three argumentative gestures. First, they typically provide an "impassioned, and highly selective history which chronicles the oppression leading to the present moment of crisis."[21] Manifestos construct a chronology that attempts to cut free from past oppression by focusing on the present in order to create a "radically different future."[22] Second, they usually supply a list of "grievances or demands or declarations which cast a group's oppression as a struggle between the empowered and the disempowered."[23] Finally, a manifesto challenges the oppressor, who might be vague or very specific, while bringing an audience together as an "oppositional collectivity" toward a common action.[24] Each of these gestures may be offered in a variety of ways, even as manifestos often cite the formal qualities of those that have come before them.

Differential Visions

In order to understand the qualities of the manifestos, it is first necessary to explain the notion of differential vision. Sandoval uses the idea of the differential in multiple ways to describe and theorize oppositional modes of consciousness and action. In portraying social movement strategies of US third-world feminists, she advances the notion of "differential consciousness," which depicts how these feminists both had to and chose to shift "between and among" ideological positions as the basis of their political enactment, "like the clutch of an automobile, the mechanism that permits the driver to select, engage, and disengage gears in a system for the transmission of power."[25] These feminists did not have the privilege of engaging in only one mode of political consciousness, nor were the predominant and hegemonic forms of feminist consciousness sufficient for resisting global capitalist, postmodern cultural conditions. Therefore, US third-world feminists enacted multiple and impure forms that enabled them to more fully utilize available resources of power. The differential form of consciousness of these feminisms insisted upon a new subjectivity, "a political revision that denied any one ideology as the final answer, while instead positing a *tactical subjectivity* with the capacity to de- and recenter, given the forms of power to be moved."[26] Differential consciousness is not merely a matter of survival; it is both mobile and principled, with the aim of achieving the end of domination and the reorganization of social relations by creating "coalitions of resistance."[27] In this way a differential consciousness does not necessitate being able to shift into any political mode, but only those that invariably seek to resist hegemonic dominance in its multiple forms. Likewise, differential visions are not compatible with just any political mode.

"Differential belonging" picks up particularly on the idea of a "tactical subjectivity," shifting from an orientation (consciousness) to the world to a mode of belonging in, and with those in, the world. Moving from a politics of location to a "politics of relation," Carrillo Rowe is interested in how social relations can be altered and coalitions can be built in the specific contexts of our various belongings—those we are born or hailed into, those we choose, and those we long for.[28] Differential belonging asks people to acknowledge how "we are oppressed *and* privileged so that we may place ourselves where we can have an impact and where we can share experience."[29] Continuing to value impurity and multiplicity, one does not have to "be" a certain identity in order to do political work. Who someone is, is constructed by where they already belong and where they choose to belong. Differential belonging also compels us to *be* longing, to desire relations across lines of difference. By so doing, individuals reveal that the divisions upheld and promoted within hegemonic constructions of belonging that put, for example, racialized minorities against sexualized minorities are not natural. Instead, differential belonging can lead to the creation of coalitional subjectivities whereby people cannot see seemingly disparate struggles as anything other than related. The resulting coalitional subjectivities provide the agency to resist in ways that are not bound by fixed identities or subjectivities as people learn to politicize their belongings and adopt impure stances that allow for further connection between individuals and groups who are very different. In different ways each manifesto discussed in this chapter reflects and points toward coalitional subjectivities.[30] Theorizing belonging at the level of the interpersonal, as Carrillo Rowe does, is crucially important. However, alone it is inadequate to understand coalitional dynamics at the organizational or group levels within the contexts of counter-hegemonic social movement. The idea of a differential vision turns back to political activism and social movement, and it requires conjoining orientation with belonging. In the next section I discuss the unique characteristics of the differential vision of queer migration politics supplied in these manifestos in order to show the intricate ways they enable the envisioning of coalition.

Differential Visions of Queer Migration Politics

The report "Family, Unvalued" and most activists working for the narrow goal of passing the UAFA or obtaining rights for binational same-sex couples rely almost entirely on a narrative strategy that normalizes these couples as good, law-abiding, personally responsible citizens (or potential citizens) who value the United States and simply want to be included in it. Differential visions challenge this approach. For instance, the ALP suggests, "When all the assimilation strategies end, there will be many of us who still do not fit. We are building a movement for every one of us." Here, the ALP directly confronts assimilationist approaches. And as Sandoval writes, the differential's "processes generate the other story—the counterpoise. Its true mode is nonnarrative: narrative is viewed as only a means to an end—the end of domination."[31] This characteristic of differential consciousness, which is also a part of differential visions, is important because it does not divide from the normative, narrative strategy. It also does not use it or entirely affirm it. The differential vision is a fusion of both political orientation and mode of belonging. In the case of the manifestos analyzed here, we gain a clear vision of the complex and perhaps competing ways activists orient to the multiple facets of queer migration politics in the contemporary milieu, and how these activists proclaim their political belongings and longings to each other.

DIFFERENTIAL POLITICAL ORIENTATION

Creating a vision requires an orientation toward politics. In "Joint Statement Continued," CDH and Wingspan state, "We ask you to continue to see the connections between the treatment of LGBTs and migrants in federal, state, and local policies." Here, these groups reflect their interlocking orientation to politics. Orientation, according to Sara Ahmed, refers to "a direction (taken) toward objects and others."[32] Although we are all oriented along many lines, orientations are compulsory when people are "*required* to 'tend toward' some objects and not others" as conditions of fulfilling the lines that have been created for them.[33] For instance, with regard to sexuality and kinship, such lines are "straight," as people are directed down the paths of adulthood, marriage, and family. Judith

Halberstam has suggested that such orientations operate through "reproductive time," where people's lifelines are imagined on a chronology oriented around reproducing the family line.[34] In this way people develop straight orientations that compel them to progress forward, making such orientations a part of the progress narratives that are so central to the construction of modernity.[35] Political orientations, even if also somewhat compulsory, differ from compulsory orientations of sexuality and kinship for obvious reasons—most notably that politics are not, in the same way, guided by reproductive temporalities. Still, politics are oriented toward and around certain lines and objects. For instance, inclusionary politics orient toward and around various forms of "straight" lines when activists orient toward and around normative belongings and identifications—whiteness, hetero/homonormativity, middle-classness, urbanity, US Americanness, monogamy. Progressive, radical, and utopian politics also orient toward and around different lines. People choose and are conditioned to take up these orientations for a variety of reasons—for example, ideological, affective, pragmatic, and economic. My objective here is not to understand the psychology of such orientations, but to note that people take up various political orientations and that such orientations are an essential part of creating political visions.

Compulsory orientations imply a progress narrative, with people being expected to move from point to point. Progress narratives participate in modernist logics. It has also been widely claimed that manifestos are distinctly modern forms, especially as they emerge out of and in line with Enlightenment thought and western development. Winkiel argues, however, that anticolonial writers and activists who are concerned with matters of racial difference offer insights into the ways that manifestos also function to disrupt modernity and supply alternatives. The political orientation that the authors of the queer migration manifestos discussed in this chapter take up offers this type of disruption because it provides a reorientation, one that does not tend toward the mainstream, inclusionary LGBT and immigration rights movements' "straight orientation" toward and around normative ideals. At the same time, these manifestos serve to invite those movements to reorient toward and around a differential vision for queer migration coalitional politics, which is what the CDH and Wingspan quotation above reflects. Furthermore, the manifestos disrupt modernist logics by locating the critique of the laws and actions of the nation-state within a history of anti-domination, anticolonial, and anti-imperial struggle, across and within national borders. The queer migration manifestos achieve a differential political orientation by centering on the most vulnerable, shifting imaginaries, achieving legislative objectives, and constructing a "gray politics."

CENTERING ON THE VULNERABLE. "No One Is Illegal" repeatedly emphasizes an oppressive system that has made certain people—LGBTSTGNC immigrants of color, especially the undocumented, sex workers, and those who have been incarcerated—the most vulnerable. This system necessitates the political orientation of this manifesto's authors. Demanding full legalization for all migrants, the manifesto proclaims, "We believe that undocumented people, low wage workers, sex workers, and unemployed workers are as important as professional workers who have had great access to visa and green card programs." The statement calls out a historical inequity that makes some migrants more desirable than others, and suggests it is toward the needs of the most vulnerable workers that we should reorient our politics. In the concluding paragraph of the manifesto, in a loud call for action, the authors ask "that our political strategies always reflect the needs of the most vulnerable segments of our communities. Making deals based on the priorities of white, professional, non-trans immigrants and citizens is undermining more than one movement." Such a call to emphasize the most vulnerable could be read as paternalistic. Given that the writers identify themselves as LGBTSTGNC immigrants and people of color and use the phrase "us," it seems instead that this particular call emerges from those with firsthand experience of the vulnerability about which they write. This call simply implies that in making a movement premised on radical change that would help those with the least, everyone will achieve rights. In other words, this sort of politics would obtain the rights that the inclusionary strategies are designed to procure and goes far beyond that for a more holistic justice. This call is coupled with the ALP's belief that "every person in the U.S. deserves access to benefits that only some enjoy." Naming welfare, education, health care, and social security, among others, the statement acknowledges that many in the LGBTSTGNC immigrant community and citizens are either excluded or at risk of exclusion from these benefits that all people deserve as a human right, and it is here where political attention should turn. Such a political orientation is differential because it is not against those seeking inclusion; in fact, as noted above, the ALP seeks "a movement for every one of us."

The ALP and HAVOQ share this perspective that centers on those they consider the most vulnerable. In "Undoing Borders" HAVOQ frames its argument for being oriented toward the most vulnerable through the language of safety and survival. They write, "We assert our inherent interconnectedness and strive to cultivate systems, strategies and tactics that create safe communities without the use of militarization by the police, ICE or other forces. We challenge the criminalization of people's survival behavior to create safe communities for themselves, such as crossing borders without documentation, sex work, gang involvement and drug dealing. We will continue to push to expand the choices we can make to not only survive, but thrive in freedom." Akin to Michael Warner's famous call that "those who care about policy and morality should take as their point of departure the perspective of those at the bottom of the scale of respectability: queers, sluts, prostitutes, trannies, club crawlers, and other lowlifes,"[36] these writers suggest that protecting and emphasizing the rights and lives of those people who are usually outside of the realms of acceptability and respectability is a paramount objective for queer migration politics. Clearly, centering on the most vulnerable insists upon a shift in the political premise of normative political orientations, but in terms of whose needs it will address, it is more inclusive than inclusionary orientations.

CHANGING LAWS, CREATING IMAGINARIES. While conventional wisdom suggests that radical and revolutionary politics do not seek change from within existing systems, the differential orientation of the queer migration manifestos reflects a call for radical change through the shifting of *rhetorical imaginaries* while simultaneously recognizing that certain legal reforms would vastly improve the lives of queers, migrants, and queer migrants. The idea of a social imaginary is often attributed to Cornelius Castoriadis. Castoriadis sought to identify alternatives to deterministic models to explain the making of social worlds.[37] As Nilüfer Göle explains, social imaginaries are "widely and commonly shared . . . embedded in the habitus of a population or carried in implicit understandings that underlie and make possible common practices."[38] The social imaginary often functions within national logics, through what Kent Ono and John Sloop call "dominant discourses," that pervade the way a national body thinks and how people act.[39] The national imaginary not only enables practices, but also, as Shane Phelan avers, it is "the persistent cluster of images and rhetoric that, however inadequately and imperfectly, signal to a population who and what it is."[40] Taken together, social imaginaries generally constitute possible practices, identities, and subjectivities, and national social imaginaries constrain and enable what a particular group of people or a nation can do and also what it can be. Because of the enabling and constraining features of the national social imaginary, and because imaginaries are, in a certain sense, fictive, it is useful to understand imaginaries as uniquely rhetorical. Rhetorical imaginaries operate in and through persuasive messages, images, and ideologies designed to move people toward particular ways of existing and envisioning themselves and others. Rhetorical imaginaries have extraordinary impacts on how people think about and treat one another—across a counter, in the street, at a rally, or in a legislative assembly. While many argue that changing laws changes imaginaries, others suggest that it is not without first altering how people think about themselves and others that true change can happen. These manifestos shift among and between both approaches.

The CDH and Wingspan preelection "Joint Statement" reflects this aspect of differential orientation because it is constructed in response to the anti-migrant and anti-LGBTQ measures on the 2006 Arizona ballot, and because it seeks to shift the imaginary by overtly linking anti-migrant and anti-LGBTQ oppression and demonstrating solidarity between two seemingly separate communities. Rather than allowing these measures to be framed as matters of law and order or protecting traditional values, the Wingspan/CDH manifesto emphasizes the racism, xenophobia, and homophobia that the two organizations suggest each of these ballot measures reflect. For instance, "Joint Statement" boldly begins:

> Coalición de Derechos Humanos and Wingspan recognize that propositions 100, 102, 103 and 300 are simply the latest in an ongoing, state- and nationwide campaign of coded racist dehumanization aimed at undocumented migrants and anyone else of color who might fit the underlying racial profile. We also recognize that proposition 107 is a continuation of homophobic attacks aimed at lesbian, gay, bisexual, and transgender people of all races, ethnicities, and nations. Using an onslaught of initiatives in multiple states, state and federal legislation, and demonizing words and images, these campaigns of dehumanization do great harm to all people.

This opening statement collapses LGBTQs, migrants, and people of color in such a way that they are all implicated in the dehumanization of one another. Such a mix centers on the coalitional subjects who are most impacted and refuses an imaginary of these groups that allows them to be separated into discrete categories or interests. Consequently, the immediate objective of stopping the ballot measures is located within a broader objective of shifting the imaginary of these groups.

HAVOQ, QEJ, and the ALP seek to change laws including, foremost, (1) approving comprehensive immigration reform at the federal level that would address the needs and concerns of the most vulnerable queer/trans migrants; (2) passing an Employment Non-Discrimination Act that is inclusive of gender identity and expression and also applies to migrants; (3) overturning/opting out of the REAL ID Act, which makes it much more difficult for trans people and migrants to obtain identification; (4) enacting labor laws that protect all people who want to unionize, including migrants; (5) stopping enforcement and policing practices, including raids, detention, and deportation, as well as local law enforcement/federal immigration relationships and the building of walls; and (6) ending the (now former) ban against migrants with HIV and provisions that make applying for and receiving asylum more difficult. Individually, the writers call for other changes in laws as well in their lists of grievances and demands. These pragmatic demands are each coupled with radical attempts to shift the rhetorical imaginary in relation to queer migrants. As will be shown below, this happens in the ways language and strategy choices are critiqued. For example, as a result of right-wing discourses that position queers and migrants in opposition to traditional values, especially so-called family values, and law and order, resisting these negative discourses has been a paramount objective for the mainstream, inclusionary LGBT and immigrant rights movements. Family values language, in particular, has dominated both of these movements. These queer migration manifestos actively challenge the value of such language at the same time that they uphold all people's right to construct families as they desire.

The manifestos also attempt to craft a new imaginary that focuses on dehumanization and exploitation, scapegoating, and diversion tactics. In demanding an end to the ban against migrants with HIV, "Queers and Immigration" acknowledges the long-standing impacts that HIV has had on queer communities, particularly queer communities of color, as well as the unmerited criminalization of a specific group of migrants. Instead of utilizing a normative discourse that tries to fit LGBT people in the framework of family values, QEJ orients its politics toward HIV-positive queers/migrants, those who cannot be subsumed by the discourse of family values. Additionally, this statement critiques the ban because it offered waivers "on the basis of qualifying familial relationships." Rather than calling for inclusion of any kind of queer kinship, the statement advocates reinstating waivers for *individual* instances of hardship. "No One Is Illegal" and "Undoing Borders" echo this call. The ALP writes frankly, "We caution our comrades around all language which can be tied to family values. While many LGBTSTGNC immigrants of color will benefit from successful family reunification measures, our lives are independently important outside of any nuclear family framework. We also caution reducing the complex needs of LGBTSTGNC immigrants of color to the singular demand for same sex marriage rights." Even as the ALP disagrees, it does not denounce or chastise those who engage in these tactics, but offers a "caution." It is certainly possible that a reader from the mainstream movement might not see the distinction between cautioning rather than chastising, yet the ALP's position does not demean or divide from the mainstream. At a basic level the authors ask the mainstream to stretch. The reason that the ALP cautions against focusing only on marriage is because it "leave[s] out vulnerable individuals and families without citizens or documented members." Although the ALP has ideological reasons for challenging a focus on marriage, here the writers offer a pragmatic reason for the warning that might make good sense to the practically minded mainstream.

In a similar way, "Queers and Immigration" challenges the generally exclusionary definitions under immigration law, which affect not only same-sex binational couples but also extended family members such as cousins. The authors write matter-of-factly that the current definition of the word "family" "is very restrictive because it leaves out most of the family structures in which LGBTQ immigrants live." They go on to explain the other limitations that result from this definition. Thus, they do not ask for inclusion, but for a broadening of the narrow definitions of what constitutes a family. This rhetorical tactic enacts a differential orientation to politics by challenging the definition of who can belong in a family. At the same time, in the list of suggested reforms the manifesto urges passage of the UAFA as a "first step in the direction of the expansion of the definition of 'family.'" The inclusion of support for the UAFA suggests that the manifesto's authors do not seek to isolate themselves from others who want rights for LGBTQ migrants, even if they disagree with their tactics and focus.[41] QEJ's differential orientation points toward a coalitional vision of politics, which reflects that issues are intertwined even as they take different approaches.

The Wingspan/CDH "Joint Statement" uses parallel structure to demonstrate how migrants, queers, and queer migrants are scapegoats who are easily blamed for a multitude of societal problems. Unlike other local immigrant rights advocates who emphasized the family values that migrants bring with them across the Southern border, such as the Catholic Church,[42] in the Wingspan/CDH "Joint Statement" analysis of the migrant-related propositions in Arizona, they refuse to use defensive rhetoric that generalizes and homogenizes migrants. Instead, "Joint Statement" takes an offensive approach that maintains that the anti-migrant measures function to (1) justify exploitation and mistreatment of migrants at the hands of employers, law enforcement, and vigilantes; (2) position migrants as a scapegoat that diverts attention from the real reasons for the current immigration situation; (3) divert attention from finding real solutions to pressing social problems like health care and government corruption; and (4) support a system in which the erosion of human and civil rights is a profit-making industry. They refuse to defend migrants by locating them within a "family values" discourse.

In the subsequent section on Protect Marriage Arizona, "Joint Statement" takes on the family values discourse directly. Repeating the structure from above, this section suggests that Protect Marriage Arizona functions to (1) argue that marriage is in crisis because of queer people; (2) scapegoat queer people for a perceived decline in traditional "family values"; and (3) use queer people to divert attention from finding real solutions to pressing social problems like health care and government corruption. This analysis attends to issues such as the problem of granting rights only through conjugal familial relationships and the fact that "family values" have always only benefited a very select few. "No One Is Illegal" shares such an analysis of scapegoating, noting, "The Bush Administration will continue to scapegoat immigrants and LGBTSTGNC people concurrently, diverting national attention away from a war waged with lies and a failing economy due to the profit driven tactics of many of its own members."

"Undoing Borders" takes the critique of family language in a slightly different direction and advocates using queer experience with radical and chosen families, "from drag houses to communes," as an alternative to the predominant discourse on family. The authors write, "As we organize together against the racist, sexist, classist and otherwise oppressive impacts of border and immigration policies, we take this redefinition of family as a model for deep solidarity, enabling us to develop networks and connections based on mutual support." Drawing from the deep well of kinship resources, which scholars such as Kath Weston have documented as central to the survival of queers,[43] HAVOQ advances a radical shift in the rhetorical imaginary that battles policy through queer kinship.

The manifestos also balance between achieving legal objectives and shifting rhetorical imaginaries in their language choices regarding the term "illegal." The deliberate choice to use phrases like "undocumented," or the even more ambiguous use of "migrant," without mention of status at all works against an emphasis on the legal system and toward changing the way people are regarded and therefore treated. These moves are significant, for as Eithne Luibhéid persuasively demonstrates, the lines between legality and so-called illegality are anything but clear. A host of factors, many outside the control of individual migrants, can, from one moment to the next, shift someone out of regularized status.[44] A legal permanent resident who is arrested for a minor infraction may be subject to deportation, a student on a visa who loses full-time status at her university may be deported, and an asylum seeker whose claim is denied is immediately put into deportation proceedings. The labels "illegal" and "legal" are inflammatory and inaccurate. Most immigration violations are civil and not criminal; civil offenses are generally administrative violations, whereas criminal offenses violate laws or statutes that prohibit conduct. These terms also do not fairly reflect the complexities of the US immigration apparatus. The ALP manifesto directly confronts the language of illegality in its title, and the remainder of the text enacts this perspective.

In critiquing the dominant themes apparent in the anti-migrant movement in Arizona, "Joint Statement" finds "repetitive use of the word 'illegal' to label human beings rather than specific actions; repeated references to undocumented migrants as 'invaders'; implicit and explicit links between speaking Spanish, lawbreaking and invasion; and unsubstantiated rhetorical links between 'illegal aliens' and ills such as violence and drug use that in truth plague all segments of society." Although specific sources are not named in the statement, politicians, media, and law enforcement as well as the discourse among average people are indicted. A brief look at the rhetoric of those who supported the migrant-related propositions demonstrates this point. As one example, Russell Pearce, the very conservative state legislator made famous for writing and advocating for Arizona's SB 1070 in 2010, wrote the following in support of Proposition 100, which denied bail to undocumented people charged with a crime:

> Illegal aliens that commit a crime are an extremely difficult challenge for law enforcement and [a] growing threat to our citizens. Large, well-organized gangs of illegal aliens have flooded many neighborhoods with violence to the point where Arizona now has the highest crime rate in the nation. With few real ties to the community and often completely undocumented by state agencies, many illegal aliens can easily escape prosecution for law breaking simply because they are so difficult to locate. HCR 2028 [the bill number in the legislature before becoming a ballot measure] would deny bail to illegal aliens when there is convincing evidence that they've committed a serious felony, keeping dangerous thugs in jail rather than releasing them onto the streets. Allowing an illegal immigrant to post bail simply gives them time to slip across the border and evade punishment for their crimes. By voting yes for this initiative, we keep more violent criminals in jail, make our homes and communities safer, and send a powerful message to illegal aliens that their crimes will not go unpunished.[45]

As the "Joint Statement" claims, Pearce repeatedly uses the phrase "illegal alien," and he makes strong connections between migration and crime. The Wingspan/CDH statement goes on to say, "This type of hateful language positions undocumented migrants—and others who might be mistaken for undocumented migrants—as both dangerous and less than human." As with QEJ's manifesto, this statement blurs the boundaries between documented and undocumented in such a way that racism and xenophobia cannot be directed only at some "foreign other." The slippage between being undocumented and "looking" undocumented makes any distinction between the citizen and the other tenuous at best.[46] The slippage reflected here in the manifestos, blurring of the boundaries between legality and illegality, leads into the last aspect of the differential orientation: the construction of gray politics.

GRAYING POLITICS, BREAKING BORDERS.   Rather than a normative orientation to politics that emphasizes only US citizens and those who embody all the characteristics of the good citizen, and upholds the legitimacy of laws that enforce borders, the manifestos demand an end to binaries, borders, prisons, and walls—literally and metaphorically. Like Audre Lorde, who declares that the most vicious of all the master's tools is that of divide and conquer, the manifestos locate divisions among groups and nations as logics of divide and conquer. The alternative orientation elsewhere has been called "curdling-separation," "mestiza consciousness," or borderlands. For instance, Gloria Anzaldúa describes a borderland as "a vague and undetermined place created by the emotional residue of an unnatural boundary. It is in a constant state of transition. The prohibited and forbidden are its inhabitants."[47] The borderland is a queer space, and in the language of "Undoing Borders" a queer orientation centers on the "gray" areas of politics and identity. Gray politics refuse divide-and-conquer strategies and insist on building critique and change from the complex interstices among nation-states, groups of people, and issues. One manifestation of gray politics can be found in how the manifestos shift away from rights based on citizenship and toward human rights and justice, regardless of citizenship. Certainly there are important critiques to be made of human rights paradigms. Very often human rights paradigms imply a liberal subject and make assumptions about who is able to count as human.[48] Furthermore, human rights discourse often operates through universalizing logics that erase the importance of cultural, local, and other specificities, subjecting all "humans" to the same framework.[49] Gray politics do not entirely escape such trappings, as if such an endeavor would be possible; however, the manifestos challenge the usual framework. For instance, as shown, these manifestos center on the most vulnerable people—those who do not conform to the typical characteristics of the liberal human subject—but do so from a perspective informed by those same people. Thus, the manifestos differ from paternalistic human rights discourses that call for the "saving" of vulnerable people who, for a host of reasons, do not live up to the western standard of the human. Given a lack of viable alternative terms, this version of human rights and justice could be said to "disidentify" with liberal definitions by working through a familiar frame but against the logics the frame usually engenders.[50]

For example, "Queers and Immigration" includes a section on "harboring provisions," which were proposed in the 2005 congressional bill HR 4437, among other places. Harboring provisions criminalize people who protect or assist the undocumented and thus potentially affect those who provide services to undocumented people, including their friends, family, or partners. Harboring provisions are designed to deter undocumented migrants by criminalizing those with whom they interact. Even political moderates often oppose these provisions because of the impact they would have on US citizens and LPRs. The QEJ manifesto mentions the sorts of people who are targeted by these provisions but does not privilege these groups over migrants. QEJ blurs the legal boundaries among those who would be criminalized, stating, "We oppose efforts to criminalize those who assist the immigrant community, their families, and loved ones through harboring provisions." In this remark it is difficult to clearly distinguish the criminalized groups from one another. The ALP and HAVOQ oppose harboring provisions on like grounds and refuse to erect a boundary between the rights of citizens and those of migrants. Also on the premise of refusing boundaries among different groups, QEJ opposes guest worker programs because they create a "two-tiered" system of immigrants "based on their income potential and class categories." QEJ's manifesto, as well as that of the ALP, suggests that guest worker programs lead to underpaying and mistreating guest workers at the same time that they undermine the labor movement in the United States. Specifically, migrant workers' rights cannot be regulated, and low-skill, low-wage workers often bear the brunt of such programs. This section again refuses to edify the distinctions among workers. It places *laborers* in solidarity with one another, regardless of citizenship, by noting that no matter what one's citizenship is, guest worker programs affect all low-wage workers. Taking this position grays the boundaries between those who might be said to "deserve" criminalization and those who do not.

Gray politics also insists on dealing with the complex, structural reasons for migration (as opposed to reducing migration to individuals' deviant choices) and overtly challenges borders, militarization, security, and enforcement. The inclusionary approach, as found in documents like "Family, Unvalued," makes an implicit normative judgment on border crossing. For instance, even though the largest number of migrants living in the United States come from Mexico and Central America, in the entire text of "Family, Unvalued" none of the migrants featured is from these locations and none has committed an offense beyond overstaying a visa.[51] The manifestos question the legitimacy of the border and its enforcement altogether, preferring instead to emphasize the blurry lines between nation-states, legal status, and survival. As Anzaldúa famously writes, "The U.S.-

Mexican border *es una herida abierta* where the Third World grates against the first and bleeds . . . Borders are set up to define the places that are safe and unsafe, to distinguish *us* from *them*."[52] The manifestos uphold the belief that borders are fundamentally designed to divide and concretely evidence the problems with the US-Mexico border, as well as the borders, boundaries, and walls that continue to move into all parts of US life with increased enforcement and militarization efforts. "Queers and Immigration" includes a significant section on "policing the border" that underscores the detrimental impacts on human lives that heightened border militarization has had, including the record number of deaths since the early 2000s. The ALP also opposes increased enforcement, noting, "We recognize that all enforcement provisions are not just a part of an increased attack on immigrants within the U.S., but part of the ongoing and expanding War on Terrorism." The authors further oppose all provisions that create more literal walls, borders, and obstacles that limit people's mobility, adding, "We recognize that when it comes to enforcement, visibly LGBTSTGNC immigrants of color, undocumented folks, low wage workers, women, youth and elders who are LGBTSTGNC POC [people of color] are exceptionally vulnerable to all facets of the detention and the prison industrial complex." As a further example of centering on the most vulnerable, the manifestos show how walls, especially those of prison cages, affect these same vulnerable people and their ability to be mobile. HAVOQ similarly insists, "The right to mobility is more than the right to cross a national boundary. It is the right to live and work where we please, including the right to stay home. It means dismantling detention centers along with the larger Prison Industrial Complex."

The manifestos also reflect a gray politics by tying the increase in borders and the squelching of mobility to free trade, profits, and privatization, further complicating migration narratives. The manifestos attend specifically to so-called free trade agreements like NAFTA (the North American Free Trade Agreement) that open borders for the movement of capital while simultaneously closing them to the movement of people. This contradictory treatment of capital and people is especially detrimental due to the negative impact of free trade on economies in countries like Mexico, where the once-thriving agricultural sector crashed after the newly opened market was completely flooded with US agricultural imports.[53] Many Mexican citizens continue to have few other options but to attempt to migrate north to find work. Furthermore, as CDH and Wingspan write, the "removal of civil and human rights within the United States is a profit-making enterprise, especially for military contractors (like Halliburton). In this system, select companies make more money from having more and more people in privately-owned prisons and detention centers, and from government contracts to increase militarization at the border." The ALP also points toward Halliburton in their critique of expansion of the Department of Homeland Security (DHS), explaining, "The Bush Administration has already allocated money to a subsidiary of Halliburton (Vice President Cheney's 'former' corporation) to launch the development of a new genre of detention centers built for the Department of Homeland Security." Large private corporations, including those with strong ties to powerful politicians, rely upon and actively promote the expansion of militarization and the prison industrial complex—both through criminal and civil detention—in order to turn record profits. These manifestos thus show that the focus on borders is not a simple matter of whether and how to increase national security and enforce existing laws; instead, the explosion of border discourse is a more complex matter, requiring a gray politics that sees the multifaceted reasons for border militarization.

QEJ also challenges the borders of US "nation-centrism" by emphasizing the terrible impacts that border militarization and proposals for border walls have for indigenous peoples whose national borders span the US-Mexico border and who are supposed to have free movement across that border. Three recognized tribes have reservations that cross the US-Mexico border, including the Tohono O'odham Reservation, which covers seventy-five miles; the Kickapoo Traditional Tribe; and the Cocopah Tribe. Members of twenty-three other tribes live near the US side of the border, with many also including members who live in Mexico.[54] In recalling the complexities of US colonial history in relation to indigenous peoples, the issue is not about who is good enough to belong to the nation, but who should even be able to make these claims. HAVOQ explicitly calls attention to this history in "Undoing Borders," arguing that the US-Mexico border has emerged from particular histories of violent land acquisition, genocide of indigenous people, unpaid slave labor, and underpaid immigrant labor. The border, HAVOQ maintains, is "rooted in the ongoing colonization, imperialism, and global economic structures that continue to dominate our world." The ALP also stands in coalition with broader movements against borders and imperialism, exclaiming, "We support the many forms of ongoing resistance, and call for widespread solidarity with worker and student walkouts, as well as connections being made in demonstrations for an end to US imperialism and the rights of immigrants domestically."

Importantly, these groups challenge metaphorical borders and boundaries that limit people's mobility and work to enact divisions. In a section titled "Policing Our Selves" in "Undoing Borders," the authors declare, "We work to expand the definitions of 'family' to include queer and other self-defined relationships. Rather than fight to extend marriage to queers, we strive to create free and inclusive communities where we do not place legal borders between coupled families and those who enjoy single, asexual or polyamorous lifestyles." The manifestos' gray politics—their insistence on both tolerance of and comfort in a host of ambiguities in order to break down divisions between people and enable freedom of movement—is a central part of their differential orientation and is a cornerstone for the differential vision that creates space and possibility for coalition. Importantly, on its own, consciousness or orientation does not suggest ways to relate to others, nor does it privilege the relational dimensions of political activism. Focusing also on the importance of belonging, and how people are able to and desire to belong with others, within the contexts of activism, helps to prevent the reduction of politics to the level of individual consciousness. It is to the question of belonging that we now return.

"FABULOSITY" AND OTHER MODES OF BELONGING

Although the idea of differential belonging could suggest that one should build strategic interpersonal alliances even across deep ideological lacunae, as seen above, differential consciousness returns us to orienting toward those with politics that resist dominant and hegemonic systems of power. Combined, they create a differential vision. The politics of belonging have always been central to activist work. Women of color, queer, and transnational feminists have contributed greatly to theorizing belonging and its relationship to identity, politics, and community. Mab Segrest invites theorists and activists to begin work not from the place of individual thought and action but from recognition of the ways we are always already "born to belonging," born into relationality and connectivity.[55] From such recognition, seeking belonging with others who are also oppressed becomes an imperative. As Elspeth Probyn writes, belonging always "expresses a desire for more than what it is, a yearning to make skin stretch beyond individual needs and wants."[56]

Belonging, then, is about desire and a longing to be, in the sense of being, but also a longing to be attached. Although being and attachment may connote stability and fixity, as Anne-Marie Fortier notes, questions of belonging also imply movement or mobility. Thus, belonging reflects a tension, perhaps making belonging into a threshold. As Probyn argues, belonging "designates a profoundly affective manner of being, always performed with the experience of being within and inbetween [*sic*] sets of social relations. It precisely emphasizes and moves with that experience."[57] To belong means that one is in a relationship already, but it also indicates a desire to continue moving further, into where one already "belongs" or into other social relations. Like Eve Kosofsky Sedgwick's understanding of queerness as movement, belonging also moves toward and away from identities, people, and politics. In fact, Probyn slides "from 'identity' to 'belonging,'" arguing that "the latter term captures more accurately the desire for some sort of attachment, be it to other people, places, or modes of being, and the ways in which individuals and groups are caught within wanting to belong, wanting to become, a process that is fueled by yearning rather than the positing of identity as a stable state."[58] Such yearnings must be located within systems of power, and no mode of desire is innocent. As Chandra Talpade Mohanty cautions, the idea that women belong to a global sisterhood created through their shared victimization under a universal patriarchy, for example, asks women to transcend their differences rather than engage them.[59] Such a yearning for a global alliance thus reinscribes imperial and colonial logics, which prevents reciprocity and deep understanding.

Thus, adopting a "praxis of belonging," as Segrest calls it, is not a simple answer to the question of how to conduct ethical activism. Yet these manifestos reflect a commitment to acknowledging the singularities of belongings—"what emerges after we have enumerated our differences—moments and movements that establish contact across a geography of division."[60] The queer migration manifestos each provide their own discussions of their commitments with belonging—in some cases who they are and their attachments, internally with each other where they already belong, and in all cases with those they long to be in relation to and want to move toward. This is accomplished most concretely in "Undoing Borders," with the discussion of "fabulosity." A playful queer form of praxis, fabulosity encompasses these activists' guiding principles to "define, build and practice how we will treat each other and work together." These principles include creating an open and inclusive language and culture, being open with one another and to new people and ideas, discovering how to be in relation with one another without reproducing marginalizing hierarchies, and building both movement and community. These principles are foremost internal ones, and they require a shifting in and out of modalities of belonging with other activists who share attachments with others in a group with unified visions and objectives. The repeated call for openness highlights a willingness to change course, should it be necessary, and to do the labor required to create a space that reflects the kind of world activists strive to build. Importantly, the HAVOQ writers acknowledge this relationship because they understand that movement building is also about internal community building. People should enjoy sharing nonwork space and time together and foster opportunities to do so. This latter point, a desire to create worlds of belonging that enable what María Lugones calls "playfulness"—or the ability to be healthy, whole, and safe—is also central to the queerness of their approach. Being healthy together within the internal community, then, prepares one for coalition building and engagement with others externally, which may happen in environments where one cannot be playful in the sense intended by Lugones.

The other manifestos do not explicitly discuss their being and their activist attachments to one another, but they emphasize activists' visions for broader community belonging and their desires for belonging across lines of difference, or coalition building. These desires involve reunifying the community by working through divisions, refusing isolation by building connections, and shifting between fostering relationships with other like-minded radicals, but also with those who have more normative aspirations for their belongings.

REFUSING DIVISIONS, REUNIFYING COMMUNITIES.   Just as the writers of "Undoing Borders" desire community and movement building, "No One Is Illegal" pronounces, "We recommit to the difficult task of reunification with the many divided parts of our communities based on race, class, ethnicity, or religion." The focus on fostering community requires differential belonging because of the depth and breadth of the divisions, real and perceived, and the already precarious nature of "community."[61] Recognizing full well the tensions between different marginalized groups, perhaps most notably among "citizens of color who are struggling to survive innumerable assaults" and "immigrants who are doing our best to survive globalization," the writers commit to "resisting the many divisive tactics of the U.S. government through dialogue, education, and action." A tall order, to be sure, given that the ALP has named its audience as both the LGBTSTGNC community and the immigrant rights community. The ALP does not name the specific divisive tactics of the US government, though because of the earlier mention that citizens of color survive assault and immigrants of color survive globalization, one can speculate on the tactics the ALP indicts. For example, predominantly white and middle-class LGBT communities have rallied around hate crime legislation that includes sexual orientation, gender identity, and gender expression as a way to ensure the safety of LGBT people who are regularly targeted with abuse and harassment for their gender and sexuality. However, not only are hate crime laws disproportionately used against people of color, including queers of color, but adding levels of severity to punishments expands the prison industrial complex, which has massively larger and more significant effects on communities of color.[62] Moreover, if one is a migrant—with or without documents—being brought into the US criminal justice system is almost a guarantee of detention and deportation, making an expanded punitive system even worse for noncitizens. Such governmental assaults are often unseen or unrecognized by many in the LGBT community and thus breed divisions. These disunions are often nearly impenetrable, but the ALP commits to finding ways to bridge them.

CDH and Wingspan also work to tear down divisions and foster connections between communities. In the 2006 election all four anti-migrant measures in Arizona passed by a three-to-one margin, and Protect Marriage Arizona lost by roughly two percentage points. LGBTQ organizations and citizens around the state and the country celebrated this historic event, and few attended to the fact that the rights of migrants, along with poor, non-English-speaking, and Latin@ citizens in the state had been severely diminished.[63] During my fieldwork this point was brought up to me by queer Latin@s, who resented the lack of reflexivity on the part of many white, citizen LGBTQ people. Some Wingspan activists recognized this brewing division and wanted to reiterate their steadfast commitment to coalition with migrant rights and justice. Thus, the second part of the Wingspan/CDH manifesto, created in response to the election, primarily (though not entirely) speaks to an audience of mostly white, LGBTQ *citizens*, perhaps especially those who were un-reflexively celebrating the election results.[64] This part of the manifesto is also written as a performative gesture of solidarity with migrant and Latin@ communities, one that disrupts the dominant LGBTQ discourse of the moment. Part two of the manifesto does not address the needs or rights of citizens, nor does it explicitly name this group as a target audience. Rather, "Joint Statement Continued," urges LGBTQ, migrant, and LGBTQ migrant communities to refuse "divide and conquer" tactics just because it seems like one movement has advanced while the other has regressed. The manifesto calls all three of the aforementioned audiences to take action by speaking out for LGBTQ and migrant rights, acknowledging the scapegoating tactics used against LGBTQs and migrants, and recognizing the people who exist within both communities. The manifesto asks all community members to shift out of either a mainstream and celebratory space or a resentful and frustrated space back into a politics of relation with one another. However, the specific action steps that the statement offers clearly target LGBTQ US citizens and encourage them to create relationships and solidarity with migrants:

1. Don't refer to migrants as "illegal." Human beings are not illegal.
2. Research the unfair global economic policies—often advocated by the U.S. government and U.S. big business—that depress economies in places like Mexico and lead to migration.
3. Research the good that migrants do for the U.S. economy and culture.
4. Join one of the many local migrants' rights organizations, work for social justice, and learn about the inhumanity caused by the militarization of the U.S.-Mexico border.[65]

These action steps reiterate themes already discussed above. Although Wingspan had made some headway in recent years with getting LGBTQ citizens to think about immigration as an LGBTQ issue, some leaders in Wingspan feared that LGBTQ community members might be inclined to distance themselves from migrant rights and justice with the defeat of Protect Marriage Arizona. The strategic centering of those individuals as an audience does not recenter citizenship as the mode of belonging; instead, it asks citizens to be agents in building connections across these lines of difference, especially when it seems there might be politically and personally expedient reasons not to.

FOSTERING RELATIONSHIPS WITH RADICALS AND LIBERALS. Closely related to the project of actively promoting belonging and connection within and across communities is a desire to reach out through ideological divisions within and between movements themselves. "Queers and Immigration" begins by affirming that in the United States there is little analysis of the intersections between queer rights and immigration. It then critiques inclusionary politics and the centering of only normative attachments by explaining how LGBTQ migrants are invisible within both movements because the migrant rights movement places undue emphasis on heteronormative family relationships and the LGBTQ movement focuses on partners of US citizens. In beginning the statement with a critique of both movements' emphasis on conventional, partnered relationships and conceptions of normality, "Queers and Immigration" not only challenges those discourses of belonging but also promotes an alternative that centers on LGBTQ immigrants no matter what their relationships are. QEJ does not deny the importance of issues like marriage or binational same-sex couples receiving immigration rights; rather, the authors of the group's manifesto encourage a more extensive approach. CDH and Wingspan utilize a similar strategy, arguing, "We believe that rights such as healthcare, childcare, and visitation should not be granted only through marital arrangements. However, we also believe that further reducing LGBT people's access to marriage or domestic partner benefits is blatantly wrong." Such statements invite those with normative aspirations to consider how their understanding of what is most oppressive (i.e., marriage inequality) actually might reinforce the oppression of others (i.e., those without conventional relationships or a desire to have them).

HAVOQ also balances on this line between declaring belonging to those with more radical thought and liberals who seek inclusion. In proclaiming their belief in access to education for all, the writers include a footnote that states: "We feel the need to say, in light of the recent failure of the Dream Act that while we believe in access to education for all, we do not believe that higher education or military service should be the only way for undocumented youth to gain residency/path to citizenship. We do not believe that we should have to concede to increased militarization to gain access to educational resources." Given the momentum behind the movement for the DREAM Act, and the delicate maneuvering for US citizens critiquing a pathway to citizenship for undocumented people—a move that has been extensively critiqued by youth activists (see chapter 3), this phrasing is key.[66] It acknowledges the need for education and pathways to citizenship, thereby aligning with the liberal aspirations of the DREAM activists, at the same time that it recognizes the more radical and progressive positions that critique the militarization of this and other similar bills.

HAVOQ enacts a comparable differential rhetoric in their position on political asylum. Like QEJ and the ALP, HAVOQ denounces the strict limitations on asylum applications and any proposals to add more restrictions. The authors then include the following footnote: "While we acknowledge that the US is not inherently any safer for queer and transgender people than the rest of the world, we . . . support the expansion of accessibility to asylum. The current 1 year deadline is particularly challenging for queer and trans people who often experience high levels of isolation and as a result do not learn about asylum options until the deadline has passed." Again, this statement suggests alliance with liberal organizations working for inclusion through asylum, and at the same time it indicates alliance with those who critique the system of asylum for the way asylum pleas often problematically position other countries as wholly non-modern and the United States as the bastion of safety for LGBT people. The inclusion of both of these previous points in footnotes as opposed to the body of the manifesto is an interesting choice. It could suggest that these points are of lesser importance. It also may mark the tension between extending a gesture of solidarity while not leaving principles behind.

These queer migration manifestos advocate differential modes of belonging within groups of activists, across communities, and across movements by looking to remain open to possibilities and to build and sustain connections and relationships even when divisions run deep and wide. These coalitional aspirations for belonging create differential visions when conjoined with differential political orientations.

Conclusions

As a product of present conditions, a differential vision describes the ways that some activists position themselves in relation to each other, to other groups, and to issues in their public proclamations designed to articulate their politics. A differential vision reflects an impure orientation, committed to a politics of rela-tion with others that may differ in their approach (i.e., inclusionary, progressive, revolutionary, or utopian), but that share a commitment to resisting hegemonic systems of power, even as they might understand that system differently. A dif-ferential vision can aid in creating, and perhaps sustaining, coalitional subjec-tivities and coalitions of resistance with both those who share the vision and those who may share only particular goals. This is because differential visions are multifaceted in how they present politics, and they also provide numerous opportunities for people to see their issues as inextricably connected. As a pub-lic proclamation, then, a differential vision theorizes, maps, and highlights the methods for differentially engaging in social movement in or toward coalition. A differential vision holds competing positions for the sake of building coali-tion, centers the perspectives of coalitional subjects, and recognizes the neces-sity of maintaining flexibility with regard to political form and relationalities. The coalitional possibilities reflected in the moments of these manifestos are vast and varied within the individual texts, but when taken together the vision is surprisingly concrete. Moreover, the manifesto has proven to be an ideal form for conveying and constructing a differential vision because the form is intended to demand an end to oppression while mapping how wrongs may be righted in clear and frank terms. Analyzing a group of thematically connected but separately generated manifestos reveals the consistency of this vision, the kinds of coali-tion imagined and practiced, and this analysis thus supplies a robust rationale for taking the charges within the texts seriously.

Still, perhaps one response to what I have just argued about the differential vision promoted in these manifestos would be to say that the vision very well points toward coalition, but that that vision of coalition is itself utopian. The ideas analyzed here have circulated within a range of communities as activists across the United States have worked to integrate dimensions of these differ-ential visions in places as wide ranging as Madison, Wisconsin, and Greens-boro, North Carolina.[67] The circulation suggests that these gestures of belonging have been heard, responded to, and even embraced by some. Yet the nature of the ideological divisions between those committed to counter-hegemonic resistance in the form of radical, progressive, and liberal thought are not easily overcome; to think otherwise would be utopian. Furthermore, one could contend that the vision of coalition will prove dissatisfying to liberals, progressives, and radicals alike. As a result, coalition, and the compromise it entails, is either a dilution of political objectives and principles or an unrealistic pipe dream that does not actually provide an alternative to utopia, as I argued in the introduc-tion. To me, such a conclusion would be premature. The rhetorical form of the manifesto is designed to rupture or intervene in history, in the present, with the aim of a better future. The intervention staged in these differential visions points toward what is possible and what is, at least in some ways, already present. For instance, while the manifestos call for modes of belonging across lines of seemingly insurmountable difference, they make that call at least in part because either the authors live within those spaces, intersections, or interstices that already bridge those differences, or they presently exist in those sites of belonging and move toward others. Also, those who produced the manifestos in varying degrees possess the differential political orientation they advocate—a fact evidenced by the multi-author, collaborative production of each manifesto. Perhaps the ironic thing that these manifestos reveal is that what is most utopian are the gestures they make toward those with inclusionary orientations and normative aspirations for belonging since the legislative objectives may be the least likely to be achieved of the many things they demand. Meanwhile, on local levels, within communities, the differential vision is already playing out. The manifestos simply name the need for wider reception and uptake for the kind of world they try to live in and make possible.

This naming also brings up another important point with regard to the unique form of the manifestos analyzed here. As stated at the outset, manifestos are not dialogic texts. Both coalitional politics and the differential visions outlined here seem to at least tend toward dialogue. Although this may indicate an irreconcilable paradox revealing that I have mistakenly categorized these statements as manifestos, I rather think that it points toward an innovation in the rhetorical form. When manifestos construct a differential vision that points toward coalition, the declaration may in fact invite dialogue, but that invitation is limited. In discussing the concept of "fabulosity" above, I did not mention the last characteristic, which is that HAVOQ members will ask for what they *want*, not just what they think they can get. This dimension of fabulosity invites approaching situations as abundant with possibility rather than scarce, which is what capitalist models have led us to believe—including promoting the belief that we do not deserve to ask in the first place, or that we should sacrifice our own desires if they are not in line with capitalist thought. In confronting this ideology, the authors who construct these differential visions are not interested in dialogue about their principles, but they do invite others invested in counter-hegemonic resistance to talk about what the differential vision means for them and how they might reorient their politics, shift their belongings, and ask for more. Whether such visions lead to more coalitions or coalitional possibilities remains to be seen.

CHAPTER 2

The Coalitional Possibility
of Radical Interactionality

Queercents is a special-interest website that features daily tips on financial matters, an LGBTQ perspective on money, and an array of stories
that are likely relevant to a middle-class, US-based LGBTQ audience.[1] Shortly
after joining as a contributor, Yasmin Nair wrote an entry about the Uniting
American Families Act. No stranger or outsider to the queer blogosphere, on
this particular occasion Nair began what was to be a series on immigration in
relation to the queer community. Queer people have financial considerations
beyond married heterosexuals when it comes to US immigration policy. Still,
many LGBT folks have framed immigration primarily as an emotional issue,
not an economic one, arguing that the laws need to be changed so that people who love each other can be together. Nair argues that she is against the
UAFA, because her concern is passing comprehensive immigration reform. In
stark contrast to most UAFA-oriented blogs, which, like other UAFA advocacy
discussed in this book so far, feature the sad stories of binational same-sex
couples,[2] Nair shifts the discussion and matter-of-factly writes: "The current
immigration crisis has come about because the United States feeds on cheap
labor and the exploitation of millions, the very people it chooses to dispose of
quickly and crudely via the mechanisms of raids and deportations. It does this
because it knows that there is more cheap labor to be had because of the conditions of 'free trade' it has created, conditions that guarantee a breakdown in
the economies of countries like Mexico. These conditions, in turn, guarantee

the flow of people desperate to find a living here."[3] For those people on the left within the immigration rights and justice movement, this analysis is not particularly radical or unusual. But such analysis is not common within the LGBT immigration rights community.

Nair, a queer woman of color and Indian immigrant who lives in Chicago, is the most consistent and persistent voice in the US activist blogosphere who writes about queer migration from a perspective that does not center on the rights of binational same-sex couples. Her work is featured on blogs and news outlets including the *Bilerico Project*, *Queercents*, *In These Times*, and the *Windy City Times*. She is also included and cited in an array of other venues, such as academic and activist essays and projects like Chicago's Gay History Project, which documents prominent gay activists in the city. Nair's larger intellectual and activist project involves writing cogent critiques of neoliberalism, particularly as it manifests among the mainstream LGBT rights community.

Just as support of "marriage equality" has become a default position for liberal and progressive LGBT rights advocates, support for the UAFA seems a logical site for these same people. Major gay and lesbian rights organizations such as the Human Rights Campaign and the National Gay and Lesbian Task Force focus almost solely on the UAFA within their immigration platforms, and these groups undeniably have a large reach among LGBT audiences in the United States. In writing about queer migration, Nair addresses her rhetoric to this type of audience. She notes, "If we as a gay and lesbian community are to speak about immigration in any form, we need to understand the larger context in which such bills operate."[4] This audience resides in the ambiguous space of likely and unlikely ally. Such audiences are likely allies with Nair because they share her political interest in the same subjects, and yet they may be unlikely allies because of the different ways they approach their politics.

Although Nair is sympathetic to the situation of binational same-sex couples, she maintains that thinking of immigration outside the framework of economics—and in this instance within the framework of love and permanent partnership—is shortsighted. In the first place, marriage (or permanent partnership) is not a magical fix for anyone's immigration status problem. It does not work that way for straight people, nor will it work that way for gays and lesbians. Since the 1996 Illegal Immigration Reform and Immigrant Responsibility Act, using marriage to obtain immigration is an increasingly difficult path even for heterosexual married people who follow proper channels, and in most cases it provides essentially no recourse if the immigrant partner is currently undocumented. Furthermore, Nair questions why anyone should advocate for a law that helps only a relatively privileged few: documented immigrants who happen to be partners of US citizens or legal permanent residents. As should be clear from the brief discussion of "Family, Unvalued" in chapter 1, numerous resources and other forms of support from major national and international rights-based organizations as well as individual LGBT people have poured into UAFA advocacy. Moreover, because the UAFA deals with couples who have based their argument on the right to be with the one they love, it is a piece of legislation that can arouse a wide range of emotions. Nair struck that emotional chord at its core. Several responses from one of her primary audiences, those who advocate for the UAFA, flooded her blog entry's comments section. Many people vehemently disagreed and often used personal anecdotes from their own binational relationship to defend their positions. Early on, Nair responded carefully and sympathetically to each person, asking them to consider her argument and not respond simply from an emotional place. Soon the "flaming" of Nair got so bad that the site's editors shut down the comments. Commenters then took their critiques to their own blogs, including one written by an especially disgruntled man that he titled "Yasmin Nair: Eat this!"[5]

Nair has amassed a body of commentary, a series of coalitional moments that repeatedly bring queer and migrant issues into each other's folds. The positions that Nair has taken on the UAFA, the relationship between queer and migrant organizing, and the relationships between migration and queer issues in the public sphere reflect an unwavering commitment to an alternative imaginary of how queer and migration politics should be enacted. Nair's activist vision is oppositional. She directly opposes the political orientation and conditions of belonging set forth by the mainstream LGBT immigration rights community, which she suggests leaves most migrants out. Nair's vision opposes normative and inclusionary politics that implicitly or explicitly include only "good" people, that divide the oppressed from one another, or that succumb to the narrow agenda of the most powerful within marginalized communities. As a result of such positions, some critics have described her politics as unrealistic and utopian. I am arguing for an alternative interpretation. The positions Nair takes engender what I call the rhetoric of *radical interactionality*, an idea that builds on the women of color feminist notion of intersectionality. It is a form of rhetorical confrontation that begins critique from the roots of a problem or crisis and methodically reveals how systems of power and oppression interact with one another in ways that produce subjects, institutions, and ideologies and that enable and constrain political response. Nair's rhetoric often focuses on constructing arguments toward the achievement of legislative ends, but the legislative frame for the rhetoric does not compel Nair to make arguments based on political expedience as might be expected.

Instead, the legislative frame merely provides the exigency for the rhetoric of radical interactionality. Such rhetoric is in opposition to how debates about legislation often unfold, where the legislation is seen as an end in itself. In this instance a conversation about legislation opens into broader discussions about other, more radical possibilities for justice and change.

Radical interactionality shifts from viewing identities as discrete and suggests that the crux of any kind of oppression is multifaceted and complex. The possibilities reflected in these coalitional moments, then, are not the sorts that ask people to strategically coalesce around temporary or politically expedient issues. Nair invites her audience to read against the grain of oppression and to understand migration and queer issues more broadly. Nair's writing asks for people to come together at the roots of their interlocking oppression. As made clear in the above story, however, heightened emotionality often characterizes how Nair's gay and lesbian audience reads her work. As will become clear in the analysis below, large swaths of her audience read her as a polemicist, as insensitive, and as failing to understand their deeply personal situations. Aimee Carrillo Rowe maintains that within transracial alliances, a primary gift that women of color have to offer is their critique of power relations, yet most white allies are not interested in receiving the gift.[6] The LGBT people to whom Nair offers her critique do not want that gift either. In this chapter I analyze Nair's rhetoric of radical interactionality, as well as the audience responses to it, in order to reveal the possibilities and difficulties these coalitional moments create. I begin with a brief discussion of Nair and her work within the context of queer and migrant activism in the United States. I then elaborate on the notion of radical interactionality through an examination of Nair's blogs and online commentary found in several queer venues. I conclude with what Nair's rhetoric offers for thinking about radical coalitional politics.[7]

Yasmin Nair: Academic, Writer, Activist, Organizer

Within the study of the rhetoric of social movements, scholars have often attended to the rhetoric of prominent movement leaders such as Martin Luther King Jr., Malcolm X, Elizabeth Cady Stanton, and César Chávez.[8] This leader-centered model for social movement or mobilizing often neglects rhetorical practices of groups, organizers, or others deemed less noteworthy.[9] This is troubling because, as Tracy Baim writes in her introduction to *Out and Proud in Chicago*, "the work of thousands of gay activists has been lost because it was never documented."[10] Nair is not a leader in the sense that King and Chávez were leaders. Her work in Chicago since the early 2000s has centered on a host of social justice issues, including prison abolition, gentrification, antiwar, queer homelessness, and immigration. Her work has existed at least partially behind the scenes, in what might be called counter-public enclaves, where activists plan, regroup, and prepare.[11] Still, Nair's writing on queer migration has garnered her significant public attention within the queer migration world. For example, Marta Donayre, a well-known activist and a co-founder of Love Sees No Borders, which since 2001 has supported and advocated for binational same-sex couples, has defended and championed Nair's work, even as they disagree about the value of the UAFA.[12] Moreover, Nair helped to write the Queers for Economic Justice Vision Statement and was featured as an expert by QEJ during their national teleconference on queer migration.

I interviewed Nair in 2007 while completing my dissertation on queer and migrant activist coalition building in southern Arizona (see chapter 4). My committee member H.L.T. Quan, who had previously lived and worked in Chicago for several years, advised me that Nair was the leading expert on queer migration activism and that she would provide an important perspective on my findings from Arizona. From the initial interview and a follow-up conducted in 2011, I learned a bit more about Nair's activist trajectory and how she has come to the particular analysis that she currently holds, and throughout this chapter I use some remarks from those interviews to contextualize her writing. Nair is a self-described "bastard child of queer theory and deconstruction," and her work, while still beholden to the potentiality and importance of the queer critique, is more centrally materialist in its orientation.

Nair has worked in various capacities with grassroots organizations, including Queer to the Left; Chicago Lesbian, Gay, Bisexual, Transgender, Questioning, and Queer Immigrants Alliance (CLIA); Gender JUST (Gender Justice United for Societal Transformation); and Against Equality.[13] She found her first political home in Chicago with Queer to the Left, a now defunct group that describes itself as "a Chicago-based multi-racial group of lesbian, gay, bisexual, transgender, and queer people committed to working in coalition with queers and non-queers to promote economic, gender, racial, and sexual justice."[14] By early 2006 Nair left Queer to the Left and began volunteering for CLIA, which is where she developed her analysis of queer migration. CLIA started in fall 2005 as an initiative of several Chicago-based organizations, and in its 2006 "CLIA Manifesto" it describes itself as "a network of advocates committed to promoting dialogue and justice within and between queer and immigrant communities." Although starting prior to 2005, CLIA gained energy to promote its immigration agenda from the 2005 bill HR 4437, and as a progressive group CLIA committed to guiding principles, including the following:

- The dominant structures of labor and immigration policies are oppressive towards immigrants, particularly LGBTQ immigrants.
- Gender, race, ethnicity, language, sexuality, and national origin are particularly significant identities that influence the opportunities of LGBTQ immigrants.
- Queer individuals of privilege, members of both immigrant and non-immigrant communities, can benefit from examining critically the politics and ideologies surrounding LGBTQ immigrants.
- The effects of rampant globalization and an unfair economy that favors profits for a few and depresses the wages of the many have harmful effects upon local and international labor forces. To demand that Americans choose between immigrant and domestic labor is to posit a false choice. A more equitable solution is to demand better working conditions and a fair living for all and to call for ending the growth of unfair US economic policies worldwide.[15]

CLIA's principles reflect an analysis similar to Nair's analysis of immigration, but as she remembers, CLIA was not always as publicly progressive. She recalls her introduction to CLIA: "They sent a call out to attend this meeting, and they only talked about binational couples. And I remember that I sent an email that said these are the problems with that, and I figured they would just say, 'Yeah, fuck you.' Instead, she invited me to the meeting. So I basically went to the meeting, and I articulated my critique, and what's interesting is that it turned out there were a whole bunch of people in the room who had felt the same but hadn't thought they could even say that out loud."[16] From there CLIA wrote its manifesto. While the CLIA Manifesto is so named and shares a lot of the political analysis of those manifestos analyzed in chapter 1, it does not actually conform to most of the expected criteria of the manifesto form. Instead it provides an introduction to CLIA, including its history, principles, and projects. CLIA also organized three public forums on various issues related to labor, sexuality, gender, and immigration. Nair was central in organizing each of them. Eventually, she recalls, CLIA dissipated. She explains that she now does a lot of similar work with Gender JUST, which is "a multi-racial, multi-ethnic, and multi-generational grassroots organization of Lesbian, Gay, Bi-sexual, Transgender, Queer, and Allied (LGBTQA) young people, LGBTQA people of color, and LGBTQA grassroots folks developing leadership and building power through organizing."[17] Nair is the unpaid policy director, and Gender JUST emphasizes a number of interrelated issues, including economic justice, racial justice, reproductive justice, and prisoner solidarity. Gender JUST's work on immigration seems to extend directly from CLIA, as its guiding principles on immigration mirror those from CLIA's manifesto. The important issues and demands pertaining to immigration also reflect those outlined in the QEJ Vision Statement, further indicating Nair's fingerprint. Gender JUST holds regular forums, arts events, organizing meetings, development seminars, and direct actions on an array of justice issues. Nair is a regular speaker and organizer at these events.

Most recently, Nair has co-founded with Ryan Conrad Against Equality, which is an online archive and writers' collective that critiques mainstream LGBT politics and seeks to ignite the queer political imaginary. Members of the collective "are committed to dislodging the centrality of equality rhetoric and challenging the demand for inclusion in the institution of marriage, the US military, and the prison industrial complex via hate crimes legislation."[18] In 2010 they published their first book, *Against Equality: Queer Critiques of Gay Marriage*, an edited collection of previously published writings of thinkers speaking against gay marriage. In 2011 they published their second book, *Against Equality: Don't Ask to Fight Their Wars*, which challenged those advocating for an end to the "Don't Ask, Don't Tell" military policy since it supports expanding militarism. The third book, *Against Equality: Prisons Will Not Protect You,* was released in the fall of 2012 and offers a critique of hate crime legislation for expanding the prison industrial complex.[19] Conrad and Nair took the first book on a national tour during fall 2010 to spring 2011, and they have been interviewed by numerous outlets, including National Public Radio affiliates, local radio stations, university and local newspapers, blogs, and journals such as *We Who Feel Differently*. As a result of getting to know Nair after moving back to the Midwest and starting to write this chapter, and later, meeting Conrad, I joined *Against Equality* in late 2011. I am now a collective member, and I write, give presentations, and do other forms of unpaid labor on behalf of the collective.[20]

In addition to taking part in grassroots organizing and activism, and as stated above, Nair has engaged in much activism in the blogosphere. "Cyberactivism" is hotly contested, as critics question whether activism on the Internet amounts to anything more than "slacktivism."[21] Others note the gendered nature of blogging, because men dominate the subgenre of political blogs.[22] Still, blogs are a participatory genre, and they have great potential to connect individuals and communities who might otherwise never interact. Robert Glenn Howard discusses the potential for agency and social change within the "vernacular web," his name for "this technology-dependent but other-than-institutional process of dynamically interconnecting discursive activity."[23] Vernacular expression challenges the power of institutions, and because of the at least theoretical openness of the web, more people potentially have access to it and can find an audience for their voices. As Barbara Warnick maintains, "A good deal of vibrant and effective public discourse in the forms of social activism and resistance occur online . . . such discourse has had noticeable effects on society"[24] Optimism does not erase the potential downsides to Internet activism, yet Merlyna Lim argues that in the contemporary era online and offline activism often go hand in hand.[25] Furthermore, whether scholars and critics champion or bemoan political participation through social media, the fact is that people in places like the United States increasingly use the Internet for political expression and information seeking.[26] Blogs, then, are important sites for analysis, and in Nair's case she uses her blog to publicly outline her political vision. In the next section I outline the concept of radical interactionality, which I then use to make sense of Nair's queer migration rhetoric as found in essays and blog entries she has written.

Radical Interactionality

Pundits, scholars, and activists often use the term "radical" synonymously with "revolutionary" and "extremist" and regularly do not define it very clearly.[27] James Klumpp describes "radicalization" as "the process of *identifying* the individual ideologically and actively with the radical movement, the radical leadership, and the radical interpretation of the situation."[28] Since in this statement he is writing about the 1968 student takeovers of Columbia University, Klumpp presumably understands the "radical interpretation" as profoundly antiestablishment and, at least nominally, revolutionary. James Darsey also associates radicalism with extremism and revolution, but he argues that radicalism "is defined by its concern with the political roots of a society, its fundamental laws, its foundational principles, its most sacred covenants. It is common for radicals to claim to be the true keepers of the faith; they oppose their society using its own most noble expressions and aspirations."[29] Darsey argues that much of the radical rhetoric in the United States stems from prophetic religious discourse, so rather than subverting or revolting against a society, radicals actually seek to recover the roots of their society. This idea resembles Robert L. Scott's depiction of the conservative impulse in radical rhetoric. Though not wanting to reduce radical rhetoric to this conservative voice, Scott claims that radicals will often claim that they more purely hold on to a given value than the hypocritical establishment does. This charge of hypocrisy comes only from suffering and division, but it utilizes the same logic of the conservative establishment by simply reversing the hierarchy.[30] Hannah Arendt, in her historical discussion of the term "revolution," notes that original uses of this term in both the American and French Revolutions did not see revolutions as starting something new, but as restoration projects.[31]

In these instances, "radical" and "revolutionary" refer to fundamentalism and purity, which positions radical rhetoric as being similar to the sorts of rhetoric it ostensibly seeks to oppose. Radicalism, in this sense, is not well suited for coalitional politics, because any political approach that insists on purity and fundamentalism, even that which is an active revolt against a current system, remains dogmatic.

Morgan Bassichis, Alexander Lee, and Dean Spade paint a somewhat different picture of radical organizing, noting that it seeks to "expand possibilities for broad-based, social justice solutions."[32] Howard Zinn put the matter simply in his play *Marx in Soho*: "to be radical is simply to grasp the root of a problem."[33] Drawing on Zinn's definition, performance studies scholar D. Soyini Madison describes a radical act as "a confrontation with the 'root' of a problem. It is to reach for the causes of an issue and not simply respond to its symptoms. It is a showdown with limitations to embrace necessary excess and to disturb a state of affairs in pursuit of confronting those root causes."[34] The word "radical" extends from the Latin *radicalis*, which pertains to "relating to or forming the root."[35] Arguably, finding "root" causes is very similar to the association of radical with fundamentalism and purity because a root may also be a fundamental or an origin. To understand the fundamental or root of a problem is not the same as promoting fundamentalism. Moreover, in some instances the metaphor of a root also refers to a rhizome, a horizontal root mass that produces new roots and shoots that can be severed and started anew.[36] As Gilles Deleuze and Félix Guattari have argued in their extension of the botanical metaphor to theory, a rhizome turns away from purity and instead highlights multiplicity—or in this case the complexity—of a problem or situation.[37] Heading too far in the direction of Deleuze and Guattari is not my interest here, except to illuminate the fact that a root is not synonymous with purity or reductionism. A radical act, then, addresses or confronts roots in their multiplicity and complexity.

I seek to conjoin this idea of radical critique with a framework that is equipped for addressing the complexity of a problem's roots, and what results I name *radical interactionality*. In the realm of social justice, the framework of intersectionality has been advanced to understand the complicated interworking of power that constitutes the situation of people who experience interlocking oppressions.[38] Intersectionality invites an understanding of how multiple oppressions (and privileges) deriving from systems such as race, class, gender, sexuality, and nation intermesh so that the experience of being a queer, working-class woman of color in the United States differs very much from being a queer, working-class white woman or any number of other women. Intersectionality works against reductionism and purity, promoting instead a perspective that accounts for the "differences that make a difference" in how people can maneuver their worlds.[39] And as David L. Eng writes, we must "insist on new approaches to intersectionality in queer studies."[40] Intersectionality has been popularized in the academy to describe the complexity of power, oppression, and identity, but it has also been critiqued for fixing the very identities and power systems it seeks to subvert and overturn.[41] Jasbir K. Puar, for instance, advises moving from intersectionality to Deleuze and Guattari's notion of the assemblage. An assemblage is a conglomeration of multiplicities, "a series of dispersed but mutually implicated and messy networks, [that] draws together enunciation and dissolution, causality and effect, organic and nonorganic forces."[42] In this way the assemblage accounts for "other contingencies of belonging" that the identity politics framework, which is allegedly upheld through intersectionality, may not account for. The assemblage emphasizes movement, flow, and affectivities. Drawing on Brian Massumi, who maintains that the notion of "positionality" suggests a "positioning on a grid,"[43] Puar suggests that intersectionality is "a hermeneutic of *positionality* that seeks to account for locality, specificity, placement, junctions."[44]

On the one hand, Puar's critique of intersectionality is unnecessarily reductionistic and builds a binary between intersectionality and the assemblage. Many intersectional theorists show specificity of oppression without essentializing identity. Kimberle Crenshaw's analysis of the erasure of women of color within political, structural, and representational realms demonstrates the particular ways that these women's experiences are negated without fixing the women or any others into such positions.[45] In a move that is similar to postmodern theorists before her, Puar uses the postmodern writing of European male theorists to critique the "theory in the flesh" of women of color theorists, which functions to simplify and negate women of color theorizing while remaining distant from the actual lived experiences of oppressed people. On the other hand, Puar and Massumi highlight the difficulty of the metaphor of intersectionality that at least implies a grid and a fixed position upon it. Puar further advocates keeping the assemblage and intersectionality in tension, and one way to do this is through *interactionality*.

Building on intersectionality, interactionality moves away from the linear metaphor and highlights the complicated and dynamic way in which identities, power, and systems of oppression intermesh, interlock, intersect, and thus interact.[46] Interactionality addresses both the mobility and complexity of bodily experience but does not negate the lived experience of oppression through seemingly fixed identities and positions within systems of power. As a resistant logic of impurity and multiplicity,[47] interactionality holds in tension both the predictable ways oppression and power manifest in relation to and upon particular bodies while also carrying possibilities for creative and complicated responses to oppression.[48] To illustrate, in a blog entry critiquing the "undocuqueer" movement—a group of young, undocumented, and queer migration rights activists who urge "coming out" as undocumented (see also chapter 3)—Nair remarks, "It is not radical to claim that the undocumented are not illegal. In fact, that is a deeply conservative point. It is far more radical to think about all of us taking on the onus of interrogating the notion of the 'illegal.' Do we, as people who believe in justice and fairness, want to leave anyone behind?"[49] In this controversial critique, Nair reveals how the rhetoric of radical interactionality addresses the complex roots of a problem without reducing experiences of oppression to fixed identities. Nair goes on to say, "When immigration becomes a matter of a declarative identity, we stop seeing and dismantling the systems we have to fight." Such rhetoric also acknowledges how systems of oppression interact in both predictable and surprising ways. In this instance Nair works against conventional wisdom on the left, which has pushed everyone to use the label "undocumented" instead of "illegal" to describe migrants who are in civil violation of immigration law. Nair claims that making "undocumented" an identity and disconnecting the problems of immigration from the system that deems some people illegal misses the roots of the issue. Her radical interactional alternative is a mode of resistance that responds through both structural critique and logics of creativity and multiplicity.

Radical interactionality is an important rhetorical resource for queer politics. As black queer materialist scholar Cathy J. Cohen writes, "It is the multiplicity and interconnectedness of our identities which provide the most promising avenue for the *destabilization and radical politicalization* of these same categories. This is not an easy path to pursue because most often this will mean building a political analysis and political strategies around the most marginal in our society, some of whom look like us, many of whom do not."[50] Cohen presumably addresses an audience of privileged queer people who may find comfort in the categories that will need to be destabilized. The radical interventions she calls for require coalition building among different and differently positioned people. The perspective engendered by such strategies must make "central the interdependency among multiple systems of domination. Such a perspective also ensures that while activists should rightly be concerned with forms of discursive and cultural coercion, we also recognize and confront the more direct and concrete forms of exploitation and violence rooted in state-regulated institutions and economic systems."[51] Importantly, then, this vision bridges between discursive and material approaches to ending oppression, recognizing both as sources that deserve attention.

Nair's rhetoric of radical interactionality integrates the kind of approach Cohen outlines and seeks to offer an alternative, oppositional vision or paradigm for queer migration activism. Her rhetoric engenders three primary characteristics: a critique of neoliberal affect and the use of personal narrative, a strategic blending of the queer and the migrant worker, and a denouncement of the ways nonprofit organizations dictate the "gay" agenda and squelch dissent from within the LGBTQ community.

THE PROBLEMS OF PERSONAL NARRATIVE

For Nair, the root of contemporary oppression of migrants, queers, and others is neoliberal capitalism and how it economically functions and becomes culturally and politically naturalized.[52] Consequently, one of her primary concerns is how labor becomes erased from both a queer and a queer migration agenda as groups instead choose to emphasize good stories as a means to achieve political ends. Because we are, in Nair's words, "all neoliberals now," left-leaning politics tends to adhere "to a sentimental and nostalgic view of the Other [that] is deeply embedded in a politics of abjection and rescue."[53] Such logic is not unique to neoliberalism or new to leftist politics. Bassichis, Lee, and Spade write, "Oppressive dynamics in the United States are as old as the colonization of this land and the founding of a country based on slavery and genocide. However, they have taken intensified, tricky forms in the past few decades—particularly because our governments keep telling us those institutions and practices have been 'abolished.'"[54] To Nair, one such "tricky form," is neoliberalism's reduction of politics to the intimate and private, an argument akin to Lauren Berlant's notion of the "intimate public sphere."[55] Within this logic, if people feel bad for someone whose situation is so terrible that they need to be rescued from it, then those people are more likely to take action. This function of narrative is long-standing. Perhaps the difference within neoliberalism is that the personal narrative and affect in the form of "feeling good" about helping an individual in a bad situation stand in place of a critique of the labor conditions and capitalist expansion that have created the bad conditions in the first place. If a feel-good story about someone's terrible personal plight can be told to persuade lawmakers to change laws that oppress people because of an identity they possess, it is a much easier strategy than offering a systemic and abstract critique of issues that would require much more radical change. Moreover, such a strategy tries to construct all who share that position as "good" and deserving of help.

A primary function of neoliberalism is to privatize financial and governmental structures,[56] which results in slashing public services and organized labor in the name of individual freedom. This has devastating material impacts on working and poor people, who are disproportionately women and people of color. The pain privatization causes has to be blunted through affective or emotional means. Nair explains that "to dull and distract from the pain of privatization, we need to feel good about ourselves as human beings and as creatures of identity, people with stories."[57] If people can relate to others, feel their plights as shared, and also feel affirmed in their identities, it makes it easier to deal with the material devastations of neoliberal privatization. The affective dulling offered through story sharing is especially devastating for immigration politics. Framing immigration as a crisis, as opposed to, say, an economic reality, creates space for the dehumanization of those who supposedly cause the crisis. In order to confront this situation, those on the political left rely on compelling stories about "good" migrants.

The need to confront dehumanization also explains why appeals to family and family reunification are so strong, because, as Nair puts it, the logic is that "the plight of the undocumented would best be alleviated if their families were allowed to join them here," and families should not be torn apart.[58] Keeping loved ones together who desire to stay together is a powerful and important goal, yet as shown in the last chapter, this rhetoric can be highly problematic. Fundamental to Nair is that the appeal to the family erases the reality that many families are not hospitable to queers or that family situations generally can be inhospitable for all of their members because of various kinds of abuse. Such rhetoric also "erases the labor issues that are integral to how families work within their adopted neighborhoods and cities." Families are not mere affective units bound by love. Instead, paid and unpaid family members often serve as the primary labor source for migrant-run business, for instance, and this is an economic consideration more than an affective one.

Moreover, such familial rhetoric often erases the migrants whose experience involves sex work, perhaps to support their family or as an only means to escape their family. Nair wonders if it is "even possible to 'tell a different story.'"[59] Writing about a forum hosted by CLIA that addressed the complicated intersections between sexuality, gender, labor, and migration issues, Nair notes that one panelist, Jessica Acee, offered a key reminder: "There can be no neat divisions between the kinds of labor performed by immigrants, and we benefit from a renewed focus on labor and its connection to issues of gender and sexuality."[60] Nair concludes, "A queer immigration reform agenda which centralizes labor has less to do with locating actual queers and narratives and more to do with the particular analytic and activist lens that's possible within a queer framework."[61] A queer framework attends specifically to gender and sexuality, but emphasizing labor decenters queer identity and narrative. This framework links differing material conditions and oppressions to sexual and gender logics. For instance, a migrant trans sex worker likely experiences unique kinds of oppression as a laborer compared to other laborers. Their situation highlights much about the way sexuality and gender interact with labor and migration to affect people's possibility for a livable life.[62] Utilizing such a framework does not make Nair anti-narrative; instead, she says, "Personal stories can help to make systemic conditions more easily understood. But is there a way to use them without buying into pathos and abjection?"[63] As is clear, Nair views capitalist exploitation as the root of oppression. She also sees that an analysis of capitalism—and in this historical period, neoliberal capitalism—necessitates an approach that concurrently attends to gender and sexuality. Yet gender and sexuality politics have too often relied only on narrative strategies and their accompanying "pathos and abjection," which distracts from capitalist exploitation and seeks to normalize and make respectable certain identity groups. In part, Nair seeks a new, more radical story.

Nair also seeks a turn to abstraction. She explained to me that she is interested in writing an essay called "The Importance of Being Abstract," a riff on Oscar Wilde's famous play *The Importance of Being Earnest*. The call for abstraction could easily be taken as a guise for another call to masculine rationality. The point of the essay, Nair claims, would be to center on issues that are fundamentally problematic regardless of whether someone feels personally connected to or impacted by them. To Nair, oppression and injustice in the abstract sense should be enough to compel to action, or at the very least they should be the foundation for creating arguments for or against a position. Without abstraction it is easy to get lost in the details of a personal situation that may or may not have relevance to the broader issue at hand. Critiquing the commonsense feminist adage "the personal is political," Nair told me, "I think the whole personal is political, that formulation of the personal as political was useful at its time, and I think in some ways it can still be critically useful, but now the personal has become the neoliberal. So I think neoliberalism now has learned how to use that formulation . . . I think the political is political. And I'm tired of this idea. I think what that has become now is, for instance, an issue of dueling stories. Whose story can be more melodramatically effective?"[64]

At least in part, Nair's analysis reflects a type of Marxist tension between structure and agency that insists that achieving liberation is a matter of changing deep structural conditions as opposed to enacting individual (or even some forms of collective) agency. In suggesting that the personal has been reduced to the neoliberal, Nair issues a sweeping and normative claim about the realm of the political, one that may be off-putting to some people. This claim also functions as a profound warning about the co-optation of stories to achieve ends that the subjects of those stories may not actually desire (e.g., maintaining capitalist exploitation of some people under the guise of achieving equality for others). At times Nair seems to negate the value of the human component to movement, which for many is what compels involvement. Furthermore, the idea of persuading people by using a plea to abstraction is somewhat utopian, given the power of stories generally and the profound role that emotions and affect play in all of our lives, including in activism. As Deborah Gould writes in her book about the role of emotion in AIDS activism, "The *movement* in 'social movements' gestures toward the realm of affect; bodily intensities; emotions, feelings, and passions; and toward uprising."[65] Here, Gould remarks upon the undeniable role that emotion plays in political life and maintains the importance of thinking through emotional processes. Nair's oppositional vision may err too much on the side of being anti-affective, but she provides an important counterpoint to the predominant narrative strategy. And in this way her vision also resonates with Chela Sandoval's claim about differential consciousness providing an alternative narrative for counter-hegemonic struggles.[66]

One way to see how Nair enacts this aspect of her vision is by examining the way she crafts her arguments about queer migration in her blog entries, specifically as she offers critiques of the UAFA and the centrality of binational same-sex couples. As I mentioned at the start of this chapter, Nair tries to offer sympathy to those in binational couples who responded to her *Queercents* blog entry. At the same time, her radical interactional rhetoric is oppositional, and she refuses to attend to issues outside of what she has identified as the roots of the problem. Nair begins with the situation of Shirley Tan and Jay Mercado that I discussed in chapter 1. The couple's situation and the use of their story illuminate precisely the point Nair wants to make about the function of narrative and affect. Nair cites a quotation from Rachel Tiven, the executive director of Immigration Equality, who said of the family, "They are exactly the kind of people you want living in this country."[67] Nair argues that Tiven's quotation implies that there are many other kinds of people you *do not* want living in this country: "the day laborers who move from job to job, underpaid and overexploited; the low-paid workers who build suburban houses for us on the cheap as opposed to living in them."[68] In other words, galvanizing around Tan and Mercado's story serves to obfuscate the reality of many migrants, including queer ones, who would not be served or helped by the narrow agenda of the UAFA.

Nair goes on to explain the many kinds of situations that the UAFA ignores and the myriad dilemmas it would seem to remedy but in actuality would not. For example, sponsorship through heterosexual marriage or engagement requires the sponsoring partner to have enough financial resources to adequately care for their partner so that the person does not become a public charge. The UAFA is no different. Similarly, heterosexual couples must show "financial interdependence," and the same would be true for same-sex couples. This sets up the dependent partner for potential exploitation and abuse, which has appeared in numerous cases within married couples and resulted in the 1994 passage of the Violence Against Women Act (VAWA). VAWA allows abused dependent spouses or minor children to self-petition for a green card without informing their abusive sponsor.[69] Nair asks, "Is this the kind of situation feminist queers fought for? Do we seriously believe that the pure love between gay and lesbian couples makes it impossible for such abuse to occur?"[70] This question—which several responders heard as an insensitive critique of the strength of their love— is designed to highlight the problems with galvanizing politics around one "good story." Nair's rhetoric does not attack Tan and Mercado or any other couple. In fact, Nair ends this particular post by saying, "So, go ahead and protest for Shirley Tan and others like her. But if you can't or won't protest on behalf of the millions of others who don't fit the cozy and unrealistic idea of 'family' as well, don't protest at all."[71] This comment insists that the coalition suggested by queer migration politics is more expansive than others seem to assume. She further notes that both relying on and rallying around one story may put some people in a position of defending ideals that they may actually oppose, such as promoting the conditions for relational abuse and coercion. In other words, Nair calls on people to consider with whom and with what politics they actually coalesce.

Some people in Nair's audience do not heed this call. To explain her critique of personal narrative and affect more fully, I show how Nair responds to two kinds of personal/affective responses from readers of her blog: first, some readers attempt to refute Nair with an argument that claims "love is all we need"; second, some readers resort to personally attacking Nair and making assumptions about her personal narrative. In responding to each kind of personal/affective response, Nair enacts a radical interactional rhetoric to try to return readers to the issues, not to focus on individuals or emotions.

"LOVE IS ALL WE NEED." The first kind of personal/emotional response Nair receives involves the individual story that makes an argument based on the premise that "love is all we need." As Sara Ahmed has similarly questioned in a different context, "What are we doing when we do something *in the name of love*?"[72] Such arguments that draw on the emotion of love attempt to privilege the emotional over the political. Nair uses such responses to help illuminate her points about the UAFA, the failures of personal narrative, and the function of affect. For example, one responder to the *Queercents* post, Angela, replies with a series of quotations taken from Nair's article and then responds to them based on her own relationship and experience. Angela writes:

"Do you really think your love would be enough?" [quoting Nair]

So you are saying it is not enough? It is not enough to love my partner from Berlin Germany and want to spend my life with her? I need something else? We both work hard for a living, lady. We're not rich people looking for handouts (bailouts). We just want to be together finally after 2 and half [*sic*] years. I have to carry the weight of all of the problems with the immigration system that I did not create in order for it to be more noble to want to be with her?[73]

Nair begins her response to Angela by assuring her that she is sympathetic to her situation, but she then returns to what she has delineated as the issues and arguments at hand. She writes, "My question, 'Did you really think your love would be enough?' was intended to make people who've been given hope by UAFA realise that it probably won't solve their problems."[74] Later, Nair further strikes at what she sees as the root of the problem and the trouble with reducing the entire situation to a matter of love. She does this through strategic use of an illustrative anecdote. Nair writes, "I once had someone with a disabled foreign partner and no insurance scream, in a comment, that their being together would solve all his problems. To which I responded: and you'll get your partner here, and then what? Two people without health insurance, in a state that will monitor your relationship and not give a damn about the myriad issues that face people in your situation?" In this comment Nair uses an anecdote that may resonate with Angela in order to turn attention back to the economic context and the health care problems in the United States, which are the realities obfuscated by both individual stories of hardship and "love is all we need" arguments. Nair's use of the anecdote also encourages Angela and others to see it as an invitation to build radical coalitions around concerns that more people face.

When confronted with an argument based on love, Nair uses this as an opportunity to identify the many other dimensions that interact with a couple's relationship, including country of origin, race, ability, and, of course, economics. In reply to an anonymous commenter who describes her partner's decision to live in the United Kingdom so that they can be together as living in "exile,"[75] Nair explains that "exile" is the wrong word to use in the situation, and then she notes:

Okay, people, from here on—if you have a personal situation, feel free to share it. But I can't and won't be responding to your individual stories (unless it connects to some kind of political point). The point I've made is simple: people in these situations deserve sympathy, but this critique is not about individual cases, it's about asking us to take a closer look at the law and understand that it is a) ineffective for many people [and] b) unsatisfactory as law because of its excessive privileging of some people over others.

> Please remember that for every case of a binational couple kept apart, there
> are probably ten who are kept apart for reasons other than their relationships.[76]

Nair highlights the flaws in this piece of legislation and what the personal discussion obscures. As this example also demonstrates, some commenters on the
blog are trying to make political points, but Nair interprets them as personal.
For instance, many people who advocate for binational same-sex couples use
the politically charged word "exile" to describe their situation of living in countries other than their country of citizenship or choice in order to be with their
partner. Because they are not forced in the sense that is usually understood to
refer to exile, Nair dismisses those who use the word, charging them with attempting to exaggerate their personal situation for political gain. This charge
has merit and also reveals Nair's unwavering focus on what she has determined
as the core or root concerns and the parameters of the political. Avoiding engagement with the personal details of a story unless she can use it to illustrate
a political point both steers the focus toward the issues and leads many readers
to assume Nair is insensitive or irrational. The frustration that this creates for
some readers can lead to a second personal/affective response, which involves
personally critiquing Nair and assuming facts about her narrative.

PERSONAL ATTACKS.   Some people simply try to diminish Nair by positioning her as misguided, others directly attack her, and some people have taken
their critiques of Nair to their blogs. As mentioned at the start of this chapter,
one responder in a binational relationship, whom Nair suggested use his own
blog because of his profuse comments, titled his entry "Yasmin Nair: Eat this!"[77]
Another appears on the blog *Lavender Newswire*.[78] Both accuse Nair of parroting
right-wing rhetoric, a common critique of Nair's analyses. Both of these authors
comment on Nair's self-description as "a queer lesbian who loves cock," and
one accuses her of having "internalized biphobia." In addition to attempting to
discredit Nair based on her sexual choices and self-identifiers, these two entries describe Nair and her work as "mean-spirited," "baseless," "insensitive,"
"senseless," and "stupid." And in a postscript on *Lavender Newswire*, the author,
who also identifies as having been in a binational relationship, writes, "May
you fall madly, hopelessly, eternally, and inextricably in love with a woman in
Iraq, or China, or Vanuatu. And that, Ms. Nair, is not a blessing, but a *curse*."[79]
This is similar to another anonymous responder who declares:

> I'm wondering what's making you so naive and unsympathetic to the people
> posting here—who's [sic] lives would be unbelievably changed by this piece of
> legislation?

Karma is a funny thing—just hope you don't fall for some nice Polish woman next week!!! and like me spend the next ten years wondering how, what, when?[80]

Each of these personal and emotional responses to Nair makes assumptions about her, ranging from challenging the authenticity of her queer identity to questioning the legitimacy of her leftist politics. Two of these posts that express the wish of a binational relationship upon her also assume that she is a US citizen or legal permanent resident. Outside of the initial *Queercents* comments, Nair also posted an entry on the *Bilerico Project* blog to talk about the ways supporters of the UAFA responded to her.[81] Although she calls attention to some of the misogyny present in questioning her sexual practices, the problems with the personal tenor of the critiques, and the nature of responding and writing on blogs, she does not challenge any of the personal attacks by offering her own personal narrative. Nair has extensive personal experience with several aspects related to the immigration system and queer negotiations of it, but she uses none of her own story as part of her argument. While in her blog post Nair used snippets from others' stories to illustrate broader political points, she refuses use of her own personal narrative so as not to reduce abstract arguments to her individual case. She avoids using her own story as the basis for an abstract critique in the same way that she denies others' stories. Ultimately she seeks to build coalition around abstract notions of justice and fairness for many people, not select couples with the right story. Women of color feminist writing on the subject of interlocking oppressions originated from a space of identity politics that involved using people's personal experiences and stories to highlight the root of oppression.[82] In neoliberalism, where Nair argues the personal has been co-opted, the queer left needs a new strategy to confront the roots of problems. In this way her radical interactional rhetoric reduces the salience of the personal and affective because people's experiences, in the case of queer migration and the UAFA, work to distract from the radical critique, for it is from that place that the richest coalitional possibility resides.

Nair's coalitional rhetoric differs widely from the way coalition has often been theorized by feminists as something personal or at least interpersonal. She offers an alternative vision of coalition building that accounts for the neoliberal conditions of the contemporary moment. This vision suggests that it is only from interrogating the roots of problems that meaningful coalition is possible. It may seem that Nair is not feminist or coalitional, or that her rhetoric isolates one of her main audiences: other people committed to LGBTQ immigration rights. Although her rhetoric may isolate some people, when looked at from the perspective of the demands and confines of neoliberalism it becomes clear that her rhetoric is coalitional in that it seeks to change the boundaries and conditions of belonging in a way that accounts for interlocking and intermeshing systems of oppression. Rather than advocating only for those with whom one has an affective bond or based on one's emotions, Nair's charge involves building relationships and connections with others and others' struggles for a radical vision of social justice. Given that many in her audience are unwilling or unable to heed this charge, the coalitional possibility may never leave the realm of the abstract. This critique of affect and personal narrative works alongside the second characteristic of the rhetoric of Nair's vision: to strategically blend the queer and the migrant worker to show the interactional nature of shared oppression and to promote a space for radical coalitional politics.

BLENDING THE QUEER AND MIGRANT WORKER

The second dimension of Nair's rhetoric builds upon the critique of the personal story and suggests that not only should those on the left be wary of the use of stories but also that we all should be cognizant of the specific ways queer and gay identities become naturalized. Nair claims that "to be gay in America is to be a separate class identity," which is largely understood as middle to upper class, and this erases the existence of poorer gays and lesbians.[83] Furthermore, in this manner of thinking, identity is separated from being a worker in such a way that "your identity as part of a social and cultural group will be protected more readily than your rights as a worker."[84] For example, the HRC Corporate Equality Index, which annually rates corporations for their LGBT-friendly policies, often highly rates corporations that have good LGBT policies like domestic partner benefits and antidiscrimination clauses even if they simultaneously engage in union busting or manufacture products that enhance border militarization, which hurts migrants and workers of all genders and sexual orientations.[85] The implications of this bifurcation between gay identity and being a worker are especially stark for migrants because it is easier "to think of immigrants as persons with stories—not as workers."[86] This emphasis on identity has created a profound disparity in the approach between LGBTQ groups who fight for immigration rights and the immigrant rights and justice community. The former has focused on binational couples, lifting the ban on migration of HIV-positive people, and the possibility to achieve political asylum on the basis of sexual orientation and gender identity. The latter is primarily focused on issues like jobs, deportation, raids, education, harassment by law enforcement, and "no-match letters" after social security numbers fail to match using the government's E-Verify program. Nair asks, "Why does it seem like queer immigrants have nothing in common with immigrants?"[87]

Nair works this question into a series of critiques of the foci of those LGBTQ groups who support queer migrant rights. In discussing asylum, for example, she echoes the same critiques we heard in many of the manifestos in chapter 1: "While it's compassionate to insist that queers need refuge in the West on account of the persecution they face, it's short-sighted to assume that asylum is the perfect solution." Nair then adds to the analysis a particular focus on coalition among people who are oppressed for a host of reasons, noting, "What concerns me is that we rush to paint all those other countries as universally hostile to queers without understanding the larger contexts in which that violence is bred . . . Do we understand the lives of persecuted queers alongside the lives of non-queers who are brutalized, physically and economically, but have no recourse to asylum?"[88] Many queer migration advocates have tirelessly worked to include gender identity and sexual orientation in national and international law as categories for which one can be persecuted and ask for political asylum.[89] Like QEJ, the ALP, and HAVOQ, Nair does not deny the importance of this work. She also challenges the emphasis on queers alone both because of the ways certain countries get imagined and then fixed as homophobic and transphobic and because of the potential erasure of the economic exploitation of queers and non-queers alike. She adds, "We ignore the economic and political circumstances surrounding anti-gay violence and persecution. For the most part, the most horrendous (reported) situations occur in countries in the global south whose economies have been wrecked by the neoliberal machinations of the developed world."[90] Even though various queer identities have increasingly become grounds for gaining asylum around the world, economic persecution remains outside the purview of asylum law. The failure to count the economic as the political prevents many people from poor countries who seek asylum from obtaining it since it is assumed they are simply seeking economic, not political, refuge. Within this dimension of immigration law, if queers are separated out from other economically oppressed people as a political group, and if many of the countries that queers name as hostile are also poor, queers become further distanced from workers generally and from migrant workers specifically. For this reason, Nair insists to queer citizens who want to ally with migrants, "We have no right to take on the cause of immigration without understanding the issues faced by immigrants themselves."[91]

Similarly, in writing about the problems with the now-ended ban on immigrants with HIV, and particularly its impact on undocumented people, Nair notes:

> There's another economic cost that comes with the creation of this group: people in such vulnerable situations, who are afraid of being outed as HIV-positive, as undocumented and, possibly, as gay/lesbian, are also among the most vulnerable

workers in the sprawling informal/shadow economy. They are most likely to end up with highly exploitative bosses. Even if not faced with unscrupulous employers, they're not able to overtly resist exploitative labor conditions and unfair wages. None of this is good for labor organizing, for undocumented immigrants, or for our cities and towns in general.[92]

Nair's concern with lifting the ban does not pertain to HIV-positive people as a queer identity group, which is sometimes how people made arguments against the ban. For example, identity largely created the ground for arguments made in the early 1990s when the US government debated whether to make an exception to the ban for HIV-positive people who wanted to visit the United States in order to participate in events such as the 1994 "Gay Games" in New York.[93] Contrary to this identity-based argument that sought to lift the ban for leisure purposes, Nair's concern is exploitation. She suggests that having HIV, especially if it exists in conjunction with being gay or undocumented, opens people to the immense possibility of exploitation. There should be no ban on HIV-positive people migrating because of the vulnerability it creates for them as workers.

Nair's radical interactional rhetoric then engages in a closing of the lacuna between queers and migrants in a way that focuses on queer migrants as unique subjects and also constructs identification (as opposed to identity) among workers. Simply put, Nair says, "I'm asking people to look at UAFA in more inclusive and contextualised terms than as just something that affects couples. I'm also asking readers to consider the arbitrary divisions we keep drawing between 'gay' and 'immigrant.' In my work with immigration rights activists, I consistently ask people to consider that immigrants are also queer/gay/lesbian. Here in a queer space, I'm asking people to consider that gays are also immigrants."[94]

In arguing for a strategic blending of the queer and migrant worker, Nair does not argue that being gay is just like being undocumented. She maintains that centering on the material realities of workers, some of whom are undocumented and queer, helps to consider how multiple dimensions of power interact to constitute the possibilities for belonging and viability. Furthermore, she criticizes a collapse of queers/migrants that ignores important differences between the material realities of many queers and migrants. In a strong critique of gay rights groups at the 2008 May Day march in Chicago, Nair notes:

> Somehow, the rights of the undocumented have become conflated with the "marriage rights/gay couples matter more than others" movement. Queer organizers insisted that their situation—as queers whose relationships aren't recognized by the state (because, apparently, only marriage can legitimize a relation-

ship)—was equal to that of the undocumented. Never mind the fact that none of them faced the harrowing issues of the undocumented.

That willingness to usurp any cause in order to further a narrow agenda is typical of those who've militantly organized over gay marriage over the last decade or so. We've allowed the loudest among us to pretend that queerness is somehow separable from the issues that affect us. We have labored over the delusion that queer love and attachment matter more than the central issue of labor—which literally organizes our daily lives.[95]

Statements such as these are certainly not without controversy because using words like "delusional" to describe the politics of many LGBT activists is provocative if not offensive. Nair's words often provoke strong response from those who feel indicted by the critique. For example, the Gay Liberation Network in Chicago, a part of the LGBT contingent at the May Day march, issued a stout response to this critique. The group argued that it does not think marriage is the only issue; rather, it has said that marriage is "the single most widespread example of legal inequality affecting LGBT people, and that addressing this inequality would give material benefits of particular importance to working class LGBT people such as health care insurance, pension and social security survivors benefits."[96] Nair has commented elsewhere on what she sees as the flaws in this logic: it assumes that people have these benefits in the first place, and it creates a system of dependency that is potentially exploitative. And she was not off the mark in her representation of the LGBT contingent's position on legality. Their publicity for the event revealed they were suggesting that being gay when sodomy was illegal is equivalent to being undocumented. The publicity, written for an LGBT audience, remarked, "It wasn't too many years ago that gays were considered 'illegal'—until the *Lawrence v. Texas* Supreme Court decision 'legalized' us."[97]

Nair has further challenged this kind of conflation between queers and migrants in a provocative analysis of American Apparel's "Legalize Gay" T-shirts, put out in 2009 to encourage the repeal of California's Proposition 8. Although the "Legalize Gay" shirts were very popular around the United States, Nair highlights an important history preceding the shirts, one that is likely less known to their wearers outside of the Los Angeles area. "Legalize Gay" was a play on an earlier shirt and campaign called "Legalize L.A.," which Nair describes as the clothing company's attempt to market itself as "an immigrants-rights-friendly entity."[98] Nair challenges the seeming parallel between the two shirts, asking, "Who, in the wake of Prop 8, is illegal for being gay?" She claims that those who are actually deemed illegal—migrants and prisoners—are "effectively erased by this t-shirt," which "allows the wearer to smugly pose as 'illegal' while cluelessly erasing the reality that millions *are* actually illegal in the terms dictated by draconian laws around immigration and the prison industrial complex."[99] The "wearer" of the "Legalize Gay" T-shirt, which at the time of this writing is available through American Apparel's online store for $17 plus $5 shipping and handling, is likely a middle-class person who can afford this luxury.[100] Such a situation is very different from the conditions of illegality Nair describes. This collapsing of the queer and migrant reduces migrants and queers to individuals with singular identities who are oppressed because of those identities. On the other hand, Nair's blending, which resembles the "gray politics" found in the queer migration manifestos since it refuses binaries and boundaries, suggests that queers and migrants are workers enmeshed in complex and oppressive systems and that this identification should create the foundations for solidarity, coalition work, and alternative imaginaries. To be sure, her tactics are imperfect. Using the descriptors "clueless" and "smug" to critique the wearers of these American Apparel shirts is not likely to intimate coalition with many of them. At the same time, Nair's oppositional approach is meant to be jarring in order to suggest the profundity of the situation.

THE "GAY NONPROFIT INDUSTRIAL COMPLEX"

The final characteristic of Nair's radical interactional rhetoric is her critique of what she describes as the "gay nonprofit industrial complex" (GNPIC). The nonprofit sector, also called the independent or third sector, has been an important part of the US service economy since the 1970s, filling a space between government and for-profit industry. Virginia Ann Hodgkinson and Murray S. Weitzman argue that the sector's growth results from federal legislation that has supported Medicare, Medicaid, education grants, and social welfare programs.[101] While some people argue that the nonprofit sector has led to better distribution of services, others worry that this sector is an instrument for privatization and social deregulation.[102] This worry prompted Miranda Joseph to suggest that in late capitalism much of what is considered "community" is promulgated by nonprofit organizations that are developed not to oppose capitalism, but rather to fill in its gaps by providing services, resources, and entertainment to local communities. By actually sustaining capitalism, in a broader sense, such "community" further disenfranchises the poor and other marginalized groups, making the idea of community something that should be critically interrogated rather than romanticized.[103] INCITE! Women of Color Against Violence's edited collection *The Revolution Will Not Be Funded*, articulates this phenomenon as the "nonprofit industrial complex" (NPIC). On one level the NPIC refers to the increased professionalization of activism and services channeled through a plethora of organizations driven by specific goals, missions, and values. Dylan Rodríguez describes the NPIC as "the set of symbiotic relationships that link together political and financial technologies of state and owning-class proctorship and surveillance over public political intercourse, including and especially emergent progressive and leftist social movements, since about the mid-1970s."[104] More specifically, both Rodríguez and Ruth Wilson Gilmore locate the NPIC as a corollary of the prison industrial complex, arguing that the latter overtly represses and brutalizes dissent while the former manages and absorbs it.[105] For its critics, additional problems with the NPIC include that it allows the state to justify its own repressive policies while appearing to have strong private-public relations. Also, since foundations serve as tax shelters, the NPIC's reliance on wealthy foundations allows the rich to avoid paying taxes to the state and then give very little, in a controlled manner, back to civil society.

The impact on social movements is most relevant to Nair's rhetoric. Tiffany Lethabo King and Ewuare Osayande argue that the logic of the NPIC is that wealthy and often white donors support a movement, and that they often donate to white-led organizations and then monitor a movement's agenda, which has a disproportionately negative impact on communities of color. Moreover, as Andrea Smith maintains, since the NPIC promotes a "careerist model" of organizing, where a small group of people get paid to do the work that it would take many more to carry out, the model is unsustainable. She further notes that the NPIC "promotes a social movement culture that is non-collaborative, narrowly focused, and competitive."[106] For Smith, this means that nonprofit organizations often end up concerning themselves with professionalization rather than grassroots organizing and with providing social services rather than engaging in direct action and advocacy. Such critiques notwithstanding, even if nonprofit organizations are helping to sustain a ruthless form of capitalism that absolves public institutions of taking care of people, nonprofits provide much-needed services, and people who work within nonprofits can and do find unique ways to challenge and subvert the constraints of the system. Furthermore, at least anecdotally speaking, many people who graduate from college with degrees in ethnic studies, American studies, or gender and women's studies find jobs in the nonprofit sector, making it an important source of labor.[107]

Nair recognizes the good that some nonprofits do, but she advances a rigorous critique of the NPIC. In both of my interviews with her, she expressed her concerns about the insidiousness of the NPIC and the ways they become the only model for politics. Moreover, she laments the single-issue focus or "purity" of such organizations that are dictated by boards of directors, funding foundations, and often highly paid and highly educated executive directors.[108] Such hierarchical structuring functions to replicate the problems found in corporations that put power in the hands of only a select few. Within the context of this broader critique, Nair also focuses specifically on the problems of the dominance of nonprofit organizations and their agenda within the supposed LGBT community. She's not the first or only one to make these critiques of the LGBT community.[109] The group Gay Shame has long criticized the dominance of large mainstream LGBT organizations, perhaps most famously in its paper *Creating Change or Creating Chains*, a critique of the NPIC generally and the NGLTF's annual Creating Change conference specifically.[110] Nair and the non-nonprofit groups she works with are responsible for the specific and public focus on the intersections between migration and queer politics. Her overarching critique of the GNPIC is quite simple: "Queer organising used to be [about] dismantling economic structures of privilege and redefining structures of kinship in ways that straights have since embraced. Somewhere along the way, we—or rather, the increasingly powerful gay organisations that speak for us and articulate 'our' agenda—have decided that we want to expand, not destroy, privilege. Instead of fighting for basic rights for everyone."[111]

In *Virtual Equality* Urvashi Vaid addresses the development of the powerful nonprofit organizations to which Nair refers, including the HRC and the NGLTF in the early 1990s.[112] Vaid further identifies the resulting "mainstreaming" of the movement and shows how certain issues like marriage, military, and hate crime legislation took precedent over others as a result of the efforts of a small group of wealthy gays and lesbians who supposedly had access to the Clinton administration and who, often behind closed doors, decided what the LGBT rights agenda would be. As these organizations have continued to grow in terms of financial and human resources, media and research capacity, and name recognition, other groups and individuals with different messages and approaches have remained less visible and influential. As Nair argues in a comment to a responder on one essay, "The problem we face is with how the queer community's collective response to issues like UAFA (and gay marriage) gets channelled via mainstream groups like HRC as well as supposedly more progressive gay groups like NGLTF and Immigration Equality. That's not the same thing as saying that queers **are** the same as HRC et al. To repeat my sentence from the entry: 'Groups like HRC and Immigration Equality have decided that UAFA is the single most important piece of immigration legislation that matters to queers.'"[113] This point is crucial for Nair, who repeatedly mentions experiences where she talks with individuals on the inside of the NPIC who share her radical analysis of issues and yet remain complicit with the mainstream agenda of their organizations. In this way organizations become more significant than the movement and people's liberation, and for Nair the impacts are most devastating for those who are already vulnerable.

Nair explains how the narrow agenda of powerful organizations exacerbates existing problems: "The problem is with what then gets *funded* as a result of gay groups organising on specific issues; what gets pushed through as legislation based on what the queer 'community' is seen as wanting; and what the gay and straight press too often picks up and disseminates as 'progressive queer politics.'"[114] For certain, numerous organizations dealing with issues outside of marriage have seen their funding take a severe downturn, even as record amounts of funding have gone into supporting same-sex marriage, including $43 million in California to defeat Proposition 8.[115] Moreover, within the queer migration realm Immigration Equality has by far the largest amount of financial and human resources, and its primary issue continues to be binational couples. Though some local nonprofit grassroots organizations like the ALP, QEJ, and the Sylvia Rivera Law Project actively work against the dominant agenda and focus on the needs and interests of the most vulnerable in their movement work, as shown in chapter 1, their reach is limited to their local communities. Their work also remains limited by what external sources are willing to fund. Nair's rhetoric points to how the NPIC limits the possibility for radical interactionality, coalition, and alliance building since the model promotes such limited focus. For queer migration activism, issues that seem unique to those with queer identities and do not expand into the realm of migrants more generally, for example, are most discernible within such a framework. Such issues do not take into account the multiple factors that interact to produce oppressive conditions.

Although Nair's position outside the NPIC does not give her access to funding, she is able to make the kinds of arguments she offers without having to answer to funders, boards of directors, or an executive director who might attempt to steer her public work toward an organization's mission. Moreover, she is able to directly confront contradictions in discourse and work out the intricacies of problems without worrying about whether she will affect the viability of an organization. In a recent interview about one of her essays, for instance, Nair explains the function of the discourse of the "good gay" and "good undocumented youth" that emerges in DREAM activism, much of which has been led by youth working under the guidance of larger nonprofit organizations. Such discourse "allows for a continued perception that only the good ones deserve 'rights'—the right to health care through marriage, the right to demand that the PIC [prison industrial complex] incarcerate more people, the right to immigration as long as normative requirements of citizenship are adhered to."[116] This argument resembles those of some academics who are also not bound by funding priorities.[117] Similarly, from outside the NPIC, Nair can level such arguments, show how the mainstream agenda has these potentially unintended long-term implications, and craft a radically alternative, even if unpopular, vision of justice that confronts the multifaceted roots of problems.

Conclusions

Nair's rhetoric of radical interactionality regularly confronts the same critique from people who disagree with her positions. As one responder simply put it, "I would like to know what you propose to do."[118] This sort of question is commonly posed to scholars writing in critical theory traditions and to activists who focus their attention on highlighting problems rather than offering their own concrete solutions. Nair has ideas about what appropriate comprehensive immigration reform and queer politics entail, and she actively advocates for these visions in her grassroots work. She is careful not to succumb to this critique, however, which distracts from the importance of the arguments she offers. In this way, Nair reflects what Raymie E. McKerrow has called a "critical rhetoric," which views discourse as material and understands critique as transformative and demystifying.[119] Nair's vision, which includes a critique of neoliberal affect and the personal narrative, strategic blending of the queer and migrant worker, and assessment of the NPIC, has transformative aims as she shows how complex the roots of the problems are for queer migrant oppression. She also reveals how those working in the service of queer migrants may very well do many of them a disservice. Because she unabashedly reveals the intricate ways that power and oppression interact across multiple registers and primarily suggests that understanding these dynamics is a major source of radical liberation, many read Nair as a polemicist.

Erin J. Rand maintains that the polemic is a queer form that engenders the following characteristics: "alienating expressions of emotion, non-contingent assertions of truth, presumptions of shared morality, and the constitution of enemies, audiences, and publics."[120] By this definition, Nair does not qualify as a polemicist. There is something to be said, however, about the parallels between the function of the polemic and the function of rhetoric of radical interactionality. The polemic is offered to incite change, and as Rand argues, it is in the space between an intending agent and the ways the polemic is taken up by others to enact change that agency exists. Yet the isolating and emotional tenor of most polemics removes them from the possibility of being a coalitional gesture or moment for the group positioned as both audience and enemy in polemical rhetoric. Rhetoric of radical interactionality is also offered to catalyze change and oppose mainstream conditions for belonging and politics, and although it is often read as isolating, it is in fact an abstract and unemotional gesture for coalition building.

The problem with the gesture is twofold. First, in minimizing the import of emotions to politics, even though there are good reasons to do so, Nair's oppositional vision may be entirely utopian and therefore unrealistic. This vision may also miss an opportunity to retool narrative and emotion in productive ways. What Gould calls "affective states" and what Raymond Williams names "structures of feeling," which may not be rationally articulable, "can shake one out of deeply grooved patterns of thinking and feeling and allow for new imaginings."[121] At the same time, as Berlant and others have so aptly demonstrated, our longings and attachments can just as easily return us to the conventional and normative,[122] a point that Nair's work evidences quite well. Still, Nair's proscription of certain modes of the political could perhaps be better served by taking more seriously, or thinking more concretely, about what *moves* people into movement and activism generally and into coalitional subjectivities specifically.

A second problem with Nair's gesture is that to take up the gesture offered would require white citizen queers, for example, to coalesce with migrants who are not their partners or lovers. It would require people to commit to comprehensive immigration reform that would radically alter the definition of family and no longer celebrate the love between two people as superior to other forms of love or relationality. It would require understanding queers and migrants not merely as people with identities and stories, but as people with material realities, as workers who are vulnerable to exploitation, and as abstract humans who deserve rights. It would require rethinking all that is familiar about the business of professional politics in the United States and actually centering on the interests, needs, and resources of queer migrants. And each of these coalitional gestures is asked for without the privilege of knowing or even liking the people with whom one would have to work or join in order to achieve such goals. Writing in the midst of second-wave feminism, Bernice Johnson Reagon explained that coalition is not at all like being in the comforts of home; it is threatening and unfamiliar.[123] If neoliberalism co-opts everything toward its own ends, it is possible that even how we envision our political belonging has to be at least strategically oppositional in order to resist its own co-optation. This sort of oppositional vision may not be comforting, but for Nair it is the only grounds for coalition that makes sense in order to challenge the way the contemporary rhetorical imaginary constitutes the existing realm of possibility. This is the sobering charge of Nair's rhetoric.

CHAPTER 3

Coming Out
as Coalitional Gesture?

The "DREAM Act 21," a group of self-identified undocumented youth activists dressed in graduation caps and gowns staged nonviolent sit-ins at the Washington, DC, offices of Senators Dianne Feinstein (D-CA), Harry Reid (D-NV), John McCain (R-AZ), Robert Menendez (D-NJ), and Charles Schumer (D-NY), on July 21, 2010.[1] All twenty-one were arrested, released within twenty-four hours, and the action attracted considerable media attention.[2] To accompany this bold and significant act of civil disobedience, a blog called *Citizen Orange* hosted a letter-writing campaign called "DREAM Now." DREAM Now featured letters written to Barack Obama by migrant youth who requested his support and advocacy of the DREAM Act.[3] *Citizen Orange*, a global justice blog committed to supporting the pro-migrant movement in the United States,[4] modeled DREAM Now after a similar letter-writing campaign by the OutServe-Service Members Legal Defense Network (SLDN). The SLDN is a group whose sole purpose was ending the military "Don't Ask, Don't Tell" policy and, now that it has ended, helping with the transition to open service. SLDN called its campaign "Stories from the Frontlines: Letters to President Barack Obama," and it ran from April 26 through May 28, 2010. It consisted of letters written to Obama each day by current and former gay, lesbian, and bisexual members of the US armed forces and their straight allies who requested the repeal of DADT.[5]

DREAM Now asserted that because its writers believed that the possibility for comprehensive immigration reform had been essentially lost, activists needed to focus on passing the DREAM Act. Originally introduced in 2001, the act would offer conditional permanent residency for a select group of undocumented young people provided they meet certain criteria, including the following: arriving in the United States before the age of sixteen, living in the United States for at least five consecutive years prior to the act's approval, possessing a clean criminal record and thus good moral standing, graduating from high school or obtaining a GED, attending two years of college or serving two years in the military within six years of the act's authorization, and being between the ages of twelve and thirty-five at the time of the act's enactment.[6] DREAM Now began on July 19 and formally ended on September 15 when Obama offered his full support for the DREAM Act; a last letter to the president appeared on September 17. *Citizen Orange* posted the letters every Monday and Wednesday, and on Friday of each week the blog posted a recap of the week's events and indicated any progress made, such as new Congress members supporting the act. Following the model of the SLDN reflected a strategic decision. As Kyle, the founder of *Citizen Orange* explains:

> As any migrant youth leader will tell you, just as racism is inextricable from nativism, so is the LGBT movement inextricable from the migrant youth movement. A disproportionate number of migrant youth leaders identify as queer.
>
> So while national immigration reform groups have sometimes made the "strategic" decision to downplay LGBT immigration concerns in order to appeal to the religious right, that has simply never been an option for the migrant youth movement. Doing so would mean neglecting the very souls of some of our strongest leaders: among them Mario Rodas, Mohammad Abdollahi, Tania Unzueta, and Yahaira Carrillo.[7]

Kyle links LGBT struggles directly with the struggles of the migrant youth movement, suggesting that the overt use of strategies from the LGBT movement is, by design, a coalitional gesture. As a result of the overt queer visibility and solidarity, popular and award-winning LGBT-oriented blogs like *Pam's House Blend* noticed and endorsed the letter-writing campaign. The SLDN also announced and backed DREAM Now.[8]

These mutual coalitional gestures, expressed through what Robert Glenn Howard calls the media's "vernacular web," evidence a powerful use of participatory social media to advance political causes and build solidarity.[9] In the past several years, migrant youth activists from an array of cultural, class, ethnic, and racial backgrounds have actively forged bonds with queer activists, issues, and politics.[10] In 2010 one of the most prominent actions that migrant youth activists conducted involved a direct appropriation of LGBTQ political strategy when activists announced a National Coming Out of the Shadows Day/Week (NCOOTSD). The NCOOTSD announcement implored undocumented youth to come out of the shadows and declare themselves "undocumented and unafraid" in order to advocate for the DREAM Act. This nationwide event functioned as a catalyst to make "coming out" a central strategy of the migrant youth movement, and such a bold appropriation of the coming out strategy is important for rhetorical analysis for several reasons.[11] First of all, it strengthens a connection between migrant rights and justice and queer rights and justice because it catapults queer migrants into the position of leaders of a national movement that has influenced public opinions and political commitments. This appropriation also provides a unique lens to understand the differences between movements, the risks and opportunities for differently positioned groups using the same strategies for different ends, and how groups imagine the conditions of their politics. Finally, it opens discursive space for the evolution of the strategy to be used toward alternative queer migration coalitions and coalitional moments, which reveals both the tenacity and flexibility of rhetorical strategies.

In this chapter I analyze a range of diverse coalitional moments to argue that migrant youth activism that uses coming out as a strategy offers a unique way for understanding how coalitional rhetorics can point to both normative and utopian politics while offering a politically impure alternative to both.[12] DREAM activism has been both highly utopian in its deployment of the "DREAM" metaphor—something that does not exist in the material world, and yet is hoped for—at the same time that it is profoundly normative because of what the DREAM Act provides and to whom it would ostensibly provide it. Still, DREAM activism is diverse in the coalitional gestures it offers through coming out, and the offshoots it has catalyzed turn toward coalition beyond the appropriation strategy. The development of the coalitional subject known as the "undocuqueer," a term attributed to San Francisco–based artist and self-identified queer, undocumented DREAM activist Julio Salgado, emerged from within DREAM activism in order to call attention to the unique situation of queers in the migrant rights movement and to emphasize queer leadership. Some young activists have come out differently altogether by defecting from DREAM activism and choosing alternative coalitions, such as those with all workers, criminalized populations, and prison abolitionists.

In the remaining pages of this chapter I supply some context for migrant youth activism in 2010 and the role of the coming out strategy. Next I move to an analysis of coming out, both coming out of the closet and coming out of the shadows, arguing that the metaphors of the closet and the shadow provide a useful lens for viewing the risks and opportunities that are at stake in the appropriation strategy. I develop this argument through an examination of the rhetorical framing of the National Coming Out of the Shadows actions as found in press releases, speeches, and public announcements. I then analyze the shift from appropriation to the development of the coalitional subject, the "undocuqueer," through an exploration of Salgado's writing and artwork. I follow with a discussion of counter–DREAM activism by analyzing activists' speeches and statements. I conclude with implications about the conditions of appropriating queer civil rights visibility politics toward the ends of attaining migrant human and civil rights, the possibilities of coalitional subjects, and thinking of an expanded rhetorical imaginary for queer migration coalitional politics.

Migrant Youth Activism, 2010

The Obama administration largely stopped the visible spectacle of apprehending migrants using workplace raids, a practice popularized during George W. Bush's years. Under Obama, the Department of Homeland Security uses strategies that are more concealed from the public, involving cooperation with law enforcement under the "Secure Communities" program and business audits. Relying on these strategies, the 2010 fiscal year ended with the highest number of migrant deportations in US history—392,000—and a record number of business audits to check the legal status of workers at more than 2,000.[13] Obama and other Democrats rationalized the enforcement approach to immigration policy, suggesting that unless they were tough on so-called security and enforcement, Republicans would never agree to comprehensive immigration reform.[14] And indeed Republicans had resisted comprehensive immigration reform as early as December 2009 with proposed legislation drafted by Rep. Luis Gutierrez (D-IL). The Gutierrez bill had problems that also prevented some Democrats like Rep. Tammy Baldwin (D-WI) from supporting it, since it left out the UAFA. The bill's failure also meant that the DREAM Act, which it had included, failed as it has every time it has been introduced. Yet another failure of the DREAM Act galvanized many migrant youth to action.

Several groups of migrant youth activist "DREAMers,"[15] already enlivened by candidate Obama's stated support of the DREAM Act in 2008, became increasingly organized, active, and visible by 2010. Largely connecting through social media and networking tools such as blogs, community portals, and Facebook, local chapters of DREAM Act coalitions formed and unified national actions began to take shape. These actions borrowed from the civil rights movement and Chican@ movement of the 1960s and evoked allusions to the struggles of other oppressed groups such as Native Americans.[16] For instance, one of the first nationally visible acts was the "Trail of Dreams," a fifteen-hundred-mile march to Washington, DC, from Miami. The march began on January 1, 2010, and culminated in DC on May 1, International Workers' Day, a holiday not celebrated in the United States but that many US migrant rights activists have reclaimed as the Day of Immigrant Rights.[17] Three undocumented college students, Gaby Pacheco, Felipe Matos, and Carlos Roa, and one legal permanent resident, Juan Rodriguez, planned and organized the march despite risking detention or deportation.[18] They joined a small group of people arrested in front of the White House, where they left their shoes as "a symbol of thousands in our communities that disappear due to our broken immigration system."[19]

Before the Trail of Dreams march ended, in April 2010 the Arizona state legislature passed and Governor Jan Brewer signed SB 1070, which requires law enforcement officials to request proof of legal status during routine stops and arrests if they reasonably suspect a person is in the United States without proper documentation. This law, which Obama called "ill-conceived," sparked protests around the United States and throughout other countries such as El Salvador and Mexico.[20] The law's backers in Arizona claimed they had to take matters into the state's hands since the federal government failed to do so, readying activists on all sides to see federal action.[21] Even with the fervor and denouncements, comprehensive immigration reform did not seriously enter the legislative agenda in that contentious election year. To many activists it seemed the DREAM Act would be the only dimension of immigration reform that still had a serious chance of garnering bipartisan support.

Some DREAM activists took further advantage of the media frenzy following the passage of SB 1070 and traveled to Arizona to call attention to the DREAM Act by donning graduation caps and gowns and conducting a May 17 sit-in at the Tucson office of Senator John McCain. Three undocumented activists, Lizbeth Mateo, Mohammad Abdollahi, and Yahaira Carrillo, all from out of state, along with an LPR from Arizona, Raúl Alcaraz,[22] were arrested on trespassing charges, risking deportation to forward their cause.[23] These traditional methods of nonviolent civil disobedience attracted significant national attention as rhetorical acts of confrontation that created "image events."[24] As Kevin Michael DeLuca and Jennifer Peeples explain, image events, or "mind bombs that expand the universe of thinkable thoughts," draw attention by rendering the familiar strange—in this instance, people in caps and gowns, a sign of achievement and respectability, being arrested.[25]

Coming Out

Time-tested civil disobedience tactics remained a crucial part of the migrant youth approach, but in 2010 a primary strategy of the LGBTQ rights movement—coming out—became an incredibly significant part of the actions that migrant youth engaged in. On February 17, 2010, the newly formed Immigrant Youth Justice League (IYJL) in Chicago first announced National Come Out of the Shadows Day,[26] to be held on March 10, exactly four years after the first of the big 2006 immigration marches. The event would begin with a rally and a march.[27] IYJL also announced a series of actions to take place from March 10 through March 21. Because Senator Dick Durbin (D-IL) is an original co-sponsor of the DREAM Act and a longtime proponent of comprehensive immigration reform, the event began in his home state of Illinois to target Durbin, Obama, and Janet Napolitano and encourage them to take action on both types of legislation. On March 5, Mohammad, a co-founder, core member, and organizer for *DreamActivist.org*, released a statement announcing National Coming Out of the Shadows Week, March 15–21, 2010. *DreamActivist.org* started in July 2009 and is a social media hub for the DREAM Act movement, as well as for those pursuing other legislation to fix the immigration system. Drawing directly from the LGBT National Coming Out Day and queer activist exhortations to be public about sexuality, this action encouraged people to come out as undocumented in a host of public forums, including in videos, at rallies, in letters to elected officials, and generally to people they know. In order to examine the rhetorical appropriation of the coming out strategy, I begin with a close examination of coming out as it pertains to the closet and to the shadow.

THE CLOSET

The metaphor of coming out of the closet and the politics of the closet have been central to contemporary western queer experiences at least since the 1960s in the United States, and perhaps earlier elsewhere.[28] The phrase "coming out of the closet" refers to the experience of coming out into a queer identity, often through a first sexual experience. It also refers to coming out into a community of other similarly identified people, which entails personal and political dimensions.[29] With regard to politics, coming out can be used toward inclusionary ends, as is often the case with the mainstream LGBT movement. Coming out can also have more radical ends, as in the politics of some queer activists who come out in order to declare their presence, demand systemic changes, and resist and disrupt the assumptions of normative culture. In this way, for some, coming out is a strategy that reflects a political orientation toward and around narrative and identity, but for others, coming out suggests being oriented toward and around systemic critique and change. Likely for many, the act of coming out is oriented toward and around a variety of objectives.

No matter the reason for coming out, some consider "the closet" mostly a negative construction. Michelangelo Signorile's "closet conspiracy" thesis alleges that within major powerful institutions in the United States, heterosexuals and homosexuals alike work to sustain the institution of the closet.[30] In 1990 Eve Kosofsky Sedgwick characterized the closet as the "fundamental feature of social life" for many gays in the twentieth century. Sedgwick does not denounce the closet as a wholly negative space, and the etymology of the term is also not bad, mostly reflecting the connection between the closet and privacy. In fact, nearly all the early usages of the term in English mention the privacy or private nature of the closet. Other definitions refer to it as a space for spiritual reflection, and others depict its function as a place for storing valuables. Only in phrases such as "skeleton in the closet" does the closet become associated with trouble or sin.[31]

Perhaps because of such multiplicity of meanings, Sedgwick carefully demonstrates how the logic of disclosing one's sexuality does not lead to necessarily predictable results, nor is being "out" of a closet an implicitly productive position. Instead, she maps the epistemologies of the closet through the operation of the homosexual/heterosexual binary in relation to a host of other binaries. Still, as Marlon B. Ross aptly notes, Sedgwick's project is an un-reflexively racialized one, and her "desire for an epistemology of sexuality necessarily draws her attention to certain subjects (elite European men) and their objects (un/closeted desires) as constitutive of all modern culture from the outset."[32] The binaries Sedgwick seeks to unpack and the construction of the closet itself rest upon unmentioned absences.

This post-structuralist approach to the metaphor of the closet, which suggests the instability of the metaphor at the same time that it explores its "mimetic relationship to social belief systems and unconscious thought," builds upon and critiques two other theories of metaphor often applied to the closet: comparison theory and interaction theory.[33] A comparison approach to metaphor assumes that two terms can be simply substituted for each other, which in this case means that being in the closet with one's sexuality is like being physically inside a closet. Interaction theory extends this literal substitution by noting a necessary interplay between the figurative and literal dimensions of a metaphor, which produces meaning. In other words, it is partially true that being in the closet is like being inside a closet, but in other ways the physical and metaphorical closet are quite different.[34] These popular usages of the closet metaphor obscure a spatial analysis upon which the metaphor relies for meaning. Geographer Michael P. Brown maintains, "It is valuable to understand the spatiality of the closet because it is important to understand the different-yet-similar material ways power works to oppress—just as it is important to see the different ways queers attempt to resist!"[35]

In the United States one of the most prominent ways that queers have responded to the oppression the closet produces is to demand that queers come out. This imperative is premised on the belief that unlike race and gender, which typically are visibly present, supposedly sexuality can be readily concealed. As Signorile writes, "Outing [public figures who remained in the closet to preserve their privilege] focused attention on the closet and what a horrible, pitiful place the closet is. Outing demands that everyone come out, and defines the closeted—especially those in power—as cowards who are stalling progress at a crucial time."[36] In this line of thinking, visibility politics, then, subverts this concealing logic.

For this reason, in 1987 members of the gay and lesbian community created National Coming Out Day (NCOD), celebrated each year on October 11. As the Human Rights Campaign narrates the history, on October 11, 1987, roughly a half a million people held the second march on Washington, DC, for gay and lesbian rights, and for the first time, they displayed the AIDS Memorial Quilt to commemorate those who had died from AIDS. After the success of the event, some leaders, including Jean O'Leary and Rob Eichberg, came up with the idea of an annual national event celebrating the importance of gay and lesbian visibility.[37] When the NCOD joined with the Human Rights Campaign Fund in 1993, leaders believed that the day could be used to have significant policy impacts.[38] And in the years since then the day has transformed into an entire project, which the HRC uses to promote coming out of the closet and to mobilize support for the annual day. The HRC also offers many resources to help people plan how to come out of the closet and live openly as LGBT people.[39]

In the US imaginary the speech act of saying, "I am gay" signals not only an emergence from the closet by acknowledging status, but it also implies an admission of engagement in certain conduct.[40] This performative act, then, marks a desire and publicizes sex. Because the desire and the acts it indicates diverge from the norm, through the speech act both the norm and the divergence become publicized in a way that they otherwise would not. Brown notes that different spaces and contexts constitute different closeting mechanisms, but as Sedgwick and others claim, if the closet is an organizing feature of life, you must continually come out, even if the spaces you exist in produce different possibilities for the speech act.[41]

As pointed to above, this construction of the closet itself reflects a particular kind of queer experience and geography, one that is representative of white, middle-class, urban, mostly US ways of regarding sexuality.[42] Carlos Ulises Decena questions the centrality and universality of the coming out queer narrative using the linguistic metaphor of the subject/verb relationship in Spanish to describe sexuality in Latin@, primarily Dominican culture.[43] In Spanish the subject (i.e., I, you, he/she, we, they) is often implied rather than stated. For example, Spanish speakers are more likely to say *voy* than *yo voy* for the phrase "I go," or *vamos* instead of *nosotros vamos* for the phrase "we go."[44] Decena argues that in a similar way knowledge of homosexuality is often understood between "gay" Dominicans and their families. Their families have tacit knowledge of their sexuality without the need for them to offer speech acts indicating it. Though some white, western critics have often described this as an example of oppressed and homophobic Latin@ culture, Decena, Lionel Cantú, and others note that this practice is culturally specific and should not need to be read within the revelation and recognition logics preferred in the west.[45] Gayatri Gopinath pushes such critiques even further, suggesting that when one starts with a queer female diasporic subjectivity, it becomes clear that home is not necessarily a place where the queer subject must leave in order to enter a supposed new queer community, which is what coming out often implies. Instead, Gopinath writes, "This queer transformation of the diasporic 'home' constitutes a remarkably powerful challenge to dominant ideologies of community and nation in ways that may very well escape intelligibility within a logic of visibility and 'coming out.'"[46] Visibility logics not only serve to render the practices, identities, and relationalities of diasporic queers as illegible, but as Monisha Das Gupta claims, the queer immigrants of color with whom she worked, "far from uncritically embracing visibility as a mode of political empowerment, inventively resisted the exposure, fixity, and linearity of mainstream calls to become politicized through 'coming out' and becoming visible."[47]

Other cogent critiques of overemphasis on visibility or "ocularcentrism" also challenge the dominant paradigm in the United States.[48] Mariam Fraser explains, for instance, that visibility politics are especially difficult to privilege when working-class identities are considered within the purview of queer because the question of visual politics and the politics of recognition can manifest very differently for these queers.[49] Eli Clare has commented that the notion of coming out among poor and working-class rural whites differs greatly from the idea among middle-class urban whites in the United States. Clare explains that although it may not be ideal, a tacit understanding of queerness often leads to a particular brand of tolerance and even acceptance of queer people and relationships within such families and communities.[50] Even though such critiques of coming out and visibility logics persist, around the world and in an array of communities within the United States, people talk about queer sexuality in terms of closets.[51] It may be too facile to say the closet is solely a western and capitalist invention, but the idea of coming out and the development of a national political holiday celebrating it are US creations, or at the very least they gained the most traction in white, middle-class, urban US contexts. The closet and the call to come out of it remain pervasive features of queer politics and life.

THE SHADOWS

A concealing logic also operates for undocumented people, who may "pass" as US citizens because of their language, culture, and lifestyle even if they lack US citizenship. But for migrants the pervasive metaphor is not the closet, but the shadows.[52] Unlike the closet, most of the etymology of the word "shadow" carries some pejorative meaning, even if it merely stems from the archetypal connection between light and dark, good and evil, and the implied racialization/racism therein. For example, the second meaning under the first definition in the *Oxford English Dictionary* references "shadow of death," and the third maintains the shadow's connection with "Gloom, unhappiness; a temporary interruption of friendship; something that obscures the lustre of a reputation."[53]

The precise origin of describing immigrants as being in "shadows" is somewhat unclear. A mention in a US newspaper occurs in 1978 where the reporter explains, "The illegal immigrant occupies *a shadow world* of fieldhands, bus boys and day laborers working, at $2 an hour or less, for employers who do not speak his or her language in jobs that most native Americans are unwilling to perform."[54] In 1981 Attorney General William French Smith described undocumented people as a "shadow population" while giving congressional testimony about the need for immigration reform.[55] Supreme Court Justice William J. Brennan picked up the term from Smith in his opinion representing the majority in *Plyler v. Doe*, which found a Texas law denying education to undocumented children unconstitutional. Brennan wrote, "Sheer incapability or lax enforcement of the laws barring entry into this country, coupled with the failure to establish an effective bar to the employment of undocumented aliens, has resulted in the creation of a substantial 'shadow population' of illegal migrants—numbering in the millions—within our borders."[56] The idea of a "shadow population" perhaps carries more severe connotation than simply living in the shadows. A shadow population *is* the shadow, which may make it more difficult for the population to relieve itself of the baggage the metaphor holds; the baggage is intrinsic.

Shadow metaphors gained prominence as comprehensive immigration reform and amnesty preoccupied the US imaginary in the mid-1980s. A statement released by the National Council of Churches, the US Catholic Conference, and the Union of American Hebrew Congregations in 1985 argued that migrants should be "removed from the shadows of undocumented status and placed under the protection and rule of law."[57] Once Congress passed and Reagan signed the 1986 Immigration Reform and Control Act, supporters touted the law for bringing people out of the shadows. Reagan extended the metaphor when he remarked, "Very soon many of these men and women will be able to step into the sunlight,"[58] and from around that point the term can be found regularly in US discourse pertaining to immigration.[59]

With the massive immigration rights marches in 2006, the phrases "coming out of the shadows" and "awakening a sleeping giant" were frequently used to talk about migrants and their potential political power. Immigration scholars have apparently said little about the function of the shadow metaphor, though many rely upon it to highlight the condition for migrants in host countries.[60] An exception is René Galindo, who explains that the shadow is a visual metaphor that is "popularly used to describe the invisibility and criminalization of undocumented immigrants."[61] Galindo argues that invisibility, or "living in the shadows," marks migrants' supposed "lack of political presence and agency," but the 2006 marches catapulted them onto the political stage. Because some people did not believe migrants belonged in the US public sphere as political actors, media attention quickly turned to migrants displaying the Mexican flag at the marches, both interpreting the symbol as suggesting allegiance only to Mexico and further marginalizing migrants.[62] For people holding such beliefs, migrants should remain in the shadows, or perhaps disappear altogether.

The fact of migrants' visibility, and at least symbolic agency, has prompted some conservative immigration pundits to take time to interrogate the metaphor and suggest its shortcomings in describing migrants' situation in the United States. One Center for Immigration Studies blogger comments that undocumented people live among the rest of us and came here by their own choice, so perhaps the only way they are in the "shadows" is psychologically, through their guilt for being here.[63] This blogger maintains that while one level of meaning refers to light and dark, the distinction between honesty and deception ultimately characterizes shadow metaphors, which further emphasizes the criminalizing dimension of shadows. These binaries, like heterosexual/homosexual, operate together within western logics to keep the second terms subservient to the first and, in this instance, to subtly encode racial superiority.[64]

Although the phrase "coming out of the shadows" in relation to migrants emerged in popular discourse separately from LGBTQ movement discourse and the closet, the mimesis of the "coming out" metaphor within the context of migrant youth activism piques interest because of the centrality of queers in the movement and because the material conditions of many citizen queers and undocumented migrants are so different. A more direct discussion of the relationship between these two kinds of coming out provides an important basis to reveal the risks and opportunities of the appropriation for migrants, even when catalyzed by migrant queers.

CLOSETS VERSUS SHADOWS

Both the metaphors and the physical objects the metaphors draw upon are visual in the sense that emergence from closets or shadows garners significance only through being seen.[65] Presumably, coming out involves being seen by an audience of those who may not have realized that people resided there at all, or even if they did see people, they had no awareness of their closeted or shadowed existence. As an intended political act (as opposed to mere personal revelation), the emergence is not just about entering a community or declaring an identity for the self and others like them.[66] The act occurs before seers who not only see but who are also potential agents of change. In this rhetorical situation the audience is comprised of only those who can remedy or rectify the exigency that demanded a rhetorical response in the first place.[67]

The closet also resembles the shadow in other important ways, as both involve hiding or concealing, darkness, conjuring a sense of fear, and perhaps being places unsuitable for sustaining life. In this way one's desire to emerge from either place would be easy to see as logical and desirable, which could be a persuasive appeal to those in the audience who could enact change. On the other hand, both closets and shadows can also provide protection from the outside world and offer an alluring gesture to venture into the unknown. This subversive and exciting aspect of closets and shadows is also what can be frightening to those who want to protect others from being lured into worlds of unspecified sin or vice. The similarities in the metaphors are important, and they point to the opportunities engendered in the appropriation. Crucial differences remain, however, that help to signal some of the risks in the appropriation strategy that migrant youth activists deploy.

Closets are necessarily human made and very often directly connected to the home. Shadows can result from human creations, such as buildings, but they can also be disconnected from civilization and organic, resulting from trees, for example. Closets are concrete, physical objects. Shadows are ephemeral and changing things. They can, quite literally, disappear. Closets imply privacy and a relatively clear distinction between the public world and the private closet (even as the threshold is a liminal space). Closets can protect. Shadows may provide privacy through obscurity, but they also blur into the public and do not conceal in the same way as closets. Shadows offer little tangible protection. Closets have a history of being spiritual spaces, places of prayer and personal reflection. Shadows connect only to the negative dimensions of spirituality, ranging from the devil and death to guilt and deception. Closets have clear utility. Shadows, aside from providing shade from the sun, and perhaps serving as a hiding place, simply exist and have no specified utility. The threat of "monsters" hiding in closets can certainly provoke fear, especially for children. The threat of "stranger danger" posed by unknown people lurking in the shadows and waiting to attack innocent passersby, anywhere and anytime, functions as a much larger discourse of fear not relegated to childhood imagination.[68] Closets are not implicitly racialized. Shadows cannot be divorced from racialization. While similar in some ways, closets, then, carry less rhetorical baggage than shadows. Shadows conjure much stronger pejorative meanings than closets; thus, defining a productive politics through shadow references may prove quite difficult.

COMING OUT LOGOS

The distinctions between closets and shadows and the different political baggage they carry can be readily seen through a brief visual comparison of the logo for NCOD and the logo for the first NCOOTSD. The famous NCOD logo developed by the now-deceased pop artist and activist Keith Haring features a bright yellow, androgynous, cartoon-like character walking, or perhaps dancing, out of a dark closet into a room with pale green walls and a bold magenta floor. The marks that indicate action following the character's extended leg and arm also potentially signal that the red door was broken open. The entire image is bright, and the message is clearly intended to be uplifting as well. Even the handwritten, bubble-letter font, which simply notes "National Coming Out Day …" is lighthearted. In this way the figure that comes out is not threatening and may in fact bring joy and happiness to the home into which it enters. The figure could also be read as not needing to be taken seriously, given that it is playful and perhaps in the home solely for entertainment.

Alternatively, the logo for the first NCOOTSD features a partial silhouette of a feminine figure that stands still on the left side as if encased by the shadow.[69] The dark figure does not act and is completely opaque. While the NCOD character is cartoonish and obviously not modeled on a real person, the NCOOTSD figure is clearly a real, or potentially real, person; the figure simply remains anonymous, standing, or perhaps lurking, in the shadow. Moreover, while the cartoon character features more centrally than the text in the NCOD logo, in the NCOOTSD logo the text, "National Coming Out of the Shadows Day," takes center stage. The only color is bright red for "Coming Out" and for the word "March," which connects to both the date, "*March* 10, 2010," and the action, "*March* for Legalization." The fonts in this image are similar to those you would find in newsprint or in formal writing, which further contributes to the somber tone of the image. Considering the etymological connection between "somber" and "shadow," the feeling of the image makes sense. For example, the word for shadow in Spanish is *la sombra*, the word in French is *l'ombre*, and the first definition for "somber" in the *OED* describes it as an adjective meaning "characterized by the presence of gloom or shadow."[70]

These logos reflect some of the stark differences outlined above between the closet and the shadow. Specifically, the NCOD logo suggests the materi-

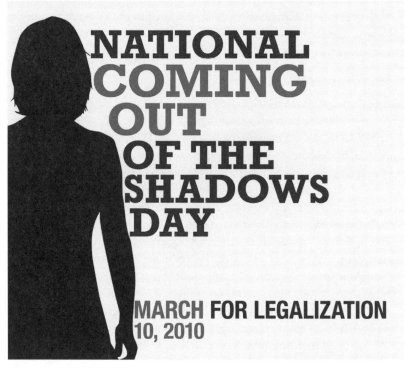

Image used by the Immigrant Youth Justice League to announce National Coming Out of the Shadows Day, March 10, 2010. Used with permission of Salvador Jiménez Flores.

ality of the closet as an object both connected to a home and from which one can emerge. At the same time, the ephemeral dimensions of the shadow come through in the NCOOTSD logo because it is not clear where the shadow comes from or if in fact the figure is the shadow. If the figure is the shadow, or simply subsumed by it, this conjures the connections between the shadow, deception, and gloom. The figure's lack of movement from the shadow further recalls some of the fears people have about what shadows obscure and the possibility of "stranger danger." The fact that this figure is anonymous, consumed by the shadow or is the shadow itself, might also function as an in-your-face political strategy, as if to say to onlookers, we're here, we're all over, and you don't even know where to look for us. Thus, the shadow could also be empowering as a place from which to hide and be ready to engage in action.

With an understanding of the operation of closets and shadows within queer and migrant-related discourse, as well as an examination of the important ways that they literally and metaphorically cohere and differ, I now turn attention to how migrant youth activists utilized coming out and visibility strategies toward the ends of advancing the DREAM Act and comprehensive immigration reform during the first coming out actions.

"UNDOCUMENTED AND UNAFRAID"

The call to action for National Coming Out of the Shadows Week on *DreamActivist.org* begins with a version of a famous quotation taken from Harvey Milk's speech "That's What America Is" given at the Gay Freedom Day Parade in San Francisco on June 25, 1978:

> Brothers and Sisters, you must come out! Come out to your parents, come out to your friends, if indeed they are your friends, come out to your neighbors, come out to your fellow workers. Once and for all, let's break down the myth and destroy the lies and distortions. For your sake, for their sake. For the sake of all the youngsters who've been scared by the votes from Dade to Eugene. On the Statue of Liberty it says "Give me your tired, your poor, your huddled masses yearning to be free." In the Declaration of Independence it is written, "All men are created equal and endowed with certain unalienable rights." For Mr. Briggs and Mrs. Bryant and all the bigots out there, no matter how hard you try, you can never erase those words from the Declaration of Independence! No matter how hard you try you can never chip those words from the base of the Statue of Liberty! That is where America is![71]

Using Harvey Milk to express the importance of coming out is central to the way that these activists position their movement. During the first action in Chicago, one IYJL activist, Tania, gave a speech called "Coming Out," designed to introduce other youth to the idea of coming out and also to inspire them to do so. Tania said, "What does it mean to come out? *¿Qué quieren decir, salir de las sombras?* Coming out means telling a friend, a loved one, a classmate, a teacher something that otherwise you would have kept private. It is using our lives, our stories as a political tool for change. For us, it is being undocumented and we are inspired by a legacy of other movements, from past immigrant rights marches, to civil rights, to gay liberation. Brothers and sisters, we must come out, said Harvey Milk in 1978."[72] Tania repeats a shorter version of the same quotation as in Mohammad's *DreamActivist.org* announcement, ending with the point about "lies and distortions." For Milk and for the undocumented youth activists, coming out begins with those who are familiar, those with whom such a story may be persuasive because they already have a personal relationship. At this point in this speech, Tania notes that Milk's words are certainly inspiring, "except that we want to make it very clear that we are not here asking for acceptance. We are asking for change. We are asking for a chance to be able to contribute fully to our communities and our societies. We are asking for legalization."

Milk also sought change in addition to acceptance; he gave this speech in the midst of California's battle over Proposition 6, the "Briggs Initiative," named after conservative state legislator John Briggs, which would have banned open gays and lesbians from teaching in the state's public schools. Yet Milk, and presumably those gays and lesbians he imagined in his audience, had the protection of legal US citizenship. Though homosexuality was not socially acceptable, and citizens could face severe legal, occupational, personal, and emotional ramifications from coming out of the closet, deportation was not one of those possibilities. In the United States the predominant narrative of coming out as a political act is a citizenship narrative, and one that is at least partially built into a belief in American exceptionalism. The argument operates in the following fashion: "I am a citizen of this country, and as a citizen I should have certain rights and protections granted to me by law. If this country is as great as it thinks it is, and is invested in individual autonomy and rights as core values, then I want to be given my rights just like other citizens. Therefore, I am coming out and demanding them."

Even though the laws often did not and do not protect gay and lesbian citizens (and the situation is worse for trans, genderqueer, and other gender-nonconforming citizens), possessing legal citizenship certainly means that garnering acceptance can be a legitimate political goal, and as stated repeatedly throughout this book, it remains a primary objective of the mainstream LGBT movement. Tania and other DREAM activists also seek acceptance, but for them, mere acceptance does nothing to alter their status. At a minimum, their goal is to change the legal immigration status quo. Tania thus marks the distinction between the paradigm of civil rights under which gay and lesbian citizen activists argue and the paradigm through which undocumented migrants must necessarily make their pleas since they do not possess a legal basis through the laws of the nation-state. Here the distinction between the shadow and the closet provides a way to understand the constraints of this strategy. A civil rights strategy like coming out makes a plea to the laws of the land, the laws of the home. Like a closet is always a part of a home, citizens, even undesirable ones, remain a part of the nation, and if they achieve a visible political voice (which is, of course, no small feat or guarantee), for the most part that voice cannot simply be erased (although it can be severely marginalized and criminalized).[73] On the other hand, despite the problems with human rights law mentioned in chapter 1, it remains true that the United States is woefully lacking in its adoption and support of international human rights law. It also lacks in its regard for justice outside of the language of rights, which severely hampers the ability of noncitizens to make legitimate rhetorical pleas. Much like a shadow can easily disappear, lacking legal status is grounds for disappearance, as happened to nearly four hundred thousand migrants in 2010. Although the idea of coming out as undocumented somewhat relies on the belief that publicity will offer protection, a key question remains: who will be protected, and who will be pushed further into the shadows or disappear altogether?

The DREAM activists do not answer this question. Tania invites the audience to join her in an exercise of utopian longing through imagining a world where they no longer have to worry about all of the problems associated with being undocumented, where they possess both human and civil rights in the United States. Tania then implores the audience, using language that parallels Milk's: "So, undocumented brothers and sisters, let's come out and organize. Come out in your church, tell your teacher, tell your friends, ask the dj for a mic at your next party and announce it over the speakers, 'I am undocumented.' Let them know that we will no longer hide in the shadows and that we are ready."[74] In some ways this challenge to come out resonates more with the "in your face" style politics of queer activism than it does mainstream LGBT politics of the contemporary moment. This is affirmed when examining another short speech given by Tania and a migrant youth named David called "Our Plaza," also given on March 10 in Chicago at the Federal Plaza. This short speech features David speaking in English and Tania offering the same message in Spanish. The speech begins, "We're about to do something radical. *Vamos a hacer algo radical.*"[75] The use of the word "radical" indicates a departure from inclusionary politics.

After explaining that many of the people who work inside the Federal Building have jobs that involve detaining and deporting the people standing in the plaza, Tania and David beseech the audience: "You have ten minutes. For the next ten minutes, Federal Plaza belongs to us. *Tienen diez minutos, por las proximas diez minutos la plaza federal es nuestro espacio.*" David then leads a call-and-response chant: "Whose plaza?" "Our plaza!" During the ten-minute takeover, the crowd breaks into small groups to meet one another, explain why they are there, tell their stories, and indicate what they will do to help with immigration reform. This takeover of government space and overt challenge to the power represented by the federal government reflects a radical strategy. Many of the actual coming out stories reify normative beliefs about inclusion, belonging, and citizenship—a strategy that is typical of migrant youth narratives.[76] Still, the youth enact their call for coming out of the shadows by placing themselves in a dangerously visible location closely connected to the state.

A radical impulse surely informs these acts, but in other ways so does a normalizing impulse. For instance, in critiquing the dominance of the coming out paradigm as "the definitive articulation of modern sexuality and progressive homosexual experience," Ross introduces the concept of "claustrophilia." He explains this idea as "a fixation on the closet function as the grounding principle for sexual experience, knowledge, and politics, and that this claustrophilic fixation effectively diminishes and disables the full engagement with potential insights from race theory and class analysis."[77] As a logic of western progress, the coming out paradigm not only levels an implicit critique on the "anachronistic" others, marked against whiteness, who have not sufficiently evolved, but it also reduces the work of challenging marginalization to the private individual. These traces are retained in the strategy in these calls to come out. Furthermore, and as we have seen elsewhere in this book, the vibrant tension between being "radical" and being "respectable" within movements emerges. In the *DreamActivist.org* announcement, after the Milk quotation the statement congratulates readers for coming out and facing their fears, and it reminds them that they are not alone. Although the announcement follows a logic that is similar to that of many support pamphlets for LGBTQ people, including resources produced by the HRC, the language reflects concerns that are unique to undocumented youth. Still, parallels to the queer plight continue: "In the same way the LGBTQ community has historically come out, undocumented youth, some of whom are also part of the LGBTQ community, have decided to speak openly about their status . . . You will be surprised how little other people know about the realities of being undocumented. People who know someone who is gay or lesbian are more likely to support equal rights for all gay and lesbian people—the same follows for people who know someone who is undocumented."[78] The weight of this argument rests upon the belief that the knowledge provided by coming out will disconfirm stereotypes that the hearer believes about the closeted group and that this will compel a change in attitude and possibly action.

The statement goes on to give youth advice about how to prepare to come out and offers "commitment" levels they can reach based on sharing their story and collecting signatures on a petition in support of the DREAM Act. In addition to the statement on the blog, a link to a document called "Coming Out, A How To Guide" provides more comprehensive descriptions of how to come out, including sample scenarios a person might create and sample actions someone might take at the higher levels. Clearly modeled after the fundraising strategies that are so popular within nonprofit organizations, it also names and provides criteria for each of the levels:

1. Dreamer "Shout It Out" level requires sharing your story with someone and getting 10 signatures on a petition to submit to Congress and the president in support of the DREAM Act.
2. Cesar Chávez and the UFW level necessitates sharing your story in video or written form with *DreamActivist.org* and collecting 25 signatures.
3. Audre Lorde "Shout It Out" level involves sharing your story in video or written form with *DreamActivist.org*, holding a coming out party, and collecting 50 signatures.
4. Rosa Parks "We Are Here, Get Used to It" level requires sharing your story in video or written form with *DreamActivist.org,* holding a coming out party that receives local press coverage, and collecting 75 signatures.
5. Harvey Milk "Out of the Closets and Into the Streets" level includes sharing your story in video or written form with *DreamActivist.org* and getting 5–7 other people to do so as well, holding a coming out party that received press coverage, and collecting 100 signatures.[79]

Notably, other than level 2, each level calls upon slogans used at various times by the LGBTQ movement, even as the slogan is associated with people affiliated with various movements, including the farmworkers' movement, feminist movement, and the civil rights movement. The pinnacle level, reflected in the figure of a white, urban gay male, Milk, is perhaps not as curious as it might seem, given Milk's overt and passionate commitment to coalitional politics across lines of difference. Yet considering Lorde's similar calls to speaking out against oppression, characterized in her famous and oft-cited quotation "your silence will not protect you,"[80] featuring Milk over Lorde certainly bespeaks a particular imaginary of LGBTQ politics and coming out of the closet.[81] As detailed above, the notion of the closet reflects a western and US imaginary of sexual identity, and "coming out" privileges the experiences of white, urban, and middle-class people. This is not to say that nonwhite, non-urban, and non-middle-class people in the United States and elsewhere do not adopt the logic of coming out as a part of their experience of sexual identity. However, the persistent marking of Milk in relation to the ideal of coming out also indicates who has access to this strategy and whose acts are considered most legitimate in the public sphere. Appropriating coming out via the figure of Milk belies the fact that the typical subject of LGBTQ politics is a white US citizen man who is only or primarily oppressed based on one thing, his sexuality, an impression also upheld in the mainstream LGBT movement. Figures like Lorde, those who experienced interlocking oppressions, also relied on visibility politics, but they spoke against several systems of power, often at once. Queer migrant youth activists like Mohammad, Tania, and other leaders also experience interlocking and intermeshing oppressions. They are clearly invested in bringing multiple facets of migrant experience out of the shadows, but their primary objective remains singular: passing the DREAM Act.[82] In this way the single-issue model of politics endures and partly explains the manner in which queer strategies are appropriated and how a coalition between queer and migrant issues is imagined. Namely, queer rights seem to be imagined as being in the purview of relatively privileged citizens who have obtained a certain level of respectability, the same kind of respectability that migrant youth hope to obtain with the DREAM Act.

In response to the calls in 2010 to come out of the shadows, dozens of undocumented youth gave speeches at the opening event in Chicago, which IYJL uploaded to its website, and others posted YouTube videos with their stories, many using the phrase "undocumented and unafraid." A number of youth wore T-shirts declaring their undocumented status with the simple phrase "I'm undocumented."[83] Newspapers and blogs ran features on undocumented youth who decided to come out of the shadows. One video, contributed by the Washington DREAM Act Coalition, includes photographs of sixty-seven youth holding signs against their chests intended for their senators, Maria Cantwell and Patty Murray. The signs say, "Change Takes Courage, My name is _____ And I am an Undocumented Student. Now is your time to lead for Comprehensive Immigration Reform," and the snapshots flash across the screen to the song "American Prayer" by Dave Stewart, created for Obama's 2008 presidential campaign. Each youth shows their face, and the signs all have their first names plainly stated in their handwriting.[84] Others gave individual "coming out" speeches, usually lasting a few minutes. The speeches, nearly all given by students or those who have had success in school and desire to continue their education, tell amazing stories of success and disappointment, with a mix of hopelessness and hopefulness. Many of the youth graduated at the top of their classes, desire to be professionals and give back to their communities, and seem to believe in the promises of the American Dream. Although coming out can have multiple objectives, as stated above, these coming out speeches and images reflect precisely the type of narrative and affective strategy that Yasmin Nair laments.[85]

Nevertheless, viewed as a tactical strategy, coupled with all the other affective and visibility tactical strategies used by these activists, it becomes easier to see that the youth are interested in building strength through their perceived weakness. Even if such strategies are imperfect and problematic, they emerge from the realities of the youths' lived experiences. These actions caught the attention of federal, state, and local governments, and the general populace. After the launch week in 2010, this brand of politics featured centrally in DREAM actions, leading up to the final vote that failed to gain the sixty votes needed in the Senate to overcome a filibuster in mid-December. Coming out has continued as a predominant strategy in various manifestations ever since these first actions.

Although the DREAM Act failed in 2010, in his 2011 State of the Union address, President Obama again reiterated his support for comprehensive immigration reform and, especially, for the DREAM Act. Then on June 15, 2012, the Obama administration announced a "Consideration of Deferred Action for Childhood Arrivals Process" (DACA), a discretionary process started on August 15, 2012, to "ensure that enforcement resources are not expended on low priority cases."[86] Essentially, DACA offers temporary relief from the threat of deportation (including both those who are currently in removal proceedings and those who are not) to those youth who qualify. It may provide access to employment authorization. DACA, which is designed to last two years (although since it is discretionary, it can end at any time at the discretion of the US Citizenship and Immigration Service) and may be able to be renewed, does not provide any access to legalization. As some activists have cautioned, it essentially puts even those undocumented folks who were not on the USCIS radar into its records with an extensive amount of information.[87] Still, migrant youth who have come out have rightly attributed this move to their tireless activism and willingness to be "undocumented, unafraid and unapologetic."

Because migrant youth who come out have done so with a primary, and in some cases sole, interest in the passage of this piece of legislation, the coalitional gesture that they offer toward queer politics, other oppressed groups (including other migrants), or other social justice projects in their appropriation of "coming out" is, in effect, fairly limited. Moreover, as I have demonstrated, the material differences between the conditions of many citizen queers and migrants, especially with regard to the matter of legal citizenship and as demonstrated through the analysis of the closet and shadow metaphors, are perhaps so vast at this fundamental level as to make this strategy profoundly risky. If people are out of the shadows and there is no move to provide them with legitimate access to a pathway to citizenship, they are increasingly vulnerable to detention and deportation, and numerous DREAMers have been detained, subjected to deportation proceedings, and then deported.[88] Furthermore, people with whom migrant youth are in contact but because of age, criminal record, or other factors have no possibility of any protection at this time may be at greater risk and live in greater fear than ever before. The strategy that pits "deserving" against "undeserving" has had this consequence.

On the other hand, in August 2012 migrant youth activists, their supporters, and families went on a fifteen-city tour with a final destination in Charlotte, North Carolina, where the 2012 Democratic National Convention would be held in early September. Animated by the coming out strategy and many DREAMers, the "Undocubus" tour, also called the "No Papers, No Fear Ride for Justice," was designed to challenge the Obama administration's criminalization of all migrants. People ranging from eighteen to sixty-five years in age made the decision to come out, including many who were not eligible for the DREAM Act.[89] This action shows a broader aim for the coming out strategy, as well as the inclusion of a more diverse constituency of political actors. Whether the risks are worth the political opportunities or whether all such actions are purely utopian is no simple question to answer.

"I Am Undocuqueer"

In spite of its risks, the coming out strategy has evolved beyond mere appropriation and away from strictly legislative ends toward other gestures that have a potentially more extensive coalitional reach. For instance, in conjunction with the Undocumented Queer Youth Collective and the Queer Undocumented Immigrant Project, Julio Salgado's "I Am Undocuqueer" art, through his tumblr (a blogging site that primarily involves posting images), Facebook, and national showings of his work, has spread rapidly through activist communities in the United States. In late 2011, Salgado shared on his tumblr site a quotation reflective of a certain kind of response that some presumably heterosexual activists in the DREAM movement offer when queers try to make queer issues central to the movement. Salgado quotes one such response: "'Don't get me wrong, but what does being a queer have anything to do with the Dream Act? Or for that matter, with being undocumented and afraid? The main purpose is to pass the Dream Act. I don't see how associating an already controversial topic to an even more controversial topic (the Dram Act [*sic*]) makes matters any easier, or gives the Dream Act a stronger argument.'"[90] Salgado responds to this by noting that the DREAM Act is not a perfect solution and that he personally has problems with it, especially with the military provision. He also recognizes that it would not help his parents even though it would help him. He then suggests that the defining characteristic of DREAM activism is empowering people and, further, that what he has learned from younger undocumented and queer activists (Salgado was twenty-eight at the time he wrote this entry) is the importance of seeing the interlocking nature of identity. Salgado concludes:

> What does being a queer (I'm pretty sure the person meant it as a slur by the way, though I cannot say for sure) have anything to do with the DREAM Act? Probably not the immediate meaning people want to see when they don't immediately understand something. It's about being part of a community that is constantly marginalized and finding strength in what others see as our weakness. It's about finding a common ground and becoming a huge fist to punch the one bully we have in common.
>
> If you cannot see the connection, I don't know what to tell you.

Shortly after this blog entry, Salgado began publishing his "I am Undocuqueer" posters and encouraging undocuqueers to send him an email with a quotation explaining what it means to them to be both queer and undocumented along with a photo of themselves from the waist up. In this response Salgado reflects a queer coalitional ethic that does not orient toward the utopian or even entirely toward the normative. In recommending using a perceived weakness for strength and common ground and becoming a "huge fist" to injure or take out shared enemies, he moves beyond the inclusionary demands of the DREAM Act toward a demand for interlocking or interactional analysis, empowerment, coalition, and justice. Moreover, in refusing to do the work of laying out all of the connections between queer justice and undocumented justice, Salgado embodies an important approach advocated by women of color feminists like Lorde, who famously said, "Because I am woman, because I am Black, because I am lesbian, because I am myself—a Black woman warrior poet doing my work—come to ask you, are you doing yours?"[91]

The "I Am Undocuqueer" posters make a similar move beyond the DREAM, even as many draw upon themes and ideals that reflect normative aspirations. Each poster features a single activist wearing a white T-shirt emblazoned with two purple-and-white badges, one reading "Undocumented and Unafraid," the mantra of DREAM activism, and the other proclaiming "Queer & Unashamed." The white T-shirts have become a symbol of the immigrant rights and justice marches, as national leaders of organizations like Somos America in 2006 asked marchers to wear the white shirts as a symbol of peaceful protest. The undocuqueers are all standing, some with microphones, others with raised fists, and still others in the midst of giving a speech or chanting. Each image of a person is set against a bright, solid-colored backdrop and beneath the words "I Am Undocuqueer." Beside the image is the individual's quotation and first name. This quotation from Jonathan (see figure below) reveals an in-your-face coalitional approach as he calls upon the famous Queer Nation slogan, "We're here, we're queer, get used to it!" Other undocuqueers also take this position, including Aidan, who begins, "I'm here and I'm undocuqueer whether you like it or not!" Others imply that the average person has no choice but to recognize undocuqueers in their midst, such as Mario, who declares, "I am undocuqueer: You will meet me sooner or later." Some undocuqueers seek to recruit others, such as Reyna W., who states, "Coming out of the shadowy closet: Undocumented and queer, join me!" Although Reyna's presumed audience is other undocuqueers who have not exited the "shadowy closet"—itself a coalitional term—her call may also remind some of ongoing fears that queers will recruit the sons and daughters of middle America.

Another key coalitional gesture reflected in many of the undocuqueer posters is a blending of linguistic culture and community, a strategy that, especially initially, has been absent in much of the national DREAM activism and in fact discouraged on some DREAM social networks.[92] For instance, Alex proclaims, "I am undocuqueer: an inspiring hue of identities. Embracing my struggle, empowering la joteria, enamoring my passions: out of the closet(s)[,] out of the shadows!" Lucinda insists, "I'm an undocuqueer mujer! Resisting self-hate was the first step to empowerment. Let your light shine. El mundo nos necesita!" These and other quotations like them insist on the interlocking identities that constitute undocuqueers—racialized, linguistic, cultural, gendered, and sexual.[93] Even as queer coalitional politics are reflected in many of the undocuqueer posters, they often simultaneously point toward more utopian and normative directions that emphasize self-empowerment, identity, and acceptance while not mentioning other issues that are common to social justice struggles, such as power, oppression, or capitalism. The reduction of undocuqueer to an identity category premised in self-acceptance and overcoming fear is, on the one hand, an important step toward developing enough pride and confidence to do the difficult work of activism, as Clare has remarked.[94] The reduction also locates the plight of undocuqueer at the level of the individual, reproducing the

Example of an "I am Undocuqueer" poster. Used with permission of Julio Salgado.

problems implied by Ross's concept of "claustrophilia."[95] Importantly, as many of the posters emphasize, the undocuqueer is positioned in community, struggle, and a broader world, and the primary goal of self-actualization certainly has a further-reaching secondary goal of liberation and legalization. Still, one of the clear implications of the coming out strategy revealed by the undocuqueer posters is that even though the undocuqueer reflects the movement from appropriation to the development of the coalitional subject, the traces of the individualism of coming out as a political strategy remain. Furthermore, given that it is not merely a shadow or a closet from which undocuqueers emerge, but a "shadowy closet," to use Reyna W.'s words, undocuqueers carry the baggage of both metaphors with the added conditions of what it means to come out in an interlocking, intermeshing way.

Forced Out and Other Coalitions

Because of the centrality of the coming out strategy for migrant youth activism and the resulting constraints suggested above regarding identity politics, personal narrative, and individualism, this strategy has also catalyzed counter-DREAM activism that works to shift the political terrain. Such activism often also relies on coming out, but typically toward alternative coalitional ends. For example, a project of the American Friends Service Committee in San Francisco called "67 Sueños" has emerged to tell stories of what the group calls "underprivileged migrant youth."[96] Claiming that those on the right side of the political spectrum have constructed the undocumented solely as criminals and that those on the left have emphasized only the most talented and successful undocumented people, 67 Sueños features the voices of those who are neither criminal nor 4.0 students. They make this move with good reason. As the educational researchers María Pabón López and Gerardo R. López note, for instance, fifteen thousand undocumented youth drop out of US high schools each year.[97] Unless these youth obtain a GED, they would have no access to the conditional residency that the DREAM Act would supply. A Migration Policy Institute study has documented that as many as 62 percent of age-eligible youth will not actually qualify for the DREAM,[98] and 67 Sueños is based on the idea that as many as 67 percent of those who are age-eligible for the DREAM Act will not qualify for other reasons, ranging from a criminal history to the inability to pay for college. This project seeks inclusion for more people in the legislative agenda and more voices in the public sphere, and it invites migrant rights and justice activists to broaden their circle of belonging. The 67 Sueños program does not challenge the basic premise of organizing around undocumented identity and the promise of publicly coming out, nor does it point to queer coalitional politics; however, it does open up different kinds of questions about who is part of this conversation in the first place.

Other activists have gone further. For example, in late 2010 Raúl Al-qaraz Ochoa, a Tucson-based migrant activist, though one with LPR status, wrote an open letter to the DREAM movement, painfully explaining why he can no longer support the movement. Al-qaraz Ochoa was formerly very involved in DREAM activism, including being arrested outside of Senator John McCain's office in Tucson during an action in the spring of 2010, as mentioned in this chapter's introduction. Although other immigration and anti-militarization activists have publicly denounced the DREAM Act, Al-qaraz Ochoa is one of the only former DREAM activists to publicly announce his removal of support for the legislation, making his letter a particularly significant document. In his letter, which subsequently went viral, he begins with a gesture of differential belonging as he lauds DREAM activists in their pursuits. Still, he maintains that he could no longer support the DREAM Act for a number of reasons, including the fact that politicians in Washington, DC, use it as an excuse not to advance comprehensive immigration reform; support for the DREAM Act implies support for the US war machine; and Democrats and other advocates "vilify and criminalize" the parents of DREAMers. Al-qaraz Ochoa's public exit from DREAM activism strikes at some of the deep, systemic problems inherent in the actual legislation and how activism in support of the DREAM Act reproduces those same systems of oppression. His letter thus approaches the rhetoric of radical interactionality. Moreover, in his exit he issues a grand call for coalition, stating, "Strong movements that achieve greater victories are those that stand in solidarity with all oppressed people of the world and never gain access to rights at the expense of other oppressed groups."[99] Like 67 Sueños, Al-qaraz Ochoa upholds the basic premises of DREAM activism, careful to indict politicians in Washington as opposed to DREAMers themselves. Moreover, Al-qaraz Ochoa says, "Passage of the DREAM Act would definitely be a step forward in the struggle for Migrant Justice." Despite Al-qaraz Ochoa's maintenance of normative aspirations, his differential orientation and call for far-reaching solidarity again pushes migrant rights and justice toward more extensive coalitions.

Thus far, those who have used or responded to the coming out strategy have sustained one of the fundamental characteristics of coming out: they have asked for inclusion in a community—and in this instance the national community. As Nair might ask, is it possible to demand, in coalitional fashion, a different narrative and a different premise altogether? To provide one answer to that question, I turn to testimony given by José Guadalupe Herrera Soto at a 2012 Chicago forum called "Forced Out: A Unity Forum at the Crossroads of Deportation and Incarceration," designed to create a community conversation about the impacts of mass detention. Herrera Soto's testimony was subsequently published on the website for the Moratorium on Deportations Campaign.[100] This campaign, based in Chicago, seeks to end all deportations, legalize all undocumented people, and put a stop to all anti-immigrant legislation. Herrera Soto does not identify as a DREAMer. His testimony does not mention the DREAM Act, even though it is clear that DREAM activism is indicted in his testimony when he states, "Today, I'm challenging the system that questions my legality in the US. I'm fighting a personal battle against immigration authorities. Despite their attempts to deport me, I continue to be part of the immigrant struggle, the struggle that fights for all people—not just for a small few who are portrayed as being worthy."[101] While clearly positioning himself in contrast to DREAM activism, Herrera Soto's testimony reflects an alternative use of coming out toward coalitional ends, even though his is not, on its surface, explicitly queer with regard to gender or sexuality. However, as Fatima El-Tayeb argued about her use of the word "queer" to explain the strategies of European activists of color, "queer" describes "a practice of identity (de)construction that results in a new type of diasporic consciousness neither grounded in ethnic identifica- tions nor referencing a mythical homeland, instead using the tension of living supposedly exclusive identities and transforming it into a creative potential, building a community based on the shared experience of multiple, contradic- tory positionalities."[102] Herrera Soto advances a different coming out, one that deconstructs identifications based on multiple and contradictory positionali- ties toward the end of forging new conditions for activism and radical coali- tion. Moreover, these identifications and coalitions he seeks are not ethnically based or located in any particular nation or culture. This type of positioning is made explicit when Herrera Soto opens his testimony by arguing that the issue of detention and deportation of immigrants must be understood in connection to the prison industrial complex.

Herrera Soto mirrors the style of coming out testimony that has become so popular in migrant youth activism by naming himself and his identities early on in his speech. Yet he shifts from the traditional structure of the coming out nar- rative in some dramatic ways. Foremost, like Nair's use of the rhetoric of radi- cal interactionality, discussed in chapter 2, Herrera Soto draws attention away from the personal and toward a systemic critique of US capitalism, imperialism, and militarization, as well as the discourse of criminality that has constituted the entire immigration debate in the United States. For instance, he states, "My name is José Guadalupe Herrera Soto; I am considered a criminal, an illegal alien, a person without proper documentation." Many DREAM activists begin their speeches offering their name and indicating their undocumented status. Herrera Soto shifts that by announcing himself as a criminal and an alien. As Nicholas de Genova argues, some of the strategies of the migrant rights and justice movement have reflected a queer approach by announcing their presence and not asking for acceptance or inclusion.[103] Herrera Soto demonstrates this profoundly in his self-introduction and pushes even further in this direction when he indicts a system of capitalism and criminalization for stigmatizing him with these labels and oppressing him with incarceration, a criminal record, and possible deportation. He frankly explains, "This system was build [*sic*] for the purpose of profiting out of the criminalization, illegalization, racialization, incarceration and deportation of human beings; a system that pushes people into breaking capitalistic laws and thus turns humans into commodities." Rather than emphasizing individual culpability or choice, Herrera Soto turns attention to the capitalist system, which limits options and compels people to break often unjust laws while creating space for corporations to make money off of their criminalization. Most DREAMer testimonies feature stories of the hardships that undocumented youth have confronted and the profound successes they have achieved even in the face of such tremendous obstacles. Herrera Soto's testimony moves in a very different direction when he tells his story of breaking "capitalistic laws" and, since he was undocumented and without a driver's license, being charged with an aggravated felony. He explains that he refused to accept a plea bargain, which meant that he served time in Cook County Jail and fought deportation.

Whereas DREAMer testimonies often involve a declaration of belonging to the United States and a desire simply to be included through being offered a pathway to citizenship, Herrera Soto notes that he is not asking for inclusion in the racist system, nor will he conform in ways that will make him more palatable to that system. Instead, he insists:

> I have been labeled a criminal; therefore I stand up and join the struggle of those who are labeled criminals. I join the struggle of fellow human beings who are struggling to survive under the racist capitalist system we live in. I join the struggle of the marginalized, of the poor, of people of color. I join the 2.3 million people, who are behind cages, and I make no distinction between them and I, we are one, we have been labeled "criminals" by the racist system, the oppressor, the one that tries to silence and destroy our communities.

Herrera Soto's words could be characterized as utopian because of his grand desire to join a "struggle of fellow human beings," and he certainly offers such a declaration with a better potential future in mind. It is the present possibility of a coalition of those whom the system has deemed criminal, leading to an end of the racist, capitalist system that Herrera Soto foremost envisions. In this way, in coming out, he does not seek personal affirmation or a politics constructed through identity. He concludes, "We humans are not commodities and will continue to fight and make alliances to combat this. I am José Guadalupe Herrera Soto and I am grateful to share my testimony with all of you here today." Herrera Soto disrupts the usual function of identity in coming out rhetoric; he queers it. This in itself may fix or reduce the identities of other activists, and it is not that Herrera Soto can completely avoid identity. In its place he seeks *identification*, but such identification is not premised on the logic of personal identity and individual worthiness.

On November 1, 2012, Herrera Soto had a court hearing with DHS in which the judge determined that removing him would cause extreme hardship for a US citizen, his son.[104] Prior to his hearing, Herrera Soto and other members of the "No Name Collective" issued a "Call for (a Different Kind of) Solidarity." In it the collective refused to ask for people to support Herrera Soto as an individual, writing, "José has asked that we use his proceedings as a call to fight against the systems that classify and divide people." The call goes on to make statements that cannot be said in the scripted space of an immigration courtroom, including that immigration laws are illegitimate and courtrooms are mere spectacles. The call ends with the following: "Our resistance must refuse the narrative of the few exceptional cases and must stand with all those labeled criminal, or illegal, or deportable. We are sending this message today because we are looking for another way to resist and another basis for solidarity. Join us!" The issue of exceptionalism and worthiness is taken on directly in the image that accompanies the text where the collective critiques the use of petitions and the emphasis on exceptional individuals, suggesting that such use of the petition is both divisive and complicit with the corrupt system. The "Biography of Worthiness" image thus mocks the familiar petitions that circulate in order to get people to rally around individual cases. Despite the efforts of Herrera Soto and his supporters to work against these scripts, he still becomes an exception. He notes this in a comment on the event's Facebook page: "I know that I'm one of the lucky few that 'made it,' however thousands in similar situation as mines [*sic*] end up being deported." He goes on to challenge the logic that says the worthiest must be helped first, insisting, "My struggle has not ended, I'll continue to advocate for justice for all. Always speaking out against injustices and being critical of the struggle, using an identity based on politics rather than politics based on identity—like always." Here, Herrera Soto flips the identity logic popularized in DREAM activism. Although he still seeks community, it is not a community of normative citizens. Although he still desires belonging, it is through alliances with others who want more than inclusion into a corrupt

ATTENTION IMMIGRANT RIGHTS ADVOCATES!

Call for (a different kind of) Solidarity

Today, November 1, 9am-noon, Homeland Security has set a court date for Jose Herrera, a member of our collective. This stage of the attack against Jose is violence in a justice costume. But this is just one small part of an ongoing nightmare that is lived every day by millions of people. This message will not tell you Jose's story and ask that you support him as an individual. Instead, Jose has asked that we use his proceedings as a call to fight against the systems that classify and divide people—which are perpetuated not only in these proceedings, but too often in our resistance to them.

Those threatened with deportation are forced to participate in this ridiculous farce, to go into courtrooms and speak the script instead of speaking their minds. There is no way to say things as they really are in the place called a courtroom, so we say them here:

1. Immigration laws are illegitimate. They use "citizenship" to create unequal and exploited people.

2. An immigration courtroom is not a place of justice. It is a spectacle set up to focus attention on people called non-citizens and to mask the inequalities and exploitation that citizenship creates.

3. Jose is one of the lucky few who has the resources to fight his deportation. But those who can fight are pitted against others. They are forced to defend themselves on the grounds that they are more worthy, that they are somehow exceptional, implying that all others are not.

4. In defending individuals, friends and advocates are forced to replicate the distinction of worthy and non-worthy. This is where solidarity can become complicity.

BIOGRAPHY OF WORTHINESS

(This is where we would typically tell you all the ways in which Jose is good and upright, unlike the "unworthy" immigrants)

(This is where we would present a photo of our friend looking "wholesome" and "American," and totally different than all of the "unworthy" immigrants)

SIGN JOSE'S PETITION

(And here, while advocating for one of "the worthy ones," you would implicitly accept the system that condemns the rest)

As friends and advocates outside the courtroom, we do not have to follow the script of worthy and unworthy. Our resistance must refuse the narrative of the few exceptional cases and must stand with all those labeled criminal, or illegal, or deportable. We are sending this message today because we are looking for another way to resist and another basis for solidarity. Join us!

-No Name Collective

Image produced by the No Name Collective for José Herrera's immigration hearing, November 1, 2012. Used with permission of the No Name Collective.

system. Herrera Soto reveals how coming out retains the traces of the queerness of the tactical strategy by showing that coming out does not have to call for an inclusionary mode of belonging. His grand coalitional gesture and emergence still remain just as risky, if not riskier, given that he declares his coming out of the shadows as a threat to the system itself.

Conclusions

Coming out of the shadows as undocumented serves political functions for migrant youth in a way that is similar to how coming out of the closet does for queer people. Coming out, on the one hand, announces a desire to belong to a community and alter that community's boundaries so as to include the requesters. On the other hand, coming out pronounces one's visibility and presence without asking to belong to the system as it is, but with the intent to radically change it. For queer people who come out in either of these ways, the political objective for coming out can be achieved, at least in part, only through a logic of legal citizenship. The demands made, whether for inclusion or systemic change, are premised upon a belief that the state and its apparatus are broken, which means the state is not protecting or providing for its citizens in the ways it should. Even as queer politics often make demands through logics of justice or international solidarity, and not rights, many of the systems that need to be radically altered are those of nation-states. So citizens target nation-states with their political actions.

Queer and queer-minded migrants who initiated the coming out strategy within the migrant youth movement seem to have understood that effective coming out required, if not citizenship, a certain amount of privilege in the eyes of the nation-state. That DREAM activists rely on the words of Milk to animate their activism evidences this fact since they could have chosen many other activists with less privilege than, and similar politics to, their primary reference point. In the thinking of strategists, the exceptional status of many DREAMers likely would serve a similar function as citizenship or other forms of privilege. Yet queer activism, most notably AIDS activism, as well as activism on behalf of poor, homeless, drug-using, gender-nonconforming, sex-working queers, especially queers of color, teaches an important lesson: the state does not protect citizens. Further, the lessons of radical Black, Chican@, and American Indian activism tell a clear story about the US nation-state: criminalized populations, especially the poor and people of color, can expect little more than further criminalization when they challenge the laws and logics of the state. The counter-DREAM activists, especially Herrera Soto, recognize this historical fact. Both by virtue of his criminal record and his solidarity with the criminalized, Herrera Soto refuses to use coming out for exceptionalist ends. Instead, without possessing the right to the state, he demands a higher order of justice, making his politics a concrete example of radical queer migration politics. A radical queer migration politics recognizes the interlocking and intermeshing nature of oppression without reducing queer or migrant to an identity. Counter-DREAM activism like Herrera Soto's does not negate the validity of identity or the individual, even as such activism simultaneously refuses to premise politics on such identities or the stories of exceptional individuals.

Still, I want to suggest that even in the coalitional moments where DREAM-ers primarily rely on identity and exceptionalism, as found in much DREAM activism and in many of the "undocuqueer" statements, these normative aspirations should be evaluated differently than if they were the aspirations of US citizens. As Judith Butler and Gayatri Chakravorty Spivak question in their book *Who Sings the Nation-State?*, what happens when people with no legal right to the state make claims to it or in its name anyway? The very terms of that nation-state are, at least in some ways, thrown into crisis.[105] The appropriation of the coming out strategy reveals such a crisis in profound ways. Yet the risk revealed should not be underestimated. I return for a moment to the metaphors of the closet and the shadow. Even as the metaphor of coming out has been applied to a variety of different identities and situations, coming out always refers, even if only tacitly, to the closet. In the shift from the material entity of the closet to the ephemeral entity of the shadow, in the same way a shadow can disappear, for some the hope is that migrants can disappear too, no matter how talented or exceptional they may be. Because of their close connection with the home, closets suggest that those who come out of them still have a strong relationship to the intimate sphere. Certainly that relationship can be violent, hostile, and generally inhospitable, but it can also suggest familiarity, intimacy, and a willingness to offer protection. The shadow engenders no such connections and no such protection. So it seems to me that lacking the protection of legal citizenship does require, at least in part, a more generous reading of DREAM activists' normative and inclusionary aspirations given what they are risking and working against. This is especially the case because of the fact that the co-alitional gesture of the coming out strategy has opened up additional space for more radical coalition building like that advocated by counter-DREAM activists. The lack of protection—which, as stated above, exists for many who are citizens, especially those who are criminalized and citizens of countries outside the United States and yet affected by US militarism—is precisely the point that some of the counter-DREAM activists seem to clearly understand. In Herrera Soto's somewhat utopian call for solidarity and coalition, he clearly sees that no matter how deserving DREAMers may be, their inclusion will ultimately be contingent because of US racism, xenophobia, and capitalism. Their inclusion will always be premised upon others' exclusion from the possibility for a livable life. This point is one that DREAMers and undocuqueers no doubt do not want to take part in, which creates an imperative for the migrant youth movement to seek queerer coalitional moments, leading to queerer coalitional politics.

CHAPTER 4

Coalitional Politics
on the US-Mexico Border

W hen Arizona voters approved Proposition 200 in 2004, requiring their fellow Arizonans to show proof of citizenship to vote or receive certain health benefits, it marked one of the first of many laws in the early twenty-first century targeting marginalized groups in the state.[1] Activists in Tucson had anticipated movement toward enacting retrograde laws that would negatively affect marginalized groups for quite some time. Following the 2004 election, two leaders, Cathy Busha, then of Wingspan, and Kat Rodriguez, of Coalición de Derechos Humanos, wrote a commentary for the *Tucson Weekly*.[2] In their piece, similar to the statements later produced in 2006 (see chapter 1), Busha and Rodriguez argue that Proposition 200, Protect Arizona Now, shared much in common with a proposed marriage amendment that was to be on the ballot for 2006—what became Proposition 107, Protect Marriage Arizona. They suggest that the scapegoating strategies that anti-LGBT and anti-migrant forces use are essentially the same and that the attack on one marginalized group should concern all marginalized groups. Busha and Rodriguez wrote this commentary based on a long history of coalition work between the two organizations they represented. In chapter 1 I analyzed rhetoric produced by Wingspan and CDH. Here, I use field data collected during my yearlong qualitative research study as an activist with and liaison between Wingspan and CDH in order to articulate how a coalition between an LGBTQ rights and justice organization and a migrant rights and justice organization emerges, the strategies they employ to sustain it, and to suggest what such coalitions articulate about new possibilities within and for US rhetorical imaginaries.[3] I argue that CDH and Wingspan reflect a political orientation and mode of belonging that actively refuses the master's tool of divide and conquer, and they show how many forms of difference can be taken up in the service of coalition.[4] Moreover, this coalition provides insight into the specific kind of strategies that local groups can utilize in order to foster unlikely political coalitions and educate communities to shift local, state, and national ways of thinking, even though these strategies are imperfect and sometimes fail.

Only one extended academic study has actively explored sustained activist coalition work between migrant rights groups and LGBTQ rights groups in the United States.[5] This study examined the different strategies that two groups—Rural Organizing Project (ROP) and CAUSA—used to defeat anti-migrant and anti-gay ballot measures proposed in Oregon. ROP is a progressive network of local organizations that often focuses on gay and lesbian rights issues because of the plethora of anti-gay measures at the state and local level in Oregon. CAUSA is a coalition of local Latino, migrant, and workers' rights organizations that serves as a "voice" for the rights of those communities.[6] In the ethnography of the collaborations between these two networks, Lynn Stephen, Jan Lanier, Ramón Ramírez, and Marcy Westerling suggest some of the strategies and tactics that activists—particularly the leaders of these networks—used in order to defeat both anti-migrant and anti-gay political actions in Oregon. For instance, in 1997 one of Oregon's senators co-authored a bill that had the essential purpose of reinstating a failed and controversial guest worker program known as the Bracero program.[7] From the perspective of the migrant rights activists, this would reinstate all the oppression that the original program perpetuated. ROP took action by writing a letter to the senator, featuring migrant rights as a central workshop at their annual caucus, and discussing the issue in the network newsletter in a way that highlighted the parallels between this proposed anti-migrant legislation and an anti-gay measure that had been proposed in 1992.[8] Such strategies, coupled with the work by migrant rights activists, eventually led to the senator's decision to propose new legislation. This is one example of the different strategies that groups use to challenge oppressive representations and policies. The information present in the Oregon study provides an important impetus to consider strategies used in coalitions as well as the intersections among queer migration politics.

I begin this chapter by first describing my research with CDH and Wingspan. I go on to articulate how activists make use of the rhetoric in their communities about queers and migrants to animate coalition. I then engage in a theoretical discussion of coalitional politics, which is integrated within an analysis of how CDH and Wingspan build and sustain their coalition. In the last part of the chapter, I turn to the difficulties that face this coalition work and discuss the dissonances and struggles that affect coalitional politics.

Working with Wingspan and CDH

I engaged in nearly a year of participant observation and activism with Wingspan and CDH in 2006–2007.[9] After seeing Busha and Rodriguez speak about their coalition at a small conference in April 2006, I immediately contacted both activists to see about conducting an activist research project regarding the coalition their organizations have built. At the time, I had been involved in and thinking about LGBTQ activism for many years, though I was just starting to think about immigration because living in Arizona had compelled me to do so. I had long been interested in thinking about and theorizing coalition, and although I knew very little about why migration activists and queer activists would coalesce with each other, I knew that such an interesting—and, to me, unexpected—connection might provide incredible insights into understanding difference and coalition. Additionally, as a queer Chicana in Arizona, I felt implicated in and by both migration and queer politics. In the summer of 2006, then, I began visiting Tucson and spending time in both Wingspan and CDH. Through my regular physical presence and participation in email conversations, after a few months people in both organizations seemed to view my involvement as ordinary. My presence was like that of many of the other volunteers and interns that routinely cycle in and out of both organizations. I was also regularly invited to engage in other forms of direct participation. Sometimes these included basic graphic design, writing, and preparing to conduct qualitative needs assessments. Other forms of direct participation involved photocopying, handing out flyers, and setting up and taking down events. I was also actively involved in both formal and informal conversations with activists that often helped inform later choices for political action. Sometimes these conversations happened during regular work hours, sometimes through email, and other times while painting houses, having drinks and dinner, or just hanging out.

I lived ninety miles away, in Phoenix, so during my routine visits to Tucson, I engaged in a range of activities, including one-on-one meetings or conversations with people at Wingspan in order to talk about upcoming events or reflect on past activities, particularly around election time. I attended Wingspan staff and intern meetings. Sometimes I spent time in the community center simply observing the people who utilized the facilities. I also volunteered at the CDH office by organizing and preparing for different mobilizations to counter anti-migrant policy and practice and promote migrant causes. I did simple tasks there such as answering phones and creating flyers. I also attended the weekly CDH meeting on Thursday evenings. As mentioned in chapter 1, I functioned as an informal liaison between the two organizations, which meant that, if needed, I had time in meetings to report on what the other was doing and how the two groups could work together on various projects.

I also engaged regularly in email conversations and the construction of documents such as joint statements, position papers, and policy papers to be sent to local elected officials. These forms of "e-participation" were invaluable ways for me to stay connected even while being physically distant. Other forms of e-participation included receiving each organization's "e-news" through email. In total I spent more than 180 hours working directly with and observing Wingspan, CDH, and the coalition. After spending seven to nine months with participants, I also conducted thirteen in-depth interviews, ranging from 30 minutes to 2 hours each, with the purpose of having people talk in more detail about the way they understand and conceptualize their experiences.[10] These varying kinds of data provided a rich understanding of the coalition between Wingspan and CDH. At the request of participants, I use actual first names unless otherwise indicated.

The Need to Coalesce

Wingspan serves a community largely comprised of LGBTQ US citizens, a majority of whom are white. CDH represents a community of mainly Latin@ migrants who identify as heterosexual. Though certainly overlaps exist, most notably queer migrants who seek support from both organizations, the majority of each group's constituency does not necessarily see itself as naturally aligned with interests or identities of the other group. In fact, most people would probably see their interests and identities as very different from each other. Unlike much of the rhetoric analyzed in this book, then, and as demonstrated via Busha and Rodriguez's choice to write a commentary in a local news outlet linking migrant and queer concerns, CDH and Wingspan insist upon the interrelatedness of their struggles without having queer migrants at the center of their rationale.[11] As Kat puts it, "It's the same shit; it's a different brand of oppression, but it's the same ingredients."[12] Kat's statement functions as a synecdoche for the bigger argument Wingspan and CDH have created in order to rhetorically justify their coalition. This rhetorical approach is long-standing. Isabel, a co-founder and co-president of CDH, marks the inception of this thinking in the early 1980s. A Metropolitan Community Church (an LGBTQ church) had collected toys to give away for Christmas, but no mainstream organizations would accept the toys from this group. Isabel laughs, telling the inception story she had probably shared many times before: "I don't know how they came upon us, but we said yes, we'll take 'em. And I remember going, being the representative. I went to some event, big party, and it was a drag night, and I got all the toys. And so we started our [relationship]; it was great. And ever since then, we know that our struggles are the same."[13] Whether this event actually had the impacts Isabel suggests is hard to say, but the story evidences the approach that she and others take to the relationship among these groups.

Much of the feminist writing on coalition building emphasizes the necessity of accounting for and wrestling with difference. As Audre Lorde matter-of-factly states, "Ignoring the differences of race between women and the implications of those differences presents the most serious threat to the mobilization of women's joint power."[14] Alternatively, the coalition between Wingspan and CDH begins with an argument about the similarities of the struggles of migrants and queers against oppression. Isabel notes the seemingly simple event of a gift drive as the marker of a long-term relationship and acknowledgment of shared marginalization and struggle. Throughout the years, at least some members of the queer community knew they had allies in people like Isabel before CDH even existed. The longevity of that unofficial relationship undoubtedly laid the foundation for the contemporary coalition work of Wingspan and CDH. Once it formally launched in the late 1980s and early '90s, Wingspan was present at CDH events. Amelia (a pseudonym), a longtime migrant rights' activist and CDH volunteer, remembers representatives from Wingspan at CDH's first human rights conference in the early '90s. The consistent approach to viewing seemingly different issues as similar and interlocking provides a foundation for the coalition. Activists invent additional robust rhetorical justifications for their coalition.

As seen in the manifestos analyzed in chapter 1, much of this justification surrounded the way in which both queers and migrants function as scapegoats, but this also extends into both groups being regular targets of physical and rhetorical abuse. Isabel contends, "Our connections with the LGBT community now are so clear because there's open, open effort to ban us, to discriminate, to abuse, to inflict violence, to permit violence, all of that. Who have been the targets in the last ten years? The LGBT community and migrants. Where you can openly—it's no longer, you know, subtle discrimination, which we're masters at—but open, open discrimination. Look at the ballot measures. You can see it openly. It's, you know, attacking who we are."[15] Empirically, queer people and migrants have probably not been uniquely targeted in ways that differ dramatically from other marginalized groups. But for Isabel, what she names as the shared position of LGBTs and migrants as targets of open discrimination and abuse serves as a justification to link the struggles. Wingspan and CDH also find and invent rhetorical rationales for coalition in various discourses such as media, law enforcement, and policy, which, they argue, position migrants and queers as deviant and criminal.

DISCOURSES OF DEVIANCE AND CRIMINALITY

Historically migrants and queers have been figured as deviants within the national rhetorical imaginary. In popular media and political rhetoric, both groups have featured as prostitutes, sex radicals, political extremists, subversives, and much more. Media provide the most robust instances of connecting deviance with migrants and queers. As one example, among the most repeated talking points on the Department of Homeland Security's website's "Enforcement News" page is the number of undocumented immigrant sex offenders that Immigration and Customs Enforcement has apprehended and deported.[16] Such discourses work to position, in this instance, migrants as deviants. Anyone who supports them, then, must possess "fringe" politics because who would support such deviant people? CDH and Wingspan rhetorically connect such persistent discourses to highlight local and contemporary manifestations of them and show how the logics of deviance relatedly impact queers and migrants. Kat, for instance, explains an example derived from local media reporting that functions to position migrants and their supporters as fringe extremists under the façade of fair and balanced reporting. She says, "One of my biggest complaints of them [the media], say, April tenth last year [2006], eighteen thousand people at a march [for migrant rights and justice in Tucson] and there were about ten or twelve, maybe—I don't even think there were that—maybe six to ten protesters maybe in the middle of that, and we were given equal time in the media. And you know, they said, 'Well, we have to be fair and unbiased,' and I challenged them and said, 'Do you really think eighteen thousand to ten is fair, is fairly balancing it?'"[17] In one way Kat's argument inadvertently supports the possibility for the tyranny of the majority simply because they are mightier—ten people's perspectives are not equal to or as important as those of eighteen thousand people. In another way Kat contends that the media's coverage of the march suggests that the extremist, anti-migrant protesters at the march were an appropriate counterpoint to those who marched and organized the march. This positions migrants and their supporters as fringe groups on the left and the protesters as fringe groups on the right. By this logic it would be possible to deduce that because migrants are extremists themselves, anti-migrant sentiment is a reasonable response. This kind of reporting also may bolster existing anti-migrant sentiment by suggesting that there are as many people who support migrants as there are who oppose them.

Such beliefs are easily upheld in a media and political climate that regularly bombards people with information about migrants that claims they are deviant or are connected to deviant behaviors. Alexis, a CDH activist who also worked for the Pima County Public Defender's Office, notes that the Border Patrol, for example, has an aggressive media department, and since the mid-1990s it shifted from issuing weekly press releases to releasing press statements almost daily "on the number of people they've arrested, the number of drugs they've seized, the number of smugglers they've charged."[18] Local media regularly utilize the Border Patrol statistics and analyses and report on them, thereby normalizing deviant discourses in relation to migrants and migration issues. Even though CDH and local immigration scholars have continually disputed the methodologies utilized to derive such numbers, the repetition of Border Patrol statistics and perspectives gives them the status of truth; meanwhile, migrant rights seem less logical because of the fact that all migrants engage in "deviant" behavior.[19]

Although it is limited and narrow, activists generally view queer representation (noting that queers are always US citizens) in the local media as more positive than representation of migrants. Still, a scandal in spring 2007 pertained to local media coverage featuring gay men as deviant. Cathy told me the following:

> So there's the recent Channel 9 sex in the park, sex-posé, and they do it every year when it's rating time. And, you know, suddenly it was painting this picture of men—you know, gay men go to parks and have sex behind bushes where little kids are playing—and it's hard to believe that that's still even acceptable as a news story. And so I think both groups [queers and migrants] very easily and quickly can be exploited during sweeps week by the media. You know, I remember a different TV station, but same time of year, doing, you know, terrorists coming across the border and showing people sneaking over in darkness at night, and it's almost similar imagery—you know, like what do they do at night when your children are sleeping—just really playing on fear.[20]

KGUN-9, an ABC-affiliated Tucson television station, featured the "sex-posé" Cathy mentions. Beforehand the reporter, Jennifer Waddell, assured Wingspan that the discussion of sex in the parks would not focus on gay men or reinforce stereotypes about gay men as deviants or predators. After it aired, however,

Wingspan condemned the report as both "sensationalistic" and "inflammatory"[21] because although the report also mentioned that married heterosexual men use parks for sexual purposes, it primarily featured gay men. It also included an interview with a gay man with his face shadowed to protect his identity. Wingspan suggests that the interview "reinforced the stereotype of gay men as hiding in dark places."[22] Based on the discussion of the shadow metaphor in the last chapter, Wingspan's alarm about the implications of the shadowing seems warranted. This sort of reporting suggests that queers engage in deviant sex practices for which they should be ashamed, and that by extension anyone who would struggle for their rights to engage in shameful behavior must engage in fringe politics.[23]

Cathy illuminates the troubling imagery for queers, and she makes a parallel with imagery used for migrants seen crossing the border at night. In highlighting the similar ways that queers and migrants can be fashioned as deviants, Cathy supplies justification for coalition building with migrant rights. Oscar, then a Wingspan activist and bilingual educator, echoes this sentiment: "This is my own personal pet peeve, when they show, they constantly show people running under borders."[24] While activists generally think queers are positioned less often as deviants than migrants, the possibility of problematic representation always exists, which is why activists also note the connections between the ways migrants and queers can be fashioned as deviant. As several activists mentioned to me, it is important to use these instances as coalitional moments that enable rhetorically building connections in community members' minds about the similarities between problematic representations, which helps to foster understanding between groups. As Kat explains, the idea of queer sex disgusts some in the migrant community, and part of her job is to demonstrate to them how what they find deviant about queers are the same things people find deviant about them.[25] If community members understand that they are not the only ones who are imagined as shadowy strangers engaging in bad behavior in the dark, then they may be more likely to challenge those representations and ideas when they see them.

One particular kind of deviance discourse that implicates both queers and migrants, and that has been discussed throughout this book, is that of criminality. At times, albeit to different degrees, both Wingspan and CDH have had tense relationships with law enforcement, including the Tucson Police Department (TPD) and, for CDH, the Border Patrol. The stressed relationship largely stems from the discourses of criminality that loom over both migrants and queers and manifest in how law enforcement often regards them. As has been increasingly demonstrated in research, queers—especially gender-variant queers, migrants, and people of color around the United States—are much more likely to be profiled, criminalized, and incarcerated than other groups.[26]

The first day I spent volunteering with CDH, Alexis told me stories about the TPD's failure to protect migrants and migrant supporters. CDH held a community forum at Armory Park, and before it began I followed Alexis around, helping to set up tables and chairs. CDH had organized a large security committee for the forum. Alexis explained that the event required so much civil security because the TPD was going to allow Roy Warden, a local vigilante and member of a group called the Border Guardians, to be present outside of the building.[27] Earlier in the year, Warden threatened Isabel with "blowing her head off," but the police did not consider his threat realistic. CDH eventually negotiated a deal with the TPD so that Warden could not be near Armory Park. During the middle of the forum, another local vigilante, Russ Dove, walked directly into the event and began yelling at the audience.[28] CDH security folks removed Dove long before the police arrived.[29] Incidences such as this one, where police ignore threats to activists' lives and refuse to enforce deals they make to protect people, reinforce the common belief among activists that members of law enforcement consider migrants and migrant rights activists criminals, or at least unworthy of protection. And those populations are very often the same populations subject to processes of criminalization.

One of the most notorious cases of migrants and supporters being framed as criminals came during the April 10, 2006, march. According to activists, the TPD failed to separate vigilantes from the marchers by allowing vigilantes to protest in the center of the street where marchers marched. As CDH activists describe the scene, when Warden and the Border Guardians decided to burn the Mexican flag amid the marchers (an act Warden is known for committing at a variety of locales in Southern Arizona), a young woman in her teens threw a bottle of water at the flag to put out the flames. Police tackled her and several youth were subsequently beaten.[30] Following the incident, members of CDH and the newly created April 10th Coalition hosted a series of events calling attention to police brutality and law enforcement criminalization of migrant communities, including a play written by high school students involved in the incident.[31]

Police abuse and harassment of migrant communities occurs in everyday situations as well, which is one of the main kinds of abuse that CDH volunteers document at regular abuse documentation sessions held at the office.[32] Law enforcement abuse has been a central concern for CDH since its creation.[33] While the actions against migrants and activists are physical as well as rhetorical, many activists contend that it is because of the convenient slippage between migrants and criminality in people's minds that such physical brutality happens and often goes unpunished.

The TPD has also positioned queers as criminal in southern Arizona, particularly in relation to public parks. At one point Wingspan members explained that the harassment was so severe that plainclothes police officers repeatedly attempted to entrap men who have sex with other men at the parks. Local residents hid in the bushes while wearing camouflage in order to catch men who they presumed were there for sex and to then call the police.[34] Police eventually stopped some of these practices and now claim they only come to a park if they get a complaint. Wingspan still receives several weekly calls alleging police harassment. This is not surprising, considering that gays (and Jews) top the list of hate crime victims in Tucson, and many report outrage at the way the police handle these incidents.[35] The association of queers with criminality is an enduring one.[36]

Migrants, queers, and queer migrants often find themselves in situations where they are not protected. Such constructions and treatment can also lead to coalition building, as evidenced by what happened after the problem with the TPD harassing gay men in public parks. Cathy explains, "And we were sort of shocked, and then we realized it's profiling, it's the same thing. So we held a community forum on profiling. And we were able to build an alliance with the NAACP, with Derechos [CDH], with Wingspan, and with a student group. And we talked about how these different groups get profiled, and what does that mean for civil rights, and how do we together address that."[37] Cathy notes that in bringing these groups together, they adopted new ways of thinking about these issues. For one, men having sex in public parks is a controversial topic within and outside of the queer community. These organizations broadened the analysis to show that the issue was not whether men are having sex in parks or whether they should be. Rather, the issue became "this is about police who have probably better ways to spend their time, harassing people in parks."[38] In a larger sense it allowed all of these different groups to understand a long shared history of being thought of, positioned as, and treated as criminals, which has material effects for how people are able to exist.

In each of the coalitional moments discussed here, activists make use of the rhetoric that exists in discourses pertaining to their communities to foster coalitional politics. Since these two groups do not begin from the needs and experiences of queer migrants, their coalition has been crafted through arguing that these supposedly separate and different groups share struggles and experience similar forms of oppression. This argument is clearly strategic and simplifies the complexities of migrant and queer experiences, perhaps so much so that the argument could be off-putting. White, middle-class, gay and lesbian citizens certainly may experience being treated as deviant, but it would be very hard to claim that this is parallel to or the same as the criminalization of undocumented working-class migrants of color. Thus, the strategy of reframing difference as similarity, as Wingspan and CDH do, is risky and could even lead to problematic analogies that could further disenfranchise vulnerable groups. This type of concern is what leads many communities of color and their allies to be wary of the analogy between "marriage equality" and black civil rights. Because the marriage movement has been widely critiqued as a concern of white, middle-class, cisgender gays and lesbians, the analogy tends to put racism as a problem of the past at the same time it positions the end of heterosexism and homophobia as the next frontiers in achieving equality.[39] Such thinking not only reinforces present-day color-blind racism, but it also further marginalizes queers of color. Wingspan and CDH's strategy of reframing difference possesses similar potential risks. Still, the strategy creates space for new imaginaries of belonging and politics that would not otherwise exist.

Sustaining a Coalition

Wingspan and CDH activists have clearly found and created numerous reasons to coalesce, but actually maintaining a coalition is perhaps less simple than justifying the need for its existence. In this section I utilize coalitional theories, mostly created by US women of color feminists, to help frame and explain the successes and difficulties of the coalition of Wingspan and CDH in the ways they express that coalition to each other and the public. These organizations use a variety of strategies and approaches toward coalition building. For example, on a very general level activists contend that the most important foundations for their coalition involve maintaining consistency in their communication about collaborative activities and constructing consensus on what should happen with specific projects. These foundations communicate trust between the organizations. Both Wingspan and CDH have the assurance that their issues are present in each other's minds and are a part of their decision making. Although Wingspan people are rarely if ever present when CDH decisions are made, and vice versa, there is confidence that one's physical absence never means an absence in mind. As Aimee Carrillo Rowe found, one hallmark of transracial feminist alliances is the promise that when a person has a relationship across differences, she will consistently think about how conversations/decisions affect the person or group with whom she is in alliance.[40]

With these foundations in mind, here I primarily focus on how activists work to build their coalition in ways that specifically strengthen their commitment to queer migration politics, which often involves speaking on behalf of the other's issue. As Linda Alcoff has famously explained, while speaking for another engenders ethical and epistemological difficulties, it is nonetheless necessary. CDH and Wingspan's speaking on behalf of each other includes checking privilege, confronting diversions, and educating each other.

CHECKING PRIVILEGE

Cathy remarks that Wingspan community members occasionally question her, through email, about Wingspan's position on immigration. Cathy responds by inviting the community member for coffee so that they can have a real dialogue about these issues face-to-face. Most people do not take her up on her offer, and Cathy makes sense of this, saying, "It's like there's sort of a level where they know it's racist to feel that way, and not wanting to sit across from somebody and have a conversation. Like, I think they almost know that they can kind of hide it behind a computer screen."[41] Though Cathy rarely has the opportunity to have open dialogue with these community members, asking someone to come out from behind the computer screen is an invitation to "check" their race and citizenship privilege. The notion of "checking privilege" is a colloquial term commonly used in antiracist and anti-sexist communities that invites members of a privileged community to reflect upon assumptions they have resulting from a position of privilege. In addition to calling the community member to check privilege, Cathy's invitation is also an assertion of the privileging of solidarity with CDH over the desires of one Wingspan community member. Though probably not always, Cathy suggests that many of these complaints come from white community members. As a white person, Cathy's attempts to dialogue with other white people about these issues are opportunities for her to educate folks so that people of color are not implored with the task.

Kat shares this sentiment, saying, "That's my job as a brown person to check my brown sisters and brothers on those issues [homophobia and heterosexism], and I don't mind it."[42] Although a number of CDH's active volunteers are queer, CDH also deals with heteronormativity and homophobia, though in my experience the manifestations among volunteers were rare. Most members of CDH use humor and direct communication to "check" each other on heteronormative comments. One example emerged from a working meeting I participated in during January 2007 with a semi-regular volunteer named Evan (a pseudonym). As we prepared flyers for an upcoming event, Evan talked about some professional football player whom "every woman in America," would love to be with. Michelle, a white CDH volunteer who identifies as lesbian, said, "Who do you think you're here with? 'Every woman in America who?'" She stared at Evan waiting for an answer as he began stammering. Nancy, a heterosexual CDH volunteer, chimed in, "And some men too," to which Evan mumbled, "Probably." The rest of us laughed. Shortly after that encounter, and in a private conversation, Michelle and I decided that we need business cards reading, "Check your heteronormativity." In order to avoid arguments with people when they display heteronormativity around us, we joked, we could just hand them a card.[43] This rather humorous encounter demonstrates the way most people in CDH—queer or otherwise—are aware of heteronormativity, at least when it is overt. In this example Michelle responded directly to Evan's assumption that he sat among heterosexuals, whereas Nancy supported Michelle's critique using humor. While Evan did not necessarily "get it" and appeared slightly uncomfortable with the interaction, he did not get to speak unchecked. Nancy and Michelle's response to Evan also resisted his assumption that he spoke for other members of the group. By challenging the assumption that everyone engages in heterosexual relationships, CDH activists check one another not only in relation to their allies but also in relation to themselves. This generally functions to create a safe space for queer people in CDH meetings and to keep sexuality at the forefront of CDH's analysis of social justice issues.[44]

There is a sense, then, that as a predominantly US citizen, white organization, Wingspan will do its best to check the race and citizenship privileges of its largely US citizen, white constituency. At the same time, CDH does its best to check the heterosexual privilege of its largely heterosexual community. The willingness to check privilege in these ways reflects Gayatri Chakravorty Spivak's distinction between the call *to* the ethical and the call *of* the ethical.[45] Cultural studies scholar Sangeeta Ray explains that a call to the ethical fails to recognize other cultural ways of knowing and doing.[46] In other words, the call *to* the ethical privileges one's own obligation to respond to another, but only through the lens of one's own world. On the other hand, the call *of* the ethical means a person understands that others have ways of knowing and doing that are different from one's own way of knowing. One does not feel obligated, however, to respond to the other on one's own terms; rather, one feels responsible to the other and understanding her as best she can. A subject is thus ethical when she responds to the call *of* the ethical, which implies a sense of responsibility to an other who is different. Checking privilege undoubtedly presents ethical concerns, but if it is done through the call *of* the ethical based on a responsibility to someone different from the self, this communicative act is ethical.

CONFRONTING DIVERSIONS

Difference is central to coalition building. It should be wrestled with and confronted rather than denied, destroyed, or diverted. Lorde writes, "Now we must recognize differences among women who are our equals, neither inferior nor superior, and devise ways to use each others' difference to enrich our visions and our joint struggles."[47] As discussed in relation to the manifestos analyzed in chapter 1, the centrality of difference to coalition work and politics generally is directly opposed to divide-and-conquer politics. Engaging in political work does not mean that people cannot use other master's tools to achieve goals, but it does mean that differences should not be used to destroy community; people must discover ways to turn them into sites of strength and empowerment.[48] As with "gray politics," Patricia Hill Collins notes in her explication of what Italian feminists coined as "transversal politics" that coalition building necessitates rejecting the binary logics such as "us" and "them" that have long been central to all kinds of oppression.[49] At the same time, such politics resist homogeneity, instead pointing toward dialogue across differential positionings.[50]

As feminists (and others) have long argued, the best diversion tactic is to maintain divisions,[51] and it is imperative that Wingspan and CDH work to challenge divisive tactics that can come from the community. Kat purports, "If you're divided by your suffering rather than what's causing your pain, that's a really ingenious distraction from questioning the system. That's like the best diversion ever. And, you know, if you're buying into that shit . . . you paid in full for a piece of crap."[52] The frankness of Kat's metaphor highlights the necessity of gray politics that confront the diversion tactic of division. One of the main reasons that both CDH and Wingspan can coalesce is because they publicly and privately challenge divisions by redirecting diversions. In part, confronting such tactics occurs through the construction of the rationale for their coalition, which reframes differences as similarities. But resisting diversion tactics also occurs in activists' micro-practices. One main way that each group challenges these tactics is by promoting the belief that rather than diluting one's struggle by acknowledging someone else's struggle, joining another's struggle strengthens one's own. This is not to suggest that either group is without its share of community members (and perhaps even activists/volunteers) who privately believe in the divisions among suffering communities and that joining another weakens one's own. For example, some of those in the migrant and Latin@ communities

CDH represents feel uncomfortable thinking of themselves in community with queer people. Usually these instances that CDH activists report emerge from a very narrow definition of who counts as part of the community. As a result, CDH activists very often attempt to redefine the community so that its rich diversity shows through. Kat, for example, happened to mention to a Latino friend that she was going to write the *Tucson Weekly* commentary with Cathy, and she relates the following about his reaction:

> He was, like, "No, don't. Don't do that, come on, what are you doing? Don't do that, don't go with them, what the hell are you doing?" And I was so shocked because I would never have thought of him as a homophobic person, but I couldn't think of any other way to identify it when he was thinking, like, "Why are you doing that, don't do that to us," and I was thinking, *Who are you? What do you mean us? What's an "us"?* And in his mind, LGBT people are in this little box, and he doesn't realize that they cross over all these other things—the poverty issue, the race issue, the class issue—all there, and you can't take that out.[53]

Kat's example indicates how queer people can be completely removed from the discourse of what it means to be Latin@ or migrant. Feminists such as María Lugones and Gloria Anzaldúa have similarly argued how nationalist logics within such communities function to erase queer belonging. Kat went on to say, "It's close-minded, but I'm willing to challenge that within my own people—like tell him, you know what, that's stupid of you, what the hell are you talking about?" Kat's example not only demonstrates the problems with divisive thinking, but it also shows how she directly confronted her friend and tried to redefine who counts as a part of "us." Alexis affirms this definitional narrowness among some community members when she notes that there is "a widespread ignorance in the migrant community about LGBT issues, about homophobia, how that impacts people. There's a lot of silence around that. And likewise, in [the] LGBT community, there's a lot of ignorance again of issues, because everyone's being subject to the same racist, homophobic media and school system."[54] Alexis and Kat both contend that people are raised in relation to the same racist and homophobic discourse, so it is not surprising that people have these views of one another. Kat's questioning of "What's an 'us'?" however, demonstrates her commitment to developing a coalitional subjectivity. It shows how she wants to talk about herself and her identity as inextricably bound to others with whom she may be in coalition at the same time that they may be dissimilar. Kat's questioning pushes her friend and others around her to challenge how people understand themselves and how they construct and treat each other. These tactics are imperfect, but the activists' commitment to challenging divisiveness provides an opportunity for different constructions of queers, migrants, and discourses of race, gender, and sexuality more generally. Though the impacts may be minimal, as a queer person of color who functioned for a short time as a liaison between CDH and Wingspan, I believe the importance of redefining belonging through the confrontation of diversions is difficult to overstate. Such tactics made me feel like a valued activist. They also afforded me the confidence to feel as though I belonged in CDH and to speak publicly to Wingspan and others about the seriousness of CDH's commitment to coalescing with Wingspan and queer rights and justice more generally.

Working to sustain the belief in interlocking struggles through privilege checking and confronting diversions is essential to the development of co-alitional subjectivities.[55] A coalitional subjectivity that is always already in relation undoubtedly furthers the ability to respond to the call of the ethical, which values another on her terms. Her terms will never become another's terms, but her terms are now woven with and productive of one's own. Even as activists undoubtedly fail at always responding to the call of the ethical, the public commitment continues to position that call as an expectation and desired objective.

EDUCATING EACH OTHER

The commitment that Wingspan and CDH have to educating their constituencies and each other is a key strategy, apparent in a joint grant proposal they wrote in 2005. Though the grant was not funded, examining the text of the grant indicates the kind of work that the groups aimed to do if they had the resources. To my knowledge, CDH and Wingspan never reapplied for the grant, perhaps making it nothing more than a symbolic performance of coalitional intent. Still, after conversing with Cathy about the proposal, I believe it was a sincere attempt at fostering coalition, and as a document it reveals the groups' shared belief in mutual education. In the proposal Wingspan and CDH set out "to empower Latino/as and LGBT and allied people to work together to examine the societal conditions affecting their lives, to think strategically about addressing those issues, and inspire them to engage in long-term social change work together."[56] In order to achieve that goal, the grant proposal suggested that the groups would start by holding two-hour educational sessions for each other about their movement's history. This strategy would encourage the development of coalitional subjectivity, or what Paul Lichterman calls "multivalent identity," where people keep several identities on the horizon and in thinking at once. It would also adopt what Lichterman describes as the "forum" quality of movements, where talk can be about practicing ideas and learning as opposed to simply strategizing for action.[57] Though the two histories represented in this grant proposal were queer and Latin@ (as opposed to migrant), because of the location in southern Arizona and the history of Latin@ struggles in the United States, migrant issues would have been central. Additionally, the proposal called for a joint forum to educate the communities at large, a joint memorial celebration of Anzaldúa, and a requirement that volunteers from each organization devote at least forty hours to the other organization's work. This volunteer work would have served the function of familiarizing staff and volunteers with the other's issue. The ultimate goal of trying to receive money to facilitate the coalition was to build understanding and communication between two groups that are often viewed as distant from each other and educate them on the relatedness of their issues. The fact that such work is imagined as being possible only with the funds to do it points to a deep problem that Andrea Smith critiques with regard to nonprofit organizations whose objectives are dictated by what wealthy foundations are willing to pay them to do.[58] It also could suggest that even though people said this was a priority, it was not enough of a priority to be part of the general operating budget.[59] Given the very small size of the CDH budget when I was working with them, and the more urgent priorities, including worker abuse and deaths in the desert, it does not seem plausible that this project could have been part of CDH's general operating budget. With Wingspan those possibilities are less clear to me, since it has a larger budget and an avowed need to reach out to more communities of color. Such tensions over priorities are common and endless within nonprofit organizations, and the tensions are likely even starker as groups attempt to coalesce with one another. Nevertheless, the effort toward further sustaining coalition is laudable. It is also somewhat utopian in that this goal was a failure in one sense but a not quite attainable potentiality in another. This strategy shows how the utopian and coalition are not always completely distinct.

Importantly, much like I mentioned in chapter 2, such coalition building is not and would not have been easy. As Anzaldúa suggests, "there is no such thing as a common ground."[60] Bernice Johnson Reagon writes of coalition work, "Most of the time you feel threatened to the core and if you don't, you're not really doing no coalescing."[61] Thus, coalition work is not like spending a lot of time with people who are very like-minded. As Johnson Reagon says, coalition work is not about feeling good—"in a coalition you have to give."[62] This all means that in a coalition there are not hard and fast agreements on every issue, and even some basic philosophies may not be shared. Yet an acknowledgment of history is essential. History must be approached in a broad sense, and the relational nature of group histories has to be a foundation to the work.[63] This is why working to educate each other's communities about history and shared struggles, in the way that Wingspan and CDH sought to do, is central to coalition building, even if it is only ever a utopian goal.

Moreover, creating opportunities to communicate in order to build bridges across lines of difference proves central to coalition building. Lugones and Elizabeth Spelman write, "Only when genuine and reciprocal dialogue takes place between 'outsiders' and 'insiders' can we trust the outsider's account."[64] Coalition building requires dialogue, but considering power differences must be a precursor to that dialogue. This implies, for example, that if white women and women of color are to engage in coalition work and white women are to understand what women of color are saying and how they experience their lives, "they must understand our communities and us in them."[65] The rhetorical silences created by discourses of privilege such as whiteness or wealth are perhaps the biggest roadblock to forging coalitions.[66] Narrow or underdeveloped perceptions of the other, especially the other who is more marginalized, cannot be tolerated in coalition work, which displays the necessity of developing and utilizing strategies that attend to power differentials and create the platform for open dialogue. For this reason, a commitment to education is paramount to building and sustaining any coalition.

CDH and Wingspan have worked to create a coalition and to foster an environment where such a coalition can continue to sustain itself. Thus far, however, I have focused on the seeming simplicity of this coalition with its management and productive use of difference. It would be disingenuous to suggest that this kind of coalitional politics is simple or that these groups do not face severe obstacles in the work they do. In the next two sections I focus on some of these difficulties. The next section draws from data collected while working with CDH, and I identify the ways that CDH in particular uses what I describe as "dissonance" to actually strengthen its coalitional commitment. The final section focuses specifically on the ongoing struggles that plague the coalition.

The Uses of Dissonance

To facilitate this discussion of dissonance, I want to take a brief theoretical diversion into musical theory because in western thought dissonance is most commonly understood as a musical term that refers to usually loud, disagreeable sounds or discord, often the opposite of harmony. Thinking about dissonance metaphorically, through the musical concept it refers to, illuminates the complex ways that dissonance operates amid a movement—both in the musical and political senses. As musical theorist Norman Cazden explains, "In musical harmony the critical determinant of consonance or dissonance is expectation of movement. This is defined as the relation of resolution. A consonant interval is one which sounds stable and complete in itself, which does not produce a feeling of necessary movement to other tones. A dissonant interval causes a restless expectation of resolution, or movement to a consonant interval."[67] Although cacophony can be disconcerting to the ear, innovative musicians such as Bach and others used dissonance to create new sounds that are all a part of the eventual harmony of a completed work. In this way dissonance both connotes something moving toward completion and something potentially, though not inherently, very displeasing. It produces the energy and anxieties that often instigate movement to some other place. As a metaphor for the utility of difference within the context of social movement, dissonance potentially causes problems for relationships within movements, but it also instigates, agitates, and informs; dissonance disturbs and creates energy around some issue so that it remains altered in our consciousness; dissonance produces the necessity for movement.[68]

Within coalitions, dissonance might emerge from an action, a stance, or another relationship that one ally possesses that could create discord among allies. Dissonance does not necessarily refer to a contradiction or opposition; instead, it suggests something that calls for attention and must be addressed or else it can create divisions that may hinder or immobilize a coalition. Political activist organizations exist within communities not as disparate entities but as embedded components of the larger whole. They function in relation to many other organizations and individuals that are simultaneously mobilizing with their objectives in mind. Sometimes these objectives converge, and despite the unlikely coalitions that are formed, activists recognize the benefit in affiliating against the divide-and-conquer mentality and toward a united position. In this section I present the dissonances that emerge for CDH's coalition with Wingspan from its affiliations with other groups. Recognizing that CDH's own beliefs and values can also be incongruous with its coalitional commitment to Wingspan, I then move to illustrate the ways CDH activists use the energy provoked by these dissonances to move and maintain the group's coalition with Wingspan.

DISSONANT AFFILIATIONS

The nurtured ties that CDH has with the Catholic Diocese of Tucson were palpable and unsettling to me when I first began my work with the organization. The Catholic Church has historically been central to immigration mobilization in the United States,[69] and if you drive around downtown Tucson communities, it is hard to go a few blocks without seeing a "Good Samaritans" sign posted in a front yard.[70] Isabel notes that the Catholic Church was the first religious body to help CDH try to stop the migrant deaths occurring in the desert, largely guided by the biblical call to help the poor and the stranger. Despite this deep commitment to migrants, as I folded pamphlets and made protest signs while sitting among banners decorated with *La Virgen de Guadalupe* and Jesus in a crown of thorns, I could not stop thinking about the havoc the Church has wreaked on the lives of queers.[71]

Most individuals or groups engage in multiple alliances or coalitions simultaneously. And it is in the multiplicity of affiliations and relations people possess that a first sort of dissonance can arise. For example, heterosexual white women's relationships with white men potentially produce fissures in their relationships with lesbians and women of color.[72] As Tricia S. Jones maintains, allying with one often means distancing from another.[73] So, although Wingspan and CDH coalesce with each other, some of the affiliations and relationships they have with other groups create dissonance between them, such as CDH's relationship with Catholicism.

The dissonance produced via CDH's relationship with the Catholic Church became tangible in 2006 when the Church condemned the four anti-migrant measures placed on the Arizona ballot while it simultaneously voiced strong support for Protect Marriage Arizona.[74] CDH needed to remain in coalition with the Church even as the Church held this problematic position, one that was potentially very damaging for Wingspan community members as well as those whom CDH serves. The strong position of the Church was not a surprise, but its persistent rhetoric against queers created a potential difficulty for CDH's relationship with Wingspan during an election year when the two organizations were actively working together to demonstrate the relationships between anti-queer and anti-migrant sentiment and politics. Wingspan also has good relationships with many churches and religious institutions in Tucson, yet during my research it seemed clear that the Catholic Church was not an ally, and the Church's support of Protect Marriage Arizona certainly demonstrated that.

Furthermore, the Church's pro-immigration rhetoric was also a source of dissonance between Wingspan and CDH. For instance, the Arizona Conference of Catholic Bishops (ACCB) recommended opposition to Proposition 200 in 2004 because, "These hardworking immigrants are people of remarkable faith and piety. Their pro-life and pro-family values can be a great asset to our culture and to our Church."[75] The Church's rationale for supporting migrants is similar to its rationale for opposing queer rights. The ACCB's statement in support of Protect Marriage Arizona invited believers to reflect on the following question: "What is marriage, its purposes, and its value to individuals, families and society?"[76] The statement goes on to suggest that while people of "homosexual orientation" must be treated with respect, the institution of marriage must be preserved for only one man and one woman for the sake of God's natural plan, society, and children. The Church's conditional support for migrants because they supposedly espouse the Church's social and moral values implicitly critiques people, such as queers, who inherently cannot uphold those values. This potentially places CDH as the Church's ally, in a difficult position in relation to CDH's other allies. This difficulty is compounded because many members of CDH either are or were affiliated with the Catholic Church. As an activist, I was concerned about the Catholic Church, as I personally have many problems with its positions, and I did not know how this relationship affected the relationship between CDH and Wingspan. I feared it created problems.

CDH's relationship with the Catholic Church certainly creates a dissonance with Wingspan that constrains the coalition. Such dissonance also prompts CDH activists to move in response to it. Specifically, activists employ the strategy of "comparison," whereby they seek to illuminate the likeness between inconsistent or conflicting positions that the Church holds in order to affirm their coalition with Wingspan and queer issues. My own discomfort with CDH's relationship to the Church enabled me to recognize these gestures as moments in which CDH activists used the energy from the dissonance to publicly and privately reinvigorate their commitment to queer people.

COMPARISON. Amelia regularly attends Mass and attempts to bring the human rights analysis that many parishioners embrace for migrant issues to their understanding of queer issues. Amelia believes that if Church members espouse a commitment to human rights and begin to see queer rights as a human rights issue, then perhaps they will alter their position on those rights. In responding to an interview question about the difficulties of bringing sexuality into the discussion of human and migrant rights, she tells of one woman who voiced support of Protect Marriage Arizona. Amelia explains that when given the opportunity, she brings it in "smoothly" to help people like this woman think "about it in terms of human rights." She says this woman is "moving along."[77] Because other parishioners trust Amelia's values and intentions, they are sometimes more willing to listen to her perspectives. When Amelia gently points out contradictions and inconsistencies by using comparisons grounded in shared values such as human rights, she utilizes language that Catholic believers can understand.

Of course, not everyone accepts the premise of CDH activists' comparison strategy that points out inconsistencies in the human rights premise. In responding to a similar interview question about the obstacles of building coalitions, Kat, who is also Catholic, tells a story of a woman who used to be a regular CDH volunteer: "She wouldn't come to our Corazón de Justicia [annual dinner to honor social justice activists on all facets of the Tucson community], because we gave an LGBT award. She thought that was wrong, and I was like, 'Oh, okay, then, we'll see you Monday.' And I would talk to her in little ways about it, but, you know, she was staunchly very, very religious."[78] Kat's example demonstrates the extent to which religion shapes people's perceptions on the issues of social justice for both migrants and queers in such a way that beliefs about one cannot be comparable with beliefs about the other. Although the woman in Kat's example is passionate enough to volunteer with a very progressive migrant rights organization, she will not attend an event honoring queer people, even for social justice work.

In situations like this, CDH activists utilize another tactical strategy of comparison: self-implication. For instance, one of the ways Kat tried to convince this woman that her position was problematic was by comparing herself, a heterosexual, to queers. Kat told the woman things she had done that she felt this woman should abhor as much as she hated homosexuality. Kat remarks, "I thought, 'If you're going to look at them as dirty, then look at me as dirty too.'"[79] Here Kat implicates herself into the discourse of "dirtiness" by sharing "dirty" things she's done in order to challenge this woman's divisions between who is dirty and who is clean, who is acceptable and who must be rejected. This strategy works to keep those boundaries unclear, which disrupts the "either/or" thinking that often characterizes the Catholic Church's positions. The disruption is especially potent in relation to discourses of "cleanliness" since much Catholic doctrine requires a constant cleansing of the soul in order to reach salvation. If a Catholic sees queerness as a taint and is called upon to look upon another heterosexual Catholic as also being tainted because of things she has done that may be equally abhorrent in the eyes of the Church, it becomes more difficult to take a selective approach as to what qualifies as clean or pure and what does not. As with all arguments made through analogy or comparison, this strategy has the potential of being read as a fallacy. If a hearer does not agree that the two things being compared are similar enough, then the argument will not be persuasive. Still, in these incidents CDH activists may be less interested in directly changing others' minds than they are in recuperating the dissonant moment to show all of their purported allies their solidarity with their queer allies.

REDEPLOYMENT.   In addition to using the strategy of comparison to confront the dissonances created by its relationship with the Catholic Church, CDH also confronts the "family values" rhetoric by redeploying the notion of family altogether so that it includes a wider array of people.[80] As discussed in the previous chapters, family is a powerful discourse within migrant, LGBTQ, and LGBTQ migrant rights and justice communities. Redeploying a powerful ideograph like "family values" is not easy since the term is so prominent in US cultural politics and carries so many assumed meanings about marriage, religion, and morality. Importantly, family discourse remains constant in CDH's thinking. Michelle works through the complexities of using family discourses: "I mean one of the things that's really struck me is the thing about family and the way that family gets used in migrant rights. Yeah, and I see it, and now that I've seen it, I started to see it even in stuff that Derechos [CDH] was putting out, and it was, like, whoa, okay. And it always kind of, like, made me think, but again that's interesting, because what you have is why is the family stuff used? Partly it's because it's reality, but partly it's because it normalizes."[81] As Michelle notes, the idea of keeping families together and giving them a fair chance at a good life realistically reflects the needs of many migrants. This is evidenced in Isabel's analysis of a ballot measure passed in 2006 denying bail to undocumented people charged with a crime. She explains that the measure was so devastating because bail functions to allow people to remain connected to their families and communities.[82] The centrality of family is also present in the program for the fourth annual Corazón de Justicia Awards Dinner program. Much of the program is dedicated to remembering those social justice heroes who have died in the past year. At the start of this section, the program reads, "We especially hold in our hearts the hundreds of men, women, and children whose lives were lost in our communities in the search to provide a better future for their families." Although this reflects the reality of many migrants' experiences, as Michelle also points out, utilizing family discourses potentially helps to normalize migrants in the eyes of some who might oppose them in order to make a claim for migrant inclusion in the nation.

The difference between CDH's use of valuing families and the Church's use of "family values" is in the deployment. When I asked Kat to explain how she sees "family values" playing out in migrant and queer rights discourse, she suggested that migrants are often seen as destructive to family values because in the minds of many "they cause jobs to be lost, families to be divided. You know they're this other, this diseased, this immoral criminal element."[83] Even as institutions such as the Church laud migrant family values, Kat provides an alternative perspective that reflects what many other US Americans may think about migrants in relation to US family structures. Additionally, Mexicans and Chican@s have historically considered family to include extended family of all kinds.[84] The living arrangements of migrants, which can involve more than the "nuclear family" that some US Americans are used to seeing living under the same roof, can be cause for alarm. Although some migrants may approximate the family values that some institutions espouse, the ideograph of family values in the United States is also enmeshed with norms of white middle-classness and US-centrism. Thus the approximation that any nonwhite and non-middle-class "family" may make to the white middle-class norm can never be complete. Kat's comments acknowledge these deeper beliefs about family, status, and nation. She goes on to challenge traditional notions through redeploying the terms: "What greater family value [is there] than [that] you'd risk your life to come to a country to fucking clean toilets and provide and send that little bit of money back. How is that not the ultimate of family values?" In this way Kat attempts to appropriate the meaning of family and family values away from the "pro-family" discourse of institutions like the Catholic Church.

By removing "family values" from moral values and emphasizing relationships, sacrifice, and financial support for loved ones as the hallmark of "family values," Kat gestures toward a broader relational politics. She does not completely delink "family values" from other related values such as hard work, responsibility, and self-sacrifice. The appropriation from conservatives like the Catholic Church, then, is only partial and could still succumb to critiques of continuing to reinscribe normativities. Still, reiterating Michelle's earlier point, Kat mentions the reality is that many migrants do come to the United States in mother-father-child familial relationships, and so in thinking about family, CDH has to consider this as well. This dissonance between the reality of migrant lives and the "family values" discourse that oppresses queers (as well as many migrants) must be dealt with delicately. I witnessed such delicate maneuvers in CDH's work. The organization's attempts to redeploy family in a way that does not negatively impact queers, while simultaneously valuing families, has to be done with the migrant constituency in mind. Even as CDH redeploys "family" in ways such as Kat does above, often in public documents and sound bites, the use of "family" may be less redeployment and more of a typical deployment that normalizes. Much as some in the LGBTQ rights movement seek to normalize themselves by forsaking migrants (and other queers), the use of family discourse can normalize migrants at the expense of queers (as well as other migrants).

While CDH works to take dissonances from a space of discord toward harmony with its queer ally, such harmony is not so easily achieved. And in some instances the dissonance, or potential dissonance, remains. However, much like dissonance is not essentially displeasing within music, within coalitions, and as these examples evidence, the existence of such dissonances promotes a heightened awareness of, and attentiveness to, the need for constant work and reflexivity. Dissonance fosters acute awareness, though sometimes without clear direction for movement from the awkward tension. Because coalitions are never merely between two entities, external relationships will inevitably create dissonances. If dissonance is designed to mark or call attention, however, then such dissonances serve an important function on their own.

The Struggle to Sustain

Even as Wingspan and CDH diligently engage in strategies that foster coalition, struggles persist, and many of these could be said to arise generally from the nature of coalition building, while others emerge specifically from the nature of the identity politics involved within both Wingspan and CDH. Feminist, human rights, and social justice organizations often seek to adopt communicative approaches that differ from traditional bureaucratic structures. As Karen Lee Ashcraft has demonstrated, however, such approaches and forms may not be completely alternative to more traditional organizational structures.[85] Rather, Ashcraft explains that many feminist organizations are in fact hybrid constructions that feature both feminist and traditional dimensions. Ashcraft's work is informative because she warns against the tendency to glorify or oversimplify the complexity of the struggles within (and, I would add, between) organizations. I now turn to some of these struggles. As one participant, Karen (a pseudonym), a semi-regular CDH volunteer and a Wingspan community member, put it, the coalition exists largely on "the level of language."[86] Though as a rhetoric scholar I initially balk at the flippant treatment of language in Karen's comments, the tensions between "talking and acting," and the belief by some activists that the coalition exists "in name only," reveal that just as communication can be a coalition's primary enabling resource, the kind and depth of communication can also constrain its effectiveness.

TALKING, NOT ACTING

Women of color feminists have consistently shown that differences in class and race, as well as education, nation, ability, gender identity, and sexuality inhibit communication and coalition building.[87] Cherríe Moraga's idea of "theory in the flesh" insists upon using facets of our lived experience like race, place, and sexuality to build politics.[88] Since people like women of color have experienced innumerable contradictions within their lives, they can perhaps more easily understand the importance of building coalitions with different people as a means of survival. From such a perspective, limited and singular definitions of identity cannot serve as a basis for politics. The Combahee River Collective maintains that oppression and privilege result from interconnected systems of racism, sexism, heterosexism, capitalism, and imperialism.[89] And an individual or a group's position within those systems can dictate, or at least constitute, how one might interact within and respond to such systems.

Despite CDH's and Wingspan's attempts to coalesce, for some people in both organizations, mostly those who identify as people of color and/or working class, actions would speak louder than words. To illustrate, when I asked Geovanna, a Chicana and Wingspan's breast health educator at the time, how she felt about the 2006 election results, she sighed and said, "I was hurt and happy, but deep inside I felt like I didn't care about 107 [Protect Marriage Arizona] . . . I thought all these fucking people are so happy because of 107, and there is no consideration of the big picture, that, hey, these others [anti-migrant measures] passed, and of course they say it, but their actions were different."[90] Geovanna implicitly critiques the postelection joint statement that CDH and Wingspan created to further link migrant and queer issues, as well as other verbal expressions of sadness or regret that Wingspan members made about the passage of the four anti-migrant measures. Geovanna finds herself strongly connected to white citizen queers, documented and undocumented straight and queer migrants, and straight and queer non-migrant people of color of differing class and education levels. These diverse belongings necessitate that she possess reflexivity about all of these communities. Based on what she witnessed, she held the perspective that many other Wingspan members who do not bridge multiple, interlocking communities did not have such reflexivity.

An overt example demonstrating Geovanna's concern occurred during CDH's December 2006 event, Comunidades sin Fronteras (Communities without Borders), which celebrated the International Day of the Migrant and International Human Rights Day. At the daylong event in Rudy Garcia Park there were several tables from different organizations and a main stage that featured music, dance, and speeches throughout the day. At one point a middle-age white volunteer from Wingspan took the stage and thanked the entire audience (which was largely Latin@ or migrant) for helping to defeat Protect Marriage Arizona. She said she knew that there was no way the measure could have been defeated without the help of these communities. She then proclaimed that Latin@s and migrants had helped the LGBT community, so now she wanted to do her part by joining "*comunidades sin fronteras*."[91] People at the CDH table audibly groaned at the Wingspan volunteer's comments. Their distaste makes sense for several reasons. First, the volunteer did not mention the anti-migrant initiatives that passed with overwhelming support at the same time the marriage amendment was defeated. By suggesting that she wanted to help out now by getting involved, she showed a lack of political awareness and no understanding that migrants lives had already been drastically affected by the recent elections, or that the two communities are not always distinct. Moreover, *"comunidades sin fronteras"* was the name given to the day's event. It does not refer to any local migrant rights organizations in Tucson. Perhaps she meant CDH. I saw that volunteer after the event at Wingspan, but I never saw her at a CDH meeting or helping with any CDH event. This story supports Geovanna's concerns and also highlights the difficulties of coalition work. What does the work really entail? Who does a coalition require commitment from—everyone involved in an organization or just key players?

When considering these situations in light of the scholarship on coalitional politics, people of color in coalition with white people experience disappointments for many reasons, one of which is because there can be a different paradigm of enacting politics.[92] As one of the few people of color in Wingspan, Geovanna supports this assertion: "Mexicans, Latinos, Native Americans, we tend to be more timid and to the point, but we perform action after that. And all these people talk all these words, and I laugh at it. And what they say doesn't mean anything, and these big-ass words say and do nothing about ending discrimination."[93] Although Geovanna reinscribes a sort of essentialism based on identity and forecloses talking as a form of action, she speaks from her experience in that she perceives the white people in her organization use large words but neglect action. She goes on: "They're [CDH] going to do it because it's right, and here [Wingspan] only 'peons' like myself stand up and do it."[94] Geovanna's analysis of people's commitment levels and politics is based on race and class. The perception of talking versus acting as an issue of white versus person of color comes up in conversation with CDH members as well; CDH members express frustration about working with white, usually middle-class people who like to spend more time sending emails than using door-to-door grassroots organizing techniques.[95] Perhaps this critique should not easily be reduced to an issue of white versus person of color, for as Anzaldúa's conceptualization of *mestiza* consciousness suggests, identity cannot be essentialized or reduced to characteristics such as race, gender, or sexuality.[96] There are certainly people of color who privilege talking and white people who privilege other forms of action, and examples exist in both organizations. Nonetheless, a number of activists depicted the talking-versus-acting divide as emerging from different identity locations, mainly related to race and class, that privilege different sorts of involvement.

"IN NAME ONLY"

At the same time that race and class positions construct differing perspectives about the effectiveness and appropriateness of the relationship between the two groups, the disparity of resources and the dissimilar class consciousness between many in Wingspan and CDH also creates a sense, for some, that the depth of the relationship between the two groups never moves beyond, as Karen put it, "the level of language." This means that although Wingspan is often committed rhetorically to CDH, much of the physical labor that enables coalition building seems to fall upon CDH activists.

One afternoon I met a Wingspan intern, Kendra (a pseudonym), for coffee at a local shop. Kendra was doing a yearlong qualitative study on queer political organizing, focusing specifically on Wingspan. During her study Kendra had the opportunity to observe Wingspan and other activists who were involved with LGBTQ politics in Tucson. Although she had heard a lot about the coalition between Wingspan and CDH, she wondered if it was a coalition "in name only."[97] I felt myself becoming defensive, because at the time of our meeting I had spent several weeks working on joint statements and voter's guides. I explained to her that I felt in part that CDH was interested in doing more but that having only one paid staff member made it difficult. She cut me off and said she believed it was Wingspan that was not willing to have more than a name-only coalition. At this point in our meeting, she had to leave for another appointment, and we vowed to continue our conversation. The only time we were able to talk again, however, was when she interviewed me for her dissertation. Then she left Tucson after finishing data collection. In an electronic conversation many months later, Kendra explained to me that she used "in name only" to refer to one specific occasion when she felt that she was being called upon by CDH to represent Wingspan's position on an issue because she was consistently the only Wingspan representative at CDH meetings. This occurrence made her wonder if, in that instance, Wingspan liked having the rhetorical connection to CDH without having to put in a lot of effort.[98]

While Kendra spoke about a particular instance, I too experienced frustration in relation to the effort I sometimes felt Wingspan put in toward CDH. Before the 2006 election it seemed that most of the final "footwork" was done by CDH volunteers. CDH volunteers brought the voter's guides to every event they attended and put the flyers on cars. Although it is possible that Wingspan staff engaged in similar behaviors, I never witnessed it. Whether this is true or perceived—and as liaison I should have asked, but did not—I felt in large part that I was doing this kind of labor in Wingspan's name alongside CDH activists who were doing their own work.[99]

I became especially frustrated after the postelection joint statement came out because CDH asked if Wingspan could translate it since CDH translated the joint voter's guide. I said that I would ask and I assumed Wingspan would find a way to do it. However, when I asked, I was told that Wingspan could not do it because Wingspan members were disagreeing on theories of translation.[100] Unfortunately, this left the document untranslated. I was frustrated because at the time, Wingspan was a multimillion-dollar nonprofit organization with multiple paid staff, whereas CDH functioned on a shoestring budget with one part-time staff member. Despite the immense resources, Wingspan could not translate what it claimed was an important document. I do not mean to minimize Wingspan's internal struggle regarding this very important issue, but as this particular situation was unfolding, I could not help but frame it within Kendra's comments about the coalition being "in name only."

Amelia explains that CDH often finds itself partnering with organizations such that CDH members end up doing more than their share of the work, which can annoy them and prevent future partnering.[101] Both organizations are members of the nonprofit industrial complex, but Wingspan has far more paid staff. Receiving more funds means an organization is far more limited in the kinds of work its members are able to do as a result of the funding restrictions. Organizations like CDH, though also part of the NPIC, already carry agendas that are far less fundable, which means it has to rely more on volunteers to accomplish its objectives. In part this means that CDH has flexibility to do different kinds of work than groups like Wingspan can do. The catch is that CDH may not always have the resources to take full advantage of such flexibilities. This point is further exacerbated in that CDH's paid staff and volunteers, mostly women, are already overworked.

CDH and Wingspan clearly offer each other rhetorical support. At a somewhat superficial level, the overemphasis on "talking" may also disallow a rigorous interrogation of the race and class disparities that largely separate the two organizations and portions of the constituencies they represent. Such interrogation on the part of both groups might foster a stronger sense of belonging for working-class people of color who are connected with Wingspan, as well as a deeper sense of trust among CDH activists in relation to their ally.

"PRINCIPLES, NOT PERSONALITIES"

A final struggle emerges in a comment by Amelia, who argues that coalition building should be about "principles, not personalities."[102] Statements that minimize the individual for the sake of the collective's principles, such as the "Black Feminist Statement" by the Combahee River Collective, evidence this point. Yet, as much organizational communication scholarship suggests, leaders maintain a great deal of influence over the direction that a particular organization takes. If leaders are the ones who are doing most of the communicating and directing of a particular message, what happens in the absence of those leaders? While a history of relationships between the two organizations—or at least an emphasis on sexuality by CDH and a continued presence at CDH events by Wingspan—suggests that this coalition is not about personalities, there is an element that is based on the people present in both organizations in this historical moment. Karen argues that the coalition has "a lot to do with personal relationships."[103] She notes that both Kat and Isabel support Wingspan, which keeps the coalition going no matter what happens.

A similar phenomenon exists in Wingspan. For instance, Kent, Wingspan's executive director until summer 2007, comments that migrant and refugee issues have always been important to him. He worked for a migrant and refugee rights organization in Mexico City before moving to Tucson, and when he arrived in Tucson he volunteered with CDH for a summer. When he came to Wingspan, he and Cathy concurred that migrant issues needed to be a part of their agenda.[104] Cathy agrees that her own interest, as well as her position in the community and relationship to Kat, fosters the coalition. She says, "We both [Kat and Cathy] seem within our communities to be gatekeepers in a way, and so if I say to someone, 'Oh, yeah, Derechos [CDH], they're great,' sometimes that has meaning for people, and my sense is that . . . when she says, 'Yeah, Wingspan, they're cool,' that means something."[105] The idea that both Cathy and Kat serve as "gatekeepers" implies that they manage which messages enter into their communities, which messages get promoted, and which ones do not receive attention. As Janet Holmes argues, organizational gatekeeping typically happens at the level of discourse and can function in a facilitative rather than obstructive manner.[106] While certainly Kat and Cathy use gatekeeping to facilitate an inclusive environment in both organizations, their position as gatekeepers may also function to silence dialogue that may contradict the position that they, as leaders, hold. Although the longevity of the organizations' relationship as well as the mission, vision, and values suggests that the coalition would, or at least could, exist without the current personalities, it did not appear to be a strategy in either organization to foster interest in the coalition among members who are not currently aware of it or involved. This suggests that potentially the coalition may be sustainable only as long as the current leadership structure remains in place.

I will further emphasize this point with an example. I conducted this research from June 2006 to May 2007. I maintained a regular relationship with both organizations until June 2008 when I left Arizona.[107] In the summer of 2007, within a few months of each other, Kent and Cathy resigned from Wingspan to pursue other opportunities. Others with whom I regularly interacted in Wingspan no longer work there. I am no longer in contact with anyone who works at Wingspan as of this writing. Since 2007 Wingspan and CDH have continued to collaborate on events and co-sponsor projects. While members of the Tucson community have privately expressed to me their opinions about whether this will last, it appears that this coalition is sustaining, in some form, after Kent's and Cathy's departures. After the passage of SB 1070 in Arizona in April 2010, Wingspan issued a statement against the law in July. However, when I attended the May Day march in Tucson in 2010, I spoke with a new employee at CDH, a young woman who had been there for just less than a year. She told me about an event that evening pertaining to queer migration and a new organization starting in Tucson. I asked her if the event had to do with the coalition between Wingspan and CDH, and she told me she was unaware that the two organizations had a stated coalition. When I told her that I had written my dissertation on the coalition, she appeared shocked and said that as far she knows the coalition no longer exists. In my conversations with activists who have been with CDH for much longer than this woman, their commitment to Wingspan and queer issues remains strong, but it is telling that a paid employee had no knowledge of such a coalition.

Rather than negating my project, perhaps this example should return us to the definitions of coalition, particularly those suggesting that coalition is always if not temporary at least precarious. When I checked Wingspan's website in the fall of 2012, I did not recognize a single name on the staff, and the staff had shrunk from more than twenty people in 2007 to eight people in 2012. A complete turnover of staff in less than five years, while not completely atypical in the nonprofit world, is certainly enough to erase institutional memory. On the other hand, given that CDH still includes nearly every staff and volunteer I worked with, the long history present in that organization may suggest that the existence of a relationship with Wingspan is simply assumed and stated outright only when it is necessary to respond to something or to take action. Coalitional politics, then, are perhaps always just a series of precarious coalitional moments that can be reenergized or recatalyzed, or that simply fade away.

Conclusions

The examination that Stephen and her colleagues made of the statewide alliance between ROP and CAUSA in Oregon also explains that much of the success of this alliance emerged from the strong leadership in both organizations. The role of leadership is certainly important, but what is perhaps more crucial to consider is what the existence of such coalitions and alliances means in terms of political possibilities. As Stephen and her colleagues conclude, "The ability of groups with different constituencies to come together and take advantage of political openings as well as the possible existence of underlying common values and political strategies is greatly needed to move progressive politics forward in the United States."[108] This study certainly lends credence to this claim. Wingspan and CDH have attempted to build unlikely connections by reframing and negotiating difference in order to shift the nature of what politics can be. Such coalitions and alliances, and the public discussion of them, are especially crucial in the current political milieu, where homonationalism and the pitting of white queers against people of color, including queers of color, manifests regularly. The aftermath of the passage of Proposition 8 in California in 2008, which took the word "marriage" away from gay and lesbian couples who had previously been given that label for their civil unions, is a case in point. Notable white gay personalities such as Dan Savage and a host of others immediately jumped to the conclusion that blacks were to blame for this outcome; meanwhile, black people reported being called the "n-word" by white gays in West Hollywood.[109] Savage stated, "I'm done pretending that the handful of racist gay white men out there—and they're out there, and I think they're *scum*—are a bigger problem for African Americans, gay and straight, than the huge numbers of homophobic African Americans are for gay Americans, whatever their color."[110] While numerous queer people of all colors stood against this sort of divisive rhetoric, it displayed openly the profound difficulties of building coalitions, or even amicable relationships based on understanding, across lines of difference.

Without activists willing to forge unlikely connections, and centering on the voices of those who reside within the intermeshing systems of identity and oppression, no radical change can ever occur. CDH and Wingspan activists intervene in the logics of the rhetorical imaginary that keep people divided as they manifest in their local context. Namely, they take up the needs they see present in their own communities that require challenging division and building relationships. Centering here on the local is especially important because it is at the level of the local where sustained coalitional politics are most likely to happen. Local interventions, however, have further-reaching implications. In this particular case, sometimes these interventions are utopian, sometimes they reinforce the normative aspirations embedded in inclusionary politics, while other times they actively challenge normativity as well as how political belonging and national belonging can happen. In this way this coalitional work is as imperfect as it is precarious. It is also vital for thinking about alternative imaginaries and alternative visions and strategies for politics.

Conclusion

Department of Homeland Security Secretary Janet Napolitano announced in late September 2012 that gay and lesbian couples would be regarded as "family relationships" in immigration deportation proceedings.[1] This means that certain gay and lesbian couples will be treated like married or engaged heterosexual couples as officials evaluate deportation cases. Put simply, a queer migrant's familial connections in the United States will be taken into consideration as federal officials make a decision about whether to deport. This decision will likely help some binational same-sex couples to remain together in the United States, and this is no doubt important for those exceptional couples. After years of labor by organizations like Immigration Equality; in the midst of a lawsuit by binational same-sex couples challenging DOMA; and, more recently, under the urging of dozens of Congress members, Napolitano made this change. Immigration Equality and advocates for binational same-sex couples should see this as a victory resulting from decades of focused work. In light of the activist rhetoric in *Queer Migration Politics*, however, it should be clear that it is a victory in a very narrow sense.

I have offered coalition here as a productive alternative to the inclusionary and normative politics of the mainstream LGBT and LGBT immigration movements and also to the utopian politics advocated in some queer theory. Activist rhetoric that both derives from and constitutes queer migration politics offers insight into coalitional possibilities. Coalition, as I offer it, sometimes involves inclusionary and utopian approaches and does not deny that there is value in them, particularly for those who espouse them. Reorienting toward coalition provides a different perspective on the present and the possibilities for a livable life that people are working to make a reality in the here and now, which has been especially clear in the last two chapters.

Moreover, while coalition has often been theorized as only a temporary and strategic relationship designed to achieve specific goals, I have built upon María Lugones to contend that coalition should not be thought of merely in these terms. Coalition is a present and existing vision and practice that reflects an orientation to others and a shared commitment to change. Coalition is the "horizon" that can reorganize our possibilities and the conditions of them. Coalition is a liminal space, necessarily precarious, and located within the intermeshed interstices of people's lives and politics. Using the analytic of the coalitional moment, I have emphasized coalition less as an existing thing or relationship, as in "a coalition," and more as a possibility for coming together within or to create a juncture that points toward radical social and political change. We can identify this possibility when two or more seemingly different and separable issues or groups come in such contact. These moments reveal and build alternative parameters for politics, belonging, and being.

The activist rhetoric of queer migration politics has provided an appropriate lens to view and understand the complexity and variety of coalitional moments. The rhetoric has also supplied a way to witness the possibilities that coalitional moments engender for practicing and envisioning politics and making lives more livable. The level of inventing arguments and creating rationales for action and publicly pronouncing positions—the rhetorical level—is an ideal site to examine how activists respond to national social imaginaries. National social imaginaries, themselves rhetorical constructions, frame and create the parameters for the possibility of belonging, being, and change. Within the coalitional moments discussed here, activists draw upon a host of rhetorical and ideological resources. These resources range from utopian longings and inclusionary strategies to radical analyses of intermeshing and interlocking oppressions and systems of power, as well as the innovative approaches to relationships found in queer and feminist politics and communities. Activists develop and deploy rhetorical visions such as the differential vision of the queer migration manifestos and Yasmin Nair's use of radical interactionality. Activists also manufacture and adopt tactical strategies such as migrant youth activists' appropriation and extension of coming out or CDH's and Wingspan's everyday practices and processes of rationalizing and engaging in coalitional politics. A number of implications of these analyses exist for politics, theory, and possibility.

First, it is important to explicate the implications of offering coalition in place of normative/inclusionary and utopian politics. More than anything else, coalition features the messiness, the impurity, and the multiplicity of subjectivity, agency, and politics that these two approaches often miss. Coalition is always in our vision, and yet as a horizon it is simultaneously beneath our bodies. Horizons are temporally and spatially tangible, and yet as thresholds between two potentially divided things they are sites of tension; they are queer. Coalition cannot be easily categorized, fit into an identity, or fixed on a map. Coalition is not comfortable. It is not home. It is scary and unpredictable. Unlike those subjects invested in inclusionary politics, coalitional subjects refuse to accept normative aspirations as the only channel for belonging and life. Like some of those espousing inclusionary politics, coalitional subjects recognize that compromise might be necessary, reform is a part of revolution, and small victories are worth celebrating. Unlike those inviting us to take up utopian politics, coalitional politics is oriented toward the present, emphasizes realms that are not only aesthetic, and refuses what cannot be practiced—while expanding the very limits of the practicable. As with utopian politics, coalitional subjects believe in the vitality of broadening imaginaries that will open possibilities for livable life. As Judith Butler remarks, "Possibility is not a luxury; it is as crucial as bread."[2]

Coalition offers a way to rethink subjectivity, agency, and possibility. Aimee Carrillo Rowe writes, "The sites of our belonging constitute how we see the world, what we value, who we are becoming. The formation of the subject is never individual, but is forged across a shifting set of relations that we move in and out of, often without reflection. The *politics of relation* is a placing that moves a politics of location through a relational notion of the subject to create a subject who recognizes and works within the coalitional conditions that creates and might unmake her—and others."[3] This has been a book about people who can be described as coalitional subjects, those people produced by their various belongings to see issues, systems of oppression, and possibilities for a livable life as inextricably bound to one another. Every action, every political choice, every coalition entered into expands the coalitional subject's understanding of how power works and how people's issues are intermeshed. For instance, Nair's radically interactional rhetoric reveals a method for accessing the complex roots of problems in order to invite others to reorient their politics and agendas to provide more life chances, to use Dean Spade's words, for more people. Nair's imperfect methods, which come off as polemical or insensitive, do not negate her critique of the dangers of affect and personal narrative in these neoliberal times. Nair, as a queer woman of color, an immigrant, a grassroots and cyber activist, a trans-generational and transracial organizer, a person with a PhD who lives in a small apartment in Chicago—among her other sites of belonging—has had her subjectivity and her political orientation produced, reproduced, and altered from within those diverse spaces. Furthermore, through the difficult coalitional moments that are her interactions with supporters of the UAFA and the rights of binational same-sex couples above other migrants, Nair is also produced, reproduced, and altered as a coalitional subject. Coalition and the perspectives that coalition enables are not simple and easy. They are laborious but worthwhile. The development and constant refinement of coalitional subjectivities reflects a profound commitment to present possibility, to the creative resources of people with whom we share space, and to refusing to give over to despair.

Second, examining coalitional moments through the lens of queer migration politics leads to several interesting implications for thinking about politics and theory. Because of the way queer migration politics have exploded onto the discursive scene in the early twenty-first century, they supply a plethora of diverse coalitional moments, junctures that point to other possibilities. Coalitional subjects have animated some of these coalitional moments when queer migrants have inserted themselves in key ways into the public sphere. Some of these coalitional moments reflect the unlikely coalescence among those identifying primarily with queer politics and those who mostly work on behalf of migration politics. Still others have advanced a queer approach to migration politics. Within the rhetoric analyzed here each kind of coalitional moment supplies a different glimpse into how migrants, queers, or queer migrants are imagined to belong. The rhetoric of queer migration politics further indicates what activists see as the conditions for their belonging and the creative resources they use to challenge those parameters. Emphasizing activist rhetoric, including publicly available texts such as speeches, blogs, statements, and posters, alongside a look at the argumentative rationales that activists create for their work, has been especially useful in understanding the myriad ways activists offer persuasive appeals and effect change.

Analyzing the rhetoric of queer migration politics also lends insight to concerns such as audience—imagined or real—and argumentative invention. Assessing these dimensions of the politics also returns to the significance of coalition and coalitional moments. As has been seen, each activist envisions a different audience for their rhetoric. Some, like the DREAM activists, target lawmakers. Others, such as Nair and some of the manifesto authors, primarily speak to specific groups of activists. Still others, such as Wingspan and CDH, look to influence the communities in which they are embedded. These envisioned audiences lead activists to use markedly different kinds of arguments and modes of communication in order to effect change. But it is also important to remember that these envisioned audiences do not manifest from thin air; instead, they emerge from the resources that activists have at their disposal, the conditions that activists seek to change, and the actors who can help them meet those outcomes.[4] Having access to an audience results from the coalitions an activist or activist organization has and creates. These relationships open doors and opportunities that are otherwise unavailable. As suggested above, relationships and work with diverse people who have diverse ideas can lead activists to the development of coalitional subjectivities. As activists begin to understand the interactions and intersections between their issues and identities and others, thereby creating coalitional subjectivities, activists have more resources for rhetorical invention. This fact serves as a call to be drawn toward others and their struggles not necessarily because we affectively want to be but because we know we politically must be. We coalesce to increase access, to alter our ability to make arguments, to broaden the resources for rhetorical invention within our reach in order to challenge imaginaries and make people's lives, our own and others, more livable.

Additionally, understanding social movements, protest, and activism in the public sphere warrants a robust connection between people's lives and the theories designed to explain and enable improvement of them. Queer women of color feminist approaches help to facilitate such seeing because those theories, with rare exception, are not interested in utopia or liberal notions of progress and change emerging from evolution. Queer women of color feminist approaches begin from the flesh to explicate the present conditions of material and symbolic oppression. From that realistic place, those explications aid in using available material resources and available means of persuasion to enact social change. Toward this end, Lugones advocates what she calls "street walker theorizing." Street walker theorizing simultaneously privileges the experience of walking in the streets—hanging out with people whose worlds we write about in their own worlds, and the experience of "walking the streets"—drawing knowledge from those, like prostitutes and hustlers, normally considered outside the bounds of intellectual production.[5] From these spaces of intermeshed bodily, emotional, intellectual, and spiritual experience, we begin to fully understand the need for an analysis of intermeshing and interlocking oppression to improve people's worlds and the tactical strategies people are already deploying to achieve such ends. People's lives are not comprised of singular identities or concerns, as so many studies of social movement would lead us to believe. Similarly, the ways belonging is rhetorically imagined in the United States is not a simple equation of exclusion and inclusion based on discrete identities. As queer women of color feminists have always shown us, oppression and privilege, power and identity, domination and liberation are experienced in people's lives in vastly complicated ways. We need equally complicated understandings of how people who are committed to social change work to confront these material and symbolic conditions. We also need to think about the courses of action that people have available to them, on the ground, as the starting points for theoretical analysis. This book provides one example.

Finally, coalitional moments have the most radical potential when the rhetoric used does not request national belonging from within the confines of existing premises. Every coalitional moment in this book was animated by dissatisfaction with existing legal conditions within the United States. Clearly, coalitional subjects speak within the nation, even as a part of its system. But coalitions or coalitional moments with only nationalist aspirations inevitably fail, or if they do not fail in terms of their stated objectives, they often reinscribe exclusionary norms with long-term impacts for people who should have supposedly benefited from the coalition in the first place. Moreover, in the context of queer migration politics, very often the national legal objectives were not the primary part of their work, nor even most interesting part. Instead, the most important thing evidenced in nearly all of these cases is the development of political orientations and modes of belonging that point toward other political possibilities. Coalitions of those strangers who threaten security and are scapegoated for the existence of a host of ills are inevitably negated, excluded, and precluded from national belonging. When activists focus on coalitional orientations and modes of political belonging rather than the goals of legal national belonging and demand radical intervention, they may still be excluded. But they imagine something different, so while the intervention at the national imaginary may be negligible, the intervention into people's local imaginations is unbounded. Given the state of LGBT immigration politics in the United States, and the exclusions it continues to perpetuate, such unbounding could not come at a more crucial time. This "victory" for US LGBT immigration politics, with which I opened this conclusion, reminds me of something my friends have been repeating lately and that the radical trans activist Mattilda Bernstein Sycamore is often credited with saying: "Our dreams have become so small." I hope *Queer Migration Politics* can be part of what changes the size of our dreams and our present possibilities.

Notes

Introduction

1. The Immigration Act of 1990 (Pub.L. 101-649, 104 Stat. 4978, enacted November 29, 1990). Despite this seeming gain, this law did not end the exclusion of HIV-positive people from migration to the United States, and did nothing to address exclusions based on having committed crimes of moral turpitude, a type of crime historically used to exclude queer people.

2. The acronym "LGBT" (lesbian, gay, bisexual and transgender) or sometimes "GLBT," did not become common until the 1990s. Prior to that, people primarily talked in terms of "lesbian and gay" or "gay community" issues. Because of the time period I am talking about in this introduction, and the language these groups used at the time, I begin to use "LGBT" only when I talk about the present.

3. The Human Rights Campaign Fund was founded in 1980 and changed its name to the Human Rights Campaign in 1995. The National Gay Task Force was founded in 1973. Its name change to National Gay and Lesbian Task Force occurred in 1985. Lambda Legal Defense and Education Fund was initiated in 1971 and incorporated in 1973.

4. Bennett and Ullman, "Clinton Reaffirms," A15.

5. "LGIRTF," March 3, 1997, http://www.qrd.org/qrd/www/world/immigration/lgirtf.html, accessed September 21, 2012.

6. "Sexual identity" essentially means gender identity, but this is the term used at the time in the case law.

7. The number set in the 1965 Immigration and Nationality Act (Hart-Celler Act, INS, Act of 1965, Pub.L. 89-236) was 74 percent. The actual percentage of people migrating through family ties varies on a yearly basis. The formula for admitting people in the various existing categories of family is very complicated and not especially relevant here. Family reunification has continued to be a contested issue, as was the case during debates leading to the 1996 changes in immigration law, in which Congress members discussed whether so much preference should be given to family reunification or if there should be a shift to focus more on those with desired labor skills. See Gerken, "Immigrant Anxieties," ch. 3.

8. Several additional grassroots organizations developed in subsequent years to advocate for binational same-sex couples, including Love Exiles, Love Sees No Borders, Out4Immigration, and others. In 2003, the Queer Immigrant Rights Project (QUIR) formed under the auspices of the American Friends Service Committee to support and advocate for LGBTQ and HIV-positive immigrants in New York. This group did not emphasize only binational couples, and in fact sought a much broader agenda. Thanks to QUIR Dallas for directing my attention to this history. See http://web.archive.org/web/20041204043443/http://www.quir.org/aboutus.php, accessed April 8, 2013.

9. In addition to what I have shared above, a quick search of popular LGBT publications like the *Advocate*, or mainstream media sources, including the *New York Times*, *Time*, or the *Huffington Post*, reveals extensive coverage of issues pertaining to binational same-sex couples and virtual silence on any other issues pertaining to LGBT immigration. Since 2010 there has been minor coverage of migrant youth who are also queer. See chapter 3.

10. Muñoz also writes against the "antirelational thesis" advocated by some queer theorists' visions of future that discount many types of relationality, more or less, altogether. See Bersani, *Homos*; Edelman, *No Future*.

11. Muñoz, *Cruising Utopia*, 16.

12. Ibid., 9.

13. See also, e.g., Floyd, "Importance of Being Childish."

14. Rosenberg and Villarejo, "Introduction: Queerness, Norms, Utopia," 11.

15. Floyd, "Queer Principles of Hope."

16. To be sure, aesthetics can be political and politics can be, and often are, aesthetic. I am not interested in reifying a binary or engaging in long-standing conversations about the relationship between the aesthetic and political. Yet there are instances when a distinction between art and performance versus activism is important and clear, such as when addressing modes of political organizing and activism that have little or no artistic dimension. For sure, some of the activism discussed in this book is both artistic and aesthetic.

17. Lugones, *Pilgrimages/Peregrinajes*, 5.

18. Alinsky, *Rules for Radicals*, 12.

19. Berlant, *Cruel Optimism*, 4.

20. I often use the terms "inclusionary," "normative," and "mainstream" interchangeably when talking about the predominant liberal agenda of both LGBT and immigrant rights. While this choice could be critiqued for conflating terms, the inclusionary and mainstreaming strategies of the LGBT, immigrant, and LGBT immigrant rights movements work through normative logics that create distinctions between "deserving" and "undeserving" people. See, for example, Batstone and Mendieta, *Good Citizen*; Duggan, *Twilight of Equality*; Gerken, "Immigrant Anxieties."

21. Throughout this book I use the word "migrant" to refer to immigrants, refugees, and asylum seekers who have crossed an international border, regardless of whether they have documents. Using "migrant" instead of marking distinctions between different types of migrants is important because, as Luibhéid has shown, a "shifting line" exists between these different statuses, as one can move from being documented to undocumented in a mere moment. See Luibhéid, "Sexuality, Migration." When organizations or individuals use "immigrant" in their rhetoric, I usually utilize their language. On occasion, when it is necessary to specify undocumented migrants, I use the adjective "undocumented." I prefer "queer" to LGBT or LGBTQ. I use "queer" in two primary ways. First, "queer" refers to LGBT people and others, such as prostitutes or "welfare mothers," who fail to conform to the conventions of heteronormativity. I also use "queer" to describe something as abjected, othered, and out of place. I recognize that both of these usages of queer do not fully account for the ways in which queer can also collude with liberal and inclusionary politics; see Eng, *Feeling of Kinship*; Puar, *Terrorist Assemblages*. When individuals or organizations use acronyms like LGBTQ or LGBT, I also often utilize their language, and in the case when I am referring to mainstream rhetoric that would not use the word "queer," I will often opt for LGBT as well. When I am referring to both queer and LGBT politics, I use the acronym LGBTQ. As should be clear, terms and their usage are slippery and messy, and there is no ideal way to use these terms. For a more elaborate discussion on the use of "queer" and "migrant" as the preferred terms within the broader field of queer migration studies, see Luibhéid, "Introduction."

22. Moraga and Anzaldúa, *This Bridge*. My approach is also influenced by "queer of color critique." See Ferguson, *Aberrations in Black*. Following Lugones, I often use the words "intermeshed" along with words like "interlocking" and "intersecting" to describe relations of power and conditions of oppression. Each of these metaphors for how power and oppression work signals something slightly different, and none captures the complexity of oppression. Lugones maintains, and I agree, that interlocking (and also intersecting) oppressions implies that types of oppression are, at some level, separable. To say that oppression and oppressing are intermeshed suggests that oppression cannot be separated or fragmented into discrete categories or parts and that people experience oppression in such a way. See Lugones, *Pilgrimages/ Peregrinajes*, 223–24, 146n1.

23. Lugones, *Pilgrimages/Peregrinajes*, ix. See also Keating, "Building Coalitional Consciousness."

24. *Oxford English Dictionary Online*, s.v. "coalition," http://www.oed.com:80/Entry/ 35074, accessed December 3, 2012. The first mention of "coalition" in the English language appeared around 1613. The first political usage appeared in 1647.

25. Ibid. The term "coalition" is preferable to "alliance" for several reasons, but foremost, in its original usage, an alliance refers to "union by marriage." Its second usage more closely relates to coalition, but it mostly refers to relationships between sovereign states. In both of these senses, then, alliance refers to a more enduring type of relationship or coming together, and one enmeshed in both heterosexuality and national sovereignty, two concepts that are centrally challenged by this monograph. *Oxford English Dictionary Online*, s.v. "alliance," http://www.oed.com:80/Entry/5290, accessed December 3, 2010.

26. Albrecht and Brewer, "Bridges of Power," 3.

27. *Oxford English Dictionary Online*, s.v. "horizon," http://www.oed.com:80/Entry/ 88458, accessed April 30, 2011.

28. Smith, *Native Americans and the Christian Right*, xxi.

29. Carrillo Rowe, *Power Lines*.

30. Van Dyke and McCammon, *Strategic Alliances*. There are also exceptions to this: Bystydzienski and Schacht, *Forging Radical Alliances*; Rich, *Politics of Minority Coalitions*. This work emerges largely from social scientific disciplines, including sociology and political science, which often approach identities as discrete or singular variables. Moreover, such scholarship often attempts to systematize or schematize coalition and alliance behavior toward predictive ends. Such work is incredibly important in highlighting the existence of coalition and alliance, but scholarship emerging from queer and feminist perspectives within the humanities is also needed to offer alternative perspectives.

31. *Oxford English Dictionary Online*, s.v. "moment," http://www.oed.com:80/Entry/ 120997, accessed April 23, 2011.

32. Freeman, *Time Binds,* "Queer Temporalities."

33. The multiple subject is not the same as the fragmented subject. See Lugones, *Pilgrimages/Peregrinajes*. The "coalitional subject" is a term Carrillo Rowe developed in *Power Lines*.

34. The immigrant rights and justice movement is certainly not alone in sometimes refusing to include questions of sexual orientation within its purview. As one reviewer of this manuscript noted, the subject of sexual identity and orientation has been viewed as a political matter in the latter part of the twentieth century, and it has often been contentious. One needs to think no further than the practice of lesbian baiting within race-based social movements, used to keep women from bringing gender and sexuality to the center of racial analysis, or to the active decision to remove leaders with homosexual indiscretions from leadership roles in the civil rights movement. Betty Freidan's infamous concern about the "lavender menace" invading the women's rights move-

ment also comes to mind. Similarly, within trade union activism and the Communist Party, nonheterosexuality has historically been minimized or demonized. Certainly this historical context makes the existence of queer migration politics all the more significant. For more, see, for example, Clarke, "Lesbianism"; D'Emilio, "Homophobia," "Homosexual Menace"; Pharr, *Homophobia*; Wolf, *Sexuality and Socialism*.

35. Marciniak, *Alienhood*; Phelan, *Sexual Strangers*. On the subject of strangers, see Bauman, *Modernity and Ambivalence*.

36. For example, Espín, *Latina Realities*; Romero, *Maid in the U.S.A.*; Hondagneu-Sotelo, *Gender and U.S. Immigration*; Fujiwara, *Mothers without Citizenship*. For an excellent review of this type of work and the move from thinking about gender explicitly in terms of heterosexual women into thinking about gender more broadly, see Manalansan, "Queer Intersections."

37. For example, Anker, "Woman Refugees"; Bhabha, "Embodied Rights."

38. For example, Asencio and Acosta, "Migration, Gender Conformity"; Cantú, *Sexuality of Migration*; Capó, "Queering Mariel"; Carrillo, "Sexual Migration"; Decena, *Tacit Subjects*; Kuntsman, "Hospitality in Flames," "Double Homecoming"; La Fountain-Stokes, *Queer Ricans*, "Cultures of the Puerto Rican Queer Diaspora"; Manalansan, "Queer Intersections"; Peña, "'Obvious Gays.'"

39. For example, M. J. Alexander, "Not Just (Any) Body"; Canaday, *Straight State*; Carrillo, "Immigration and LGBT Rights," "Leaving Loved Ones Behind," "Imagining Modernity," "Sexual Migration"; Francoeur, "Enemy Within"; Lewis, "Lesbians under Surveillance"; Luibhéid, "Sexuality, Migration," "Heteronormativity, Responsibility," "Introduction," *Entry Denied*; McKinnon, "(In)Hospitable Publics"; Minter, "Sodomy"; Reddy, "Asian Diasporas, Neoliberalism"; J. M. Rodríguez, *Queer Latinidad*; Shah, *Stranger Intimacy, Contagious Divides*; Simmons, "Sexuality and Immigration"; Solomon, "Trans/Migrant"; Somerville, "Queer *Loving*," "Notes toward a Queer History," "Sexual Aliens"; Stein, "All the Immigrants Are Straight"; Stychin, "Stranger to Its Laws."

40. Such overall suspicion of migrant populations also led to the policing of migrants for engaging in "vagrancy" and objectionable sexual behavior. Nayan Shah, for instance, reveals how migrant men in the western part of the United States and Canada were regularly policed and criminalized for same-sex sexual encounters in the first two decades of the twentieth century. Shah, *Stranger Intimacy*.

41. Pérez, "Queering the Borderlands," 126.

42. Ibid. See also Ordover, *American Eugenics*; Somerville, *Queering the Color Line*.

43. Carrillo Rowe, *Power Lines*, "Whose 'America'?" See also M. J. Alexander, *Pedagogies of Crossing*; Somerville, *Queering the Color Line*.

44. For more on the unique study of trans migration and migrant identities, see, for example, Aizura, "Transnational Transgender Rights"; Cantú, Luibhéid, and Stern, "Well-Founded Fear"; Chávez, "Spatializing Gender Performativity"; Cotten, *Transgender Migrations*, see especially Aizura and Haritaworn in the collection; D. Morgan, "Not Gay Enough"; J. M. Rodríguez, *Queer Latinidad*; Yue, "Queer Asian Mobility."

45. The prefix "cis-" means "on the side of" and has been taken up by trans scholars and activists to describe people whose biological sex matches their gender identity. See Stryker, *Transgender History*.

46. Aizura, "Transnational Transgender Rights."

47. I use the word "politics" here to refer generally to those often agonistic, and sometimes antagonistic, practices of and relationships between people in a given society that are designed to impact public opinion and state affairs and enact social change. Activism is a particular form of politics that is explicitly designed to effect social change with a specific agenda, usually enacted outside traditional, deliberative modes of decision-making conducted within established institutions. See I. M. Young, "Activist Challenges." The very few exceptions of scholars who have examined various intersections of queer and migration activism or politics include Brady, "Homoerotics of Immigration Control"; Haritaworn, Tauqir, and Erdem, "Gay Imperialism"; Kuntsman, "Between Gulags," "Queerness as Europeanness"; Luibhéid and Khokha, "Building Alliances"; Puar, *Terrorist Assemblages*; Stephen, Lanier, Ramírez, and Westerling, "Building Alliances." Although not directly about queer migration—but certainly in conversation with the scholarship—Scott Lauria Morgensen's work also informs this book as he explores how settler colonialism produces queer politics and theory and examines the alliances and relationships among native and non-native queer activists in the United States within that context. See Morgensen, *Spaces between Us*.

48. Spade, *Normal Life*.

49. Duggan, "New Homonormativity." See also Duggan, *Twilight of Equality?*

50. Puar, *Terrorist Assemblages*.

51. Haritaworn, Tauqir, and Erdem, "Gay Imperialism." Importantly, the publication of this essay caused quite a controversy in the United Kingdom, indicating what is at stake by making such connections between xenophobia and homophobia and constructions of national identity that call out racism, xenophobia, or imperialist complicity within queer or LGBT rights movements. Peter Tatchell, the founder of OutRage!, an LGBT organization in London, is the center of critique in this article because of his representations of Islamic countries, his implicit promotion of Islamophobia to advance queer rights, and his silencing of Muslim queers in the process. Tatchell was outraged at the claims in the chapter and subsequently started a campaign against the chapter and book. In 2009 Raw Nerve Books complied with pressure and issued an apology to Tatchell and took the book out of print. See Kuntsman and Miyake, *Out of Place*. It seems to be unavailable from any seller in the United States or United Kingdom, despite being one of the first and only collections to directly address the political intersections between queer politics and race politics, including migration politics.

52. Kuntsman, "Queerness as Europeanness."

53. El-Tayeb, *European Others*.

54. Das Gupta, *Unruly Immigrants*, 163.

55. Ibid.

56. For example, Bosniak, *Citizen and the Alien*; Del Castillo, "Illegal Status"; Dickinson, "Selling Democracy"; T. Miller, *Well-Tempered Self*; Ong, "Cultural Citizenship"; Richardson, "Locating Sexualities," "Claiming Citizenship?"; Rosaldo, "Cultural Citizenship, Inequality," "Cultural Citizenship"; Tang, "Diasporic Cultural Citizenship."

57. Brandzel, "Queering Citizenship," 174.

58. Ibid.; Brandzel, "Haunted by Citizenship."

59. Morgensen, *Spaces between Us*. See also, for example, Driskill, "Doubleweaving"; Smith, "Queer Theory and Native Studies."

60. For example, Berlant, *Queen of America*; Brandzel, "Queering Citizenship."

61. For example, B. Anderson, *Imagined Communities*; Billig, *Banal Nationalism*; Calhoun, *Nationalism*.

62. W. Brown, *Walled States, Waning Sovereignty*; El-Tayeb, *European Others*.

63. Arendt, *Origins of Totalitarianism*.

64. Carrillo, "Sexual Culture, Structure"; Carrillo and Fontdevila, "Rethinking Sexual Initiation"; Carrillo, Fontdevila, Brown, and Gómez, "Risk across Borders"; Organista and Ehrlich, "Predictors of Condom Use"; Organista, "Towards a Structural-Environmental Model"; Organista, Carrillo, and Ayala, "HIV Prevention"; Organista, Organista, Garcia de Alba, Castillo Morán, and Ureta Carrillo, "Survey of Condom-Related Beliefs"; Organista and Organista, "Culture and Gender Sensitive."

65. Examples of such ethnographic analyses include Cantú, *Sexuality of Migration*; Das Gupta, *Unruly Immigrants*; Decena, *Tacit Subjects*; Kuntsman, *Figurations of Violence*; Manalansan, *Global Divas*. Examples of literary analyses include Gopinath, *Impossible Desires*; La Fountain-Stokes, *Queer Ricans*; Puar, *Terrorist Assemblages*; Tinsley, *Thiefing Sugar*; Yue, "What's So Queer."

66. Lugones, *Pilgrimages/Peregrinajes*.

67. The term "rhetoric of the streets" was first used in Haiman, "Rhetoric of the Streets." On the dominance of public rhetoric in social movement studies, see Chávez, "Counter-Public Enclaves"; Stewart, "Internal Rhetoric." See also Cox and Foust, "Social Movement Rhetoric."

68. N. Fraser, "Rethinking the Public Sphere"; Mansbridge, "Using Power"; Squires, "Rethinking the Black Public Sphere."

69. Archibold, "Lawmakers Want Look," 12A. For a comprehensive listing of participating agencies, see Immigration and Customs Enforcement, "Fact Sheet: Delegation of Immigration Authority Section 287(g) Immigration and Nationality Act," http://www.ice.gov/news/library/factsheets/287g.htm, accessed January 4, 2013.

70. Immigration and Customs Enforcement, "Secure Communities," http://www.ice.gov/secure_communities, accessed September 22, 2012.

71. I use the @ in Latin@ and Chican@ as opposed to the slash "a/o" or other forms of gender-inclusive writing following Sandra K. Soto. Soto maintains that the @ signals a departure from mastery and wholeness and disidentifies with legible gender norms. In a queer text this usage is most appropriate. See Soto, *Reading Chican@*.

72. Weston, "Get Thee to a Big City."

73. Clare, *Exile and Pride*; Gray, *Out in the Country*; Tongson, *Relocations*.

74. Halberstam, *Queer Art of Failure*.

75. "Tactical strategy" is a term I borrow from Lugones, who seeks to disrupt the dichotomy between tactic and strategy that Michel de Certeau creates. For de Certeau, strategies are used by those in power within a proper place, while tactics are used by the weak, who have no proper space of their own. As Lugones claims, strategy then stands for distance, whereas tactics imply a lack of distance. Lugones collapses the two into a tactical strategy, noting, "For the tactical strategist resisting ↔ oppressing has volume, intricacy, multiplicity of relationality and meaning, and it is approached with all the sensorial openness and keenness that permits resistant, liberatory, enduring, if dispersed, complexity of connection." *Pilgrimages/Peregrinajes,* 215. For the sake of ease, in chapters 3 and 4 I often continue using the word "strategy," even as I sometimes mean "tactical strategy." When it is clear that an action needs to be understood as a unique tactical strategy, I will use that term. See also de Certeau, *Practice of Everyday Life*.

76. Lorde, "Master's Tools."

Chapter 1. The Differential Visions of Queer Migration Manifestos

The plural of manifesto can be spelled either "manifestos" or "manifestoes." I opt for the former, though some of the scholars I cite opt for the latter.

1. This happened most famously when *People* ran a feature on the couple, which was then taken up by numerous news outlets and blogs. S. Young, "Gay Mom Faces Deportation."

2. "Testimony of Shirley Tan," United States Senate Committee on the Judiciary, June 3, 2009, http://tinyurl.com/bzljo8e, accessed January 5, 2013.

3. A few examples, drawn from the many media stories about the couple, include "Is Shirley Tan out of Options to Stay in the U.S.?" *Queerty* (blog), April 2, 2009, http://www.queerty.com/is-shirley-tan-out-of-options-to-stay-in-the-us-20090402, accessed May 8, 2013; Preston, "Bill Proposes Immigration Rights"; Ralls, "We Are Tearing Families Apart"; S. Young, "Gay Mom Faces Deportation."

4. Long, Stern, and Franceour, "Family, Unvalued."

5. Importantly, "Family, Unvalued" is also lauded on the blog site of the Independent Gay Forum, which is, according to Lisa Duggan, the quintessential homonormative organization. See Richard J. Rosendall, "Love and the Border Crossing," *Independent Gay Forum*, May 18, 2006, http://igfculturewatch.com/2006/05/18/love-and-the-border-crossing, accessed January 3, 2013.

6. Nair, "Nair Views: Gay Immigration (and) Inequality," "Viewpoints: Queer Immigration."

7. As mentioned in the introduction, when referring to mainstream organizations that I argue engage in normative discourses of belonging, I generally use LGBT. I use the acronym LGBTQ, where the Q stands for "queer," when that is the term organiza-

tions use in their writings, or in times when I am referring to both mainstream and progressive organizations.

8. I have written extensively about "Family, Unvalued" elsewhere. See Chávez, "Border (In)Securities."

9. Most of these manifestos can be found online, and they are all fairly short. With the exception of "Undoing Borders," the others do not include page numbers. As a result, I list the references for each of the manifestos here and then cite the author and/or title in the text throughout the remainder of this chapter. Audre Lorde Project, "Statement: For All the Ways They Say We Are, No One Is Illegal," April 21, 2006, http://alp.org/whatwedo/statements/nooneisillegal, accessed October 6, 2012; Coalición de Derechos Humanos and Wingspan, "Joint Statement: Continued Stand against Racism and Homophobia," November 28, 2006, http://wingspan.org/content/news_wingspan_details.php?story_id=359, accessed December 1, 2006 (URL is no longer active; I retain a copy in my files); "Joint Statement: Stand against Racism and Homophobia," October 24, 2006, http://wingspan.org/content/news_wingspan_details.php?story_id=353, accessed December 1, 2006 (URL is no longer active; I retain a copy in my files); HAVOQ, "Undoing Borders: A Queer Manifesto," April 2011, https://undoingborders.wordpress.com/undoing-borders, accessed January 4, 2013; Queers for Economic Justice, "Queers and Immigration: A Vision Statement," *Scholar and Feminist Online* 6, no. 3 (2008), http://sfonline.barnard.edu/immigration/qej_01.htm, accessed January 4, 2013.

10. Lyon, *Manifestoes*.

11. Sandoval, *Methodology of the Oppressed*; Carrillo Rowe, *Power Lines*.

12. There is no easy way to distinguish between the gradations of perspectives on the political left. It is easiest to characterize liberals, who, in line with liberal political and philosophical traditions, value inclusion through the achievement of rights, recognition, and equality. Liberal perspectives are reflected in the mainstream of the immigrant rights movement, the LGBT rights movement, and the LGBT immigrant rights movement because these mainstream proponents seek inclusion in the existing system through primarily legal means and often rely on a normative vision of politics and belonging. Progressives and radicals are more difficult to distinguish from each other since both seek significant change of the system as it is and their challenge is to existing norms. The difference between a progressive and radical position could be as simple as this: progressives are more likely to believe that we can use the existing system to change, even if what is needed is radical, whereas radicals are more likely to suggest complete overthrow of the existing system in order to start anew. Utopian politics share with radical politics a desire for something completely different but are more difficult to connect with existing political systems, thought, and practice since they often emphasize the aesthetic/artistic realms.

13. Pearce, "Radical Feminist Manifesto," 307. Manifestos have also been taken up primarily as an aesthetic form, including the 1918 Dada Manifesto and others.

14. Lyon, *Manifestoes*, 3.

15. This list did *not* include the Human Rights Campaign, the National Gay and Lesbian Task Force, or Immigration Equality, despite that an Immigration Equality representative, Francoeur, was a writer.

16. Proposition 107, Protect Marriage Arizona, sought to include an amendment to Arizona's state constitution that defined marriage as between one man and one woman and denied any non-married state employees—homosexual or heterosexual—access to domestic partner benefits. The anti-migrant measures included provisions that (1) prohibit any undocumented person charged with a felony offense from posting bail (Proposition 100); (2) make it impossible for undocumented migrants to receive punitive damages after winning a claim in civil court (Proposition 102); (3) name English as the official language of the state for all official government business (Proposition 103); and (4) prevent undocumented people from taking adult education classes or receiving child-care assistance, scholarships, grants, tuition assistance, or in-state tuition (Proposition 300).

17. During my yearlong qualitative research project studying the coalition between Wingspan and CDH, I was on the committee that produced both of the joint statements. As a committee member, I read drafts and inputted changes that members of the organizations desired. As someone fairly new to these issues at the time, even though I coordinated much of the logistics in preparing the statements, I offered less input on their rhetoric.

18. Lyon, *Manifestoes*, 12.

19. Cormack, Introduction to *Manifestos*, 2; emphasis in original.

20. Winkiel, *Modernism, Race, and Manifestoes*, 1.

21. Lyon, *Manifestoes*, 14.

22. Winkiel, *Modernism, Race, and Manifestoes*, 12.

23. Lyon, *Manifestoes*, 15.

24. Ibid.; Winkiel, *Modernism, Race, and Manifestoes*, 12.

25. Sandoval, *Methodology of the Oppressed*, 58.

26. Ibid., 59.

27. Ibid., 64.

28. Carrillo Rowe, *Power Lines*.

29. Carrillo Rowe, "Be Longing," 35; emphasis in original.

30. The viability of differential belonging can certainly be critiqued for its utopian leanings because it is, at least in part, premised on the assumption that one has access to people who are different whom they can relate to, as well as the time to foster connection over deep-seated divisions, and that one can and should develop a desire to belong to those who one does not know or know well, or worse, those who could potentially cause harm for the sake of coalitional possibility and alliance. Additionally, at times Carrillo Rowe seems to assume that feminists will share some grounds or values that will make it easier for feminists, even those who share little else, to desire belonging to and with one another. Such assumptions of feminists sharing

anything in common, a hope of many western feminists, has been repeatedly shown to be a utopian longing. See Mohanty, *Feminism without Borders*. Carrillo Rowe also addresses this concern in a later work, "Moving Relations." She primarily theorizes the politics of the interpersonal because she is interested in how individual feminists engage with and negotiate professional relationships and alliances with feminists and nonfeminists alike, within the structural conditions of academic institutions. My friend Kimberlee Pérez reads Carrillo Rowe in a slightly different way than I do, suggesting that she sees Carrillo Rowe as *most* interested in relationships among those who declare themselves feminists and so, presumably, also share some premises. I believe this is at times true, given that Carrillo Rowe's foremost interest is in transracial feminist alliances. On the other hand, Carrillo Rowe relies on metaphors like the bridge to describe how people like her—biracial, racially ambiguous, queer, but with ambiguous sexual identity (i.e., she is cisgender and can pass for straight)—can create links between very different ways of thinking. And she further suggests that sometimes shifting into relationships with, say, white men who are not feminists is an important aspect of bridge work. So it seems to me that this slippage in Carrillo Rowe's theorizing lends itself to both readings.

31. Sandoval, *Methodology of the Oppressed*, 63.

32. Ahmed, *Queer Phenomenology*, 85.

33. Ibid.; emphasis in original.

34. Halberstam, *In a Queer Time*.

35. This is in part an argument about agency. An elaborate description of my theory of agency is beyond the scope of this book, but I tend to adopt a post-structuralist conception of agency. To me, this means that agency and subjectivity are discursively constituted. Discourse does not refer here only to language because the material and the metaphysical are also symbolic and therefore discursive. Discourse does not determine agency, but it does provide us with the resources from which we must act. In this sense, choice is not completely a matter of free will because there is never an infinite number of choices in front of us, especially with regard to those very entrenched discourses such as gender, sexuality, and race. Yet people still make choices in the sense that they take up some discourses and not others, even if they are often required or conditioned to do so. See Butler, "Contingent Foundations."

36. Warner, *Trouble with Normal*, ix.

37. Castoriadis, *Imaginary Institution of Society*; Gaonkar, "Toward New Imaginaries." In his *Imagined Communities* Benedict Anderson also provided an influential thesis about the construction of nationalisms through his idea that communities are imagined.

38. Göle, "Islam in Public," 176. See also Taylor, "Modern Social Imaginaries."

39. Ono and Sloop, *Shifting Borders*.

40. Phelan, *Sexual Strangers*, 7.

41. In a conversation with an author of the statement, Yasmin Nair (see also chapter 2), she explained that some of the creators did not want to include the reference to the

UAFA, but they included it to try to build bridges with organizations like Immigration Equality. In the end, and as mentioned in a previous note, even with the inclusion of the UAFA in the statement, Immigration Equality did not sign on as a supporter. This brief example shows the complexity of differential belonging.

42. "Arizona Catholic Conference Bishops Oppose Proposition 200," Roman Catholic Church of Phoenix, 2004, www.voiceofthepoor.org/News/ACConProp200.pdf, accessed June 10, 2007.

43. Weston, *Families We Choose*.

44. Luibhéid, "Sexuality, Migration."

45. "Arizona Bailable Offenses—Proposition 100 (2006)," http://ballotpedia.org/wiki/index.php/Arizona_Bailable_Offenses,_Proposition_100_%282006%29, accessed January 1, 2013.

46. As a number of scholars have suggested, in the United States this slippage between citizen and alien is historically prominent. See Haney-López, *White by Law*; Luibhéid, "Sexuality, Migration." This is perhaps especially difficult for Latin@s, who not only get lumped into a homogenized group but are also assumed to be Mexicans, the ideal "illegal aliens." See Mendieta, "Becoming Citizens, Becoming Hispanics"; Ngai, *Impossible Subjects*.

47. Anzaldúa, *Borderlands*, 25.

48. For example, Butler, *Precarious Life*; Grewal, "Women's Rights"; Hull, "Political Limits of Rights."

49. W. Morgan, "Queering International Human Rights Law." Despite the critiques of human rights discourse, it is also important to mention, as Carl F. Stychin argues, that a universal or global human rights approach has been successfully utilized by local gay rights activists. See Stychin, "Same-Sex Sexualities." Furthermore, as Wayne Morgan insists, despite the trappings of human rights discourse in western thought, many human rights activists, especially those outside of the west, adamantly challenge and retool the discourse.

50. Muñoz, *Disidentifications*.

51. For more on this point, see my essay "Border (In)Securities." The 2002 case of Mexican gay asylum seeker José Soto Vega is briefly mentioned ("Family, Unvalued," 80), but is not featured as one of the primary stories in the report and is simply used as an example of the difficulty for people in binational same-sex couples to use asylum as a method of attaining legal immigration status.

52. Anzaldúa, *Borderlands*, 25; emphasis in original.

53. Faux, "How NAFTA Failed Mexico," 35. See also Bacon, *Illegal People*; K. Johnson, "Free Trade and Closed Borders"; Randolph, "Plowed Under."

54. Innes, "Security Fence May Split Tribes."

55. Segrest, *Born to Belonging*.

56. Probyn, *Outside Belongings*, 6.

57. Ibid., 12–13.

58. Ibid., 19.

59. Mohanty, *Feminism without Borders*.

60. Probyn, *Outside Belongings*, 13.

61. Joseph, *Against the Romance of Community*.

62. Stanley and Smith, *Captive Genders*.

63. For example, "GLAAD Was There: 2006," Gay and Lesbian Alliance Against Defamation (GLAAD), http://www.glaad.org/2007/2007PDFS/Accomplish2006.pdf, accessed May 23, 2007 (URL is no longer active); "2006 Elections Analysis," Arizona Human Rights Fund (now Equality Arizona), http://eqfed.org/ahrf/notice-description .tcl?newsletter_id=3760591, accessed May 23, 2007 (URL is no longer active); "Anti-gay Candidates Suffer Stinging Defeats, Arizonans Reject Anti-Gay Initiative," Human Rights Campaign, November 8, 2006, http://preview.hrc.org/your_community/1254 .htm, accessed January 5, 2013.

64. Since I was present and a part of these conversations during my fieldwork, and was also on the committee that produced "Joint Statement Continued," I know this was central to the thinking of Wingspan activists, particularly Cathy, with whom I shared emails about this matter.

65. This joint statement drew largely from similar action steps that appeared in an unpublished statement issued by members of the People of Color Caucus of the National Gay and Lesbian Task Force's Creating Change conference in 2006.

66. Perez, Guitierrez, Meza, and Dominguez Zamarano, "DREAM Movement."

67. I include these two cities because I am aware of the impacts firsthand. I live in Madison, and the Wisconsin Network for Peace and Justice Immigration Working Group, of which I am a part, has attended to these arguments in relation to its positions. Similarly, Southerners on New Ground has been using the HAVOQ manifesto as its inspiration for creating its own queer approach to immigration reform. I learned this when I visited and spoke at one of its meetings in November 2012.

Chapter 2. The Coalitional Possibility of Radical Interactionality

1. According to *StatShow*, a site that collects statistics on website traffic, www.queercents .com receives on average over half a million visitors and well over a million page views each year. It also has more than ten thousand indexed pages in Google, Yahoo, and Bing. This is not a huge amount of traffic, as it is certainly a special-interest blog, but it is enough to indicate that the site is regularly visited. See http://www.statshow.com/ queercents.com, accessed June 6, 2011.

2. Here is a short list of blogs pertaining to binational same-sex couples that rely on stories of couples' trials due to discriminatory immigration laws: *BiNational Same Sex Couples*, http://binationalcouples.blogspot.com; *Uniting American Families*, http:// www.unitingamericanfamilies.net; *Out4Immigration*, http://out4immigration.blogspot .com; *Canadian Hope*, http://canadianhope.blogspot.com; *Preparing Our Exile*, http:// preparingourexile.blogspot.com; *Steven's Life of Gorgeousness*, http://stevendrowe .org/wp/category/immigration; *Writing Down the Distance*, http://writingdownthedistance

.blogspot.com; *Immigration Equality Action Fund*, http://immigrationequalityactionfund
.org/blog; *Love Exiles Foundation*, http://loveexiles.wordpress.com. All accessed on March
6, 2013.

3. Yasmin Nair, "Uniting American Families Act: Facts, Fiction, Money and Emotions," *Queercents* (blog), May 4, 2009, http://queercents.com/2009/05/04/uniting
-american-families-act-facts-fiction-and-emotions, accessed February 1, 2011.

4. Ibid.

5. Madison Reed, "Yasmin Nair: Eat This!" *Lotus Opening* (blog), May 7, 2009,
http://blog.lotusopening.com/2009/05/yasmin-nair-eat-this.html, accessed January 5, 2013.

6. Carrillo Rowe, *Power Lines*.

7. For a fairly extensive archive of Nair's public writing, speeches, and appearances,
visit www.yasminnair.net.

8. Hammerback and Jensen, "Rhetorical Works"; *Rhetorical Career of César Chávez*;
Poirot, "(Un)Making Sex, Making Race"; Skinnell, "Elizabeth Cady Stanton"; Terrill,
"Protest, Prophecy"; Vail, "'Integrative' Rhetoric"; Wilson, "Interpreting the Discursive
Field."

9. DeLaure, "Planting Seeds of Change"; Jensen and Hammerback, "'Your Tools are
Really the People,'" "Working in 'Quiet Places.'"

10. Baim, "Introduction," 6.

11. Chávez, "Counter-Public Enclaves"; Mansbridge, "Using Power"; Squires, "Rethinking the Black Public Sphere."

12. Marta Donayre, "Censorship and Name Calling Are Simply Perturbing: Let Yasmin
Talk . . . Err . . . Blog!" *mdonayre* (blog), May 19, 2009, http://www.martadonayre.com/
index.php/component/components/index.php?option=com_idoblog&task=viewpost
&id=56&Itemid=0, accessed May 15, 2011 (URL is no longer active; I retain a copy of
the post in my files).

13. None of these organizations is a 501(c)3 nonprofit group.

14. *Queer to the Left*, http://www.queertotheleft.org, accessed January 2, 2013.

15. CLIA, "CLIA Manifesto," from the papers of Yasmin Nair.

16. Nair, interviews with author, July 2007 (phone interview) and May 2011, Chicago, IL.

17. Gender JUST, "Mission and Vision," *Gender JUST*, http://www.genderjust.org/
about/mission-vision, accessed January 1, 2013.

18. Against Equality, "About," *Against Equality*, http://www.againstequality.org, accessed January 1, 2013.

19. Conrad, *Queer Critiques of Gay Marriage, Don't Ask to Fight Their Wars, Prisons Will
Not Protect You*.

20. While all of the research and nearly all of the writing of this chapter were completed before I joined Nair in our shared activist pursuits, clearly the fact of my joining
suggests my own political leanings and undoubtedly affects the analysis. Fortunately,
as feminists, postcolonial scholars, and others have taught us, all perspectives are

always and already partial. I have done my best to fairly represent Nair's work, its strengths and weaknesses.

21. For example, Christensen, "Political Activities"; Morozov, "Brave New World of Slacktivism."

22. Herring, "Gender and Power"; Herring and Paolillo, "Gender and Genre Variations."

23. Howard, "Electronic Hybridity," 195. See also Howard, "Vernacular Web."

24. Warnick, *Rhetoric Online*, 3. See also Kahn and Kellner, "New Media and Internet Activism."

25. Lim, "Clicks, Cabs."

26. Xenos and Moy, "Direct and Differential Effects."

27. Chesebro, "Rhetorical Strategies"; Darsey, *Prophetic Tradition*.

28. Klumpp, "Challenge of Radical Rhetoric," 146; emphasis in original.

29. Darsey, *Prophetic Tradition*, 9.

30. Scott, "Conservative Voice," 135.

31. Arendt, *On Revolution*.

32. Bassichis, Lee, and Spade, "Building an Abolitionist Movement," 17.

33. Zinn, *Marx in Soho*, 46.

34. Madison, *Acts of Activism*, 18.

35. *Oxford English Dictionary Online*, s.v. "radical," http://www.oed.com:80/Entry/157251, accessed May 24, 2011.

36. *Encyclopedia Britannica*, s.v. "rhizome," http://www.britannica.com/EBchecked/topic/501483/rhizome, accessed May 24, 2011.

37. Deleuze and Guattari, *Thousand Plateaus*.

38. Crenshaw, "Mapping the Margins"; Combahee River Collective, "Black Feminist Statement"; Lorde, "Age, Race, Class, and Sex." Numerous US third-world feminist scholars and activists have articulated positions on intersectionality, interlocking oppressions, and related concepts.

39. I heard the black feminist communication scholar Brenda J. Allen use this phrase in a talk she gave on intersectionality at the 2009 National Communication Association convention. However, it is probably attributable to many sources.

40. Eng, *Feeling of Kinship*, 49.

41. For additional critiques of intersectionality, see Lugones, "Heterosexualism," "Toward a Decolonial Feminism." Lugones maintains that "once intersectionality shows us what is missing, we have ahead of us the task of reconceptualizing the logic of the intersection so as to avoid separability. It is only when we perceive gender and race as intermeshed or fused that we actually see women of color." "Heterosexualism," 193. In other words, intersectionality is a descriptive tool and does not actually have liberatory capacity in and of itself because the idea of the intersection still implies that gender and race are, at least analytically, separable. This is similar to Lugones's concern about interlocking oppression. See my introduction, note 22.

42. Puar, *Terrorist Assemblages*, 211.

43. Massumi, *Parables for the Virtual*, 2.

44. Puar, *Terrorist Assemblages*, 212; emphasis in original.

45. Crenshaw, "Mapping the Margins."

46. My friend Shanara Reid-Brinkley and I have been talking about the possibility and utility of a concept of interactionality for years, and she is developing her own conceptualization in current writing. I have also benefited greatly in my thinking on this from conversations with my friend Sirma Bilge.

47. Lugones, *Pilgrimages/Peregrinajes*.

48. To be clear, one of the weaknesses in the concept I am developing here is that I don't fully take into account Lugones's discussion of the "coloniality of power" and the fact that gender is not something that women of color had during colonial times and in colonial ways of thinking because they were, in fact, animals. The idea of gender itself, then, is a colonial idea, and one that describes what white women or other women of privilege possessed. I have not figured out how to integrate Lugones's complex philosophy into my work on activist rhetoric in the United States.

49. Yasmin Nair, "Undocumented vs. Illegal: A Distinction without a Difference," *Yasmin Nair* (blog), December 2012, http://www.yasminnair.net/content/undocumented-vs-illegal-distinction-without-difference, accessed December 16, 2012.

50. Cohen, "Punks, Bulldaggers," 460; emphasis in original.

51. Ibid., 442.

52. For an extensive of how "post-Fordist capitalism" becomes naturalized politically and culturally, see Jakobsen, "Can Homosexuals End Western Civilization?"

53. Yasmin Nair, "What's Left of Queer? Immigration, Sexuality, and Affect in a Neoliberal World," *Immigrant City Chicago*, 2010, http://www.uic.edu/jaddams/hull/immigrantcitychicago/essays/nair_leftofqueer.html, accessed January 4, 2013.

54. Bassichis, Lee, and Spade, "Building an Abolitionist," 20.

55. Berlant, *Queen of America*.

56. Harvey, *Brief History of Neoliberalism*.

57. Nair, "What's Left of Queer?"

58. Ibid. For more on how family rhetoric works in immigration rights movement, see Luibhéid, "Heteronormativity, Responsibility"; Gerken, "Neo-Liberalism and Family Values."

59. Nair, "What's Left of Queer?"

60. Ibid.

61. Ibid.

62. I am using "their" in the singular sense, as a gender inclusive/ambiguous form of "he" or "she." Using "their" as a singular pronoun is an increasingly common practice in trans and trans-allied communities.

63. Nair, "What's Left of Queer?"

64. Nair, interview, May 2011.

65. Gould, *Moving Politics*, 3; emphasis in original.

66. Sandoval, *Methodology of the Oppressed*.

67. Quoted in Nair, "Uniting American Families."

68. Ibid.

69. Importantly, it is very difficult for dependents to file successful petitions on the basis of VAWA. In 2012 VAWA was almost not renewed due to Republican opposition to the protection it provides to undocumented migrants in abusive relationships and also that it extends some protections to same-sex couples. See Weisman, "Women Figure Anew." In early 2013, congressional Republicans voted not to renew VAWA, based on Republican opposition to provisions that would expand protections for undocumented migrants, LGBT people, and Native Americans. See Holpuch, "US House Votes." Finally, in March 2013, congressional Republicans allowed a vote on VAWA, which passed, and Obama signed it into law. The law included protections for undocumented migrants, LGBT people, and Native Americans. See Goodman, "New Violence Against Women Act."

70. Nair, "Uniting American Families."

71. Ibid.

72. Ahmed, *Cultural Politics of Emotion*, 124; emphasis in original.

73. Nair, "Uniting American Families," Response #4, Angela.

74. Ibid., Response #5, Yasmin.

75. Ibid., Response #17, Anonymous.

76. Ibid., Response #18, Yasmin.

77. Reed, "Yasmin Nair: Eat This!"

78. Sapphocrat, "Who Is Yasmin Nair, and Why Does This Alleged 'Queer Lesbian' Parrot Right-Wing Anti-Gay Talking Points?" *Lavender Newswire* (blog), May 20, 2009, http://news.lavenderliberal.com/2009/05/20/who-is-yasmin-nair, accessed February 1, 2011 (URL is no longer active; I retain a copy in my files).

79. Ibid.; emphasis in original.

80. Nair, "Uniting American Families," Response #36, Anonymous.

81. "'Yasmin Nair: Eat This!' Or: How to Leave Comments without Going up in Flames," *Bilerico Project* (blog), May 19, 2009, http://www.bilerico.com/2009/05/yasmin_nair_eat_this_or_how_to_have_conv.php, accessed February 1, 2011.

82. Combahee River Collective, "Black Feminist Statement."

83. Nair, "What's Left of Queer?"

84. Ibid.

85. On the first point, as one example, Whole Foods, which has been notorious in preventing its workers from creating unions, has earned a respectable 85/100 from the HRC. On this last point, for example, Raytheon builds defense and aerospace systems, cites homeland and border security as one of its key markets, and benefits from the military industrial complex as a whole. Raytheon generally has good LGBT policies, earning it a perfect score on the 2011 index. See Human Rights Campaign, "Corporate Equality Index 2011," http://www.hrc.org/files/assets/resources/CorporateEqualityIndex_2011 .pdf, accessed January 3, 2013.

86. Nair, "What's Left of Queer?"

87. Ibid.

88. Nair, "Views: Gay Marriage."

89. Currently sexual orientation and gender identity are not protected categories under the United Nations definition of a refugee, which is a person who flees their country because of a "well-founded fear of being persecuted for reasons of race, religion, nationality, membership of a particular social group, or political opinion." Most countries, including the United States, address these cases under the "social group" and "political opinion" categories. Numerous scholars have discussed the different dimensions of LGBT asylum. For example, Cantú, Luibhéid, and Stern, "Well-Founded Fear"; Franke, "Not Meeting the Standard"; Landau, "'Soft Immutability'"; McKinnon, "(In)Hospitable Publics."

90. Nair, "Views: Gay Marriage."

91. Ibid.

92. "The Real Costs of the HIV Ban," *Queercents* (blog), May 18, 2009, http://queercents.com/2009/05/18/the-real-costs-of-the-hiv-ban, accessed April 17, 2011.

93. Greenhouse, "Visa Ban," B4.

94. "Nair: Eat this!" Comment, Yasmin, June 3, 2009.

95. Nair, "Views: Gay Marriage."

96. Gay Liberation Network, "Immigration/Marriage."

97. LGBT Contingent, "LGBT Groups Mobilize for Big Immigrant Rights March," Gay Liberation Network, April 17, 2008, http://preview.tinyurl.com/b9lqfej, accessed January 2, 2013.

98. American Apparel agrees, noting its continued support of immigrant rights and immigration reform and its donation of 100 percent of its proceeds from the Legalize L.A. shirts to local immigration rights organizations. See *American Apparel*, http://americanapparel.net/contact/legalizela, accessed January 2, 2013.

99. Yasmin Nair, "Legalize Gay, Or: So You Think You're Illegal?" *Queercents* (blog), July 6, 2009, http://queercents.com/2009/07/06/legalize-gay-or-so-you-think-youre-illegal, accessed April 17, 2011; emphasis in original.

100. After Proposition 8 passed, American Apparel handed out more than fifty thousand shirts for free at cities around the United States. They also explain the campaign on their website, saying, "We hope that you can understand that we're sincere about this and that we think it's important, just like we are about Legalize LA." See *American Apparel*, http://americanapparel.net/legalizegay, accessed December 29, 2012.

101. Hodgkinson and Weitzman, "Overview."

102. Defourny, "From Third Sector."

103. Joseph, *Against the Romance of Community*.

104. D. Rodríguez, "Political Logic," 21–22.

105. Ibid.; Gilmore, "In the Shadow."

106. Smith, "Introduction," 10.

107. I am not sure of the specific numbers on this, but with gender and women's

studies in particular, nearly every website I searched mentioned that many gradu-
ates will find work in the nonprofit sector. Having been around GWS programs and
departments for more than a decade, I know there is a widespread understanding
that the nonprofit sector is one of the key sites of job placement for those with GWS
bachelor's and master's degrees.

108. As one example from the LGBT nonprofit world, according to its 2008 tax
returns, the annual base salary of the HRC's then executive director, Joe Solomnese,
was $291,177, and thirteen other "highest compensated employees" made more than
$119,000 per year as a base salary.

109. For example, Gay Shame has been leading the charge against the GNPIC.
See Ryan Conrad, "Creating Change or Creating Chains? A Fierce Look at the Non-
Profit Industrial Complex," *Bilerico Project* (blog), July 23, 2010, http://www.bilerico
.com/2010/07/creating_change_or_creating_chains.php, accessed April 17, 2011.

110. Gay Shame, "Creating Change or Creating Chains?" *Gay Shame*, http://www
.gayshamesf.org/creatingchains.html, accessed January 2, 2013.

111. Yasmin Nair, "Queers and Immigration Reform: Where Do We Stand?" *Bilerico Project* (blog), January 10, 2008, http://www.bilerico.com/2008/01/queers_and_
immigration_reform_where_do_w_1.php, accessed April 17, 2011.

112. Vaid, *Virtual Equality*.

113. Nair, "Queers and Immigration Reform," Comment, Yasmin, January 10.

114. Ibid.; emphasis in original.

115. Dettmer, "Beyond Gay Marriage," 34–37. See also Conrad, "Against Equality,
in Maine and Everywhere."

116. Jessica, "Contributors to Captive Genders Take on Policing, the LGBT Mainstream, and the Re-Writing of Queer History," *Revolution by the Book: The AK Press
Blog*, June 28, 2011, http://www.revolutionbythebook.akpress.org/contributors-to
-captive-genders-take-on-policing-the-lgbt-mainstream-and-the-re-writing-of
-queer-history, accessed July 1, 2011.

117. For example, Batstone and Mendieta, *Good Citizen*; Duggan, *Twilight of Equality?*

118. Nair, "Uniting American Families," Comment, Sam, May 6, 2009.

119. McKerrow, "Critical Rhetoric."

120. Rand, "Inflammatory Fag," 301.

121. Gould, *Moving Politics*, 27.

122. Berlant, *Cruel Optimism*. See especially chapter 5.

123. Johnson Reagon, "Coalition Politics," 356.

Chapter 3. Coming Out as Coalitional Gesture?

1. David Bennion, "DREAM Act 21 Arrested on Capitol Hill," *Citizen Orange* (blog),
July 22, 2010, http://www.citizenorange.com/orange/2010/07/dream-act-21-arrested
-on-capit.html, accessed January 26, 2011. With regard to the DREAM activism in this
chapter, I focus primarily on initial actions taken in 2010. Much action has been taken

and continues to take place, and migrant youth activists are constantly changing their strategies and approach. This work is fascinating, but a comprehensive look at DREAM activism is beyond the purview of this chapter.

2. Bahrampour, "Students Raise the Stakes"; Ruiz, "'No Papers' but Endless Courage."

3. Migrant youth activists use information communication technologies in innovative ways, which scholars are noting. See, for example, Costanza-Chock, "Digital Popular Communication"; Seif, "'Unapologetic and Unafraid.'" Megan Morrissey, a graduate student on whose committee I serve, has an essay on the DREAM Now letters featured in a special issue of the *Journal of International and Intercultural Communication* that I edited on "queer intercultural communication" (2013, 6, no. 2). See Morrissey, "DREAM Disrupted."

4. See Citizen Orange, "About," *Citizen Orange*, http://www.citizenorange.com/about2.html, accessed October 10, 2010.

5. See OutServe-Servicemembers Legal Defense Network, "Stories from the Frontline: Letters to President Barack Obama," 2010, *OutServe-SLDN*, http://www.sldn.org/blog/c/letters/P20, accessed January 3, 2013. As stated in the description of the SLDN (which, after the repeal of DADT, is now called OutServe-SLDN) campaign, its primary aim was to apply pressure on the Senate to attach the DADT repeal to the Defense Authorization Bill because the network argued it was "the best legislative vehicle to bring repeal to the president's desk." See the description on the last day of the campaign, "Stories from the Frontline: A Love Letter to a G.I.," May 28, 2010, *OutServe-SLDN*, http://www.sldn.org/blog/archives/stories-from-the-frontlines-a-love-letter-from-a-soldier, accessed January 3, 2013.

6. *Development, Relief, and Education for Alien Minors Act of 2009*, 1st sess., S. 729, 111th Congress. The information cited here refers to the 2009 version of the act, which differs slightly from other versions.

7. Kyledeb, "DREAM Now Recap—Latino, LGBT, Migrant Youth, and Progressive Bloggers Lead for the DREAM Act," *Citizen Orange* (blog), August 20, 2010, http://www.citizenorange.com/orange/2010/08/dream-now-recap-letters-led.html#more, accessed February 1, 2011. A great example of the shying away from LGBT issues comes from 2009. After Catholic supporters of immigrant rights applied much pressure, Rep. Luis Gutierrez (D-IL) removed LGBT rights provisions from his immigration bill, Comprehensive Immigration Reform for America's Security and Prosperity Act of 2009. See Worley, "Activists Disappointed with Immigration Bill."

8. Daniel Hennessey, "The Dream Letters Campaign Kicks Off," *Frontlines Feed: The Latest from SLDN* (blog), July 19, 2010, http://www.sldn.org/blog/archives/the-dream-letters-campaign-kicks-off, accessed January 5, 2013. Not all felt this way, as noted in a comment by John Desselle in this entry that proclaims, "undocumented immigrant = illegal immigrant" and "all of these undocumented immigrant people need to be taken back to where they came from." Still, DREAMers also had a chance encounter with Lt. Dan Choi, who, after coming out as gay on the *Rachel Maddow Show* in the spring of 2010 and being discharged from the army, became the poster boy

for the DADT repeal. Both Choi and four DREAMers attended and disrupted a talk given by Senator Harry Reid at the Netroots Nation Convention in order to hold him to his word to advance both the DADT repeal and the DREAM Act. Choi and the four DREAMers—Matias Ramos, Yahaira Carrillo, Prerna Lal, and Lizbeth Mateo—had a chance to exchange their support for each other's causes on this occasion. See David Bennion, "DREAMers Pressure Senator Reid at Netroots Nation, Meet American Hero Dan Choi," *Citizen Orange* (blog), July 28, 2010, http://www.citizenorange.com/ orange/2010/07/dreamers-pressure-senator-reid.html, accessed April 6, 2013.

9. Howard, "Vernacular Web."

10. Three examples are worth mentioning. First, in July 2010, simultaneous to the DREAM 21 arrests, queer undocumented youth in California engaged in a hunger strike both to urge Senator Feinstein to move forward on the DREAM Act and to encourage the LGBTQ community to actively support the DREAM Act. See La Macha, "Queer Undocumented Youth Participate in a Hunger Strike and Urge All LGBTQ Communities to Support Their Fasting for Their Dreams," *Vivir Latino* (blog), July 23, 2010, http:// vivirlatino.com/2010/07/23/queer-undocumented-youth-participate-in-a-hunger -strike-and-urge-all-lgbtq-communities-to-support-their-fasting-for-their-dreams .php, accessed April 6, 2013. Second, when Lady Gaga became an outspoken advocate of repealing DADT, migrant and queer youth activists in Arizona met with her before the concert that she refused to cancel as part of the boycott of the state after SB 1070 was passed. Playing on her concern for the LGBT community, they talked with her about the problems for gay undocumented people and why she should also put her support behind immigration rights, especially the DREAM Act. Gaga offered her support and announced the need to stand for immigrant rights during the concert. See Maria, "Lady Gaga Supports the DREAM Act," *DreamActivist* (blog), August 4, 2010, http://www.dreamactivist .org/lady-gaga-dream-act, accessed April 6, 2013. Third, in 2009 migrant queer youth activist Prerna Lal wrote an impassioned essay that details the many concerns that undocumented queer youth face over and against the concerns of undocumented heterosexuals. She indicates the importance for undocumented people to come out and the necessity for the immigrant rights movement to reconsider many of its heteronormative pro-family strategies that marginalize queer migrants. See Prerna Lal, "What Constitutes Gay Immigration Politics—Notes from a Queer Immigrant Organizer," *Change.org* (blog), April 2, 2009, http://news.change.org/stories/what-constitutes-gay-immigration -politics-notes-from-a-queer-immigrant-organizer, accessed February 3, 2011 (URL is no longer active despite being listed on the author's website; I retain a copy in my files). In this entry Lal also cites *DreamActivist.org* as an "LGBT undocumented students collective." This site now describes itself as "the social media hub for the movement to pass the DREAM Act," but Lal's essay points to the centrality of queers in this movement.

11. On appropriation, see Shugart, "Counterhegemonic Acts."

12. I use the word "youth" throughout this chapter, because this is the way that many of these young activists often self-identify and are identified by others in the immigration movement as well as those in the mainstream media. "Youth" is not necessarily

an accurate descriptor for many of these activists because many are in their mid to late twenties, and some are even older. Investigating the deployment of youth would be an analysis all to itself, and it does not feature centrally in this chapter.

13. Department of Homeland Security, "Secretary Napolitano Announces Record-Breaking Immigration Enforcement Statistics Achieved under the Obama Administration," press release, October 6, 2010, http://www.dhs.gov/ynews/releases/pr_1286389936778.shtm, accessed November 1, 2010. Slevin, "Deportation of Illegal Immigrants," A1. In the 2012 fiscal year, the Obama administration set another record, deporting 409,849 people, up from 396,906 in 2011. See Foley, "Deportation Hits Another Record."

14. Mascaro, "Border Security Bill," A8.

15. "DREAMer" is a name that many undocumented youth involved in the movement use to describe themselves. Some in the movement, however, disidentify with the term, so I try to use it sparingly in this chapter. See, for example, Tania A. Unzueta, "How I Stopped Believing in CIR and Learned to Love 'Piecemeal' Legislation," *Immigrant Youth Justice League* (blog), December 14, 2012, http://www.iyjl.org/how-i-stopped-believing-in-cir-and-learned-to-love-piecemeal-legislation, accessed December 15, 2012.

16. Importantly, many of these tactics did not originate with these movements; nonviolent acts of civil disobedience have been central to movements around the world, including, perhaps most famously, Gandhi-led movements in India and the method known as *satyagraha*. See, for example, Bondurant, *Conquest*.

17. Dwyer, "Illegal Immigrants Make 1,500-Mile March."

18. Two of the young men on the trip are also romantic partners, which further shows the importance of queer leadership in the migrant youth movement.

19. "Notes from the Trail," *Trail of Dreams* (blog), May 2, 2010, http://www.trail2010.org/blog/2010/may/2/may-1, accessed January 5, 2013.

20. Barack Obama, "Remarks by the President on Comprehensive Immigration Reform," *Washington Wire* (blog), 2010, http://blogs.wsj.com/washwire/2010/07/01/transcript-of-obamas-immigration-speech, accessed January 5, 2013; Cattan, "Black Eyed Peas Join Mexico."

21. The Supreme Court decided on SB 1070 in *Arizona v. the United States* in June 2012, reiterating that immigration is a federal matter but that the controversial "show your papers" provision of SB 1070 did not violate the Constitution nor interfere with federal jurisdiction.

22. This is the name that was in media reports. He writes the blog *Un Pueblo Sin Fronteras* and uses the name Raúl Al-qaraz Ochoa.

23. Preston, "Illegal Immigrant Students Protest." One other undocumented youth, Tania Unzueta, also participated in the sit-in, but the group designated her their spokesperson, so she was not arrested.

24. DeLuca, *Image Politics*; Scott and Smith, "Rhetoric of Confrontation."

25. DeLuca and Peeples, "From Public Sphere," 144.

26. The word "Come" instead of "Coming" was used in this original announcement, even though "coming out" became the language thereafter.

27. IYJL, "National Come out of the Shadows Day!" *Immigrant Youth Justice League*, February 17, 2010, http://www.iyjl.org/?p=368, accessed February 2, 2011. Early on, it seemed these actions were coordinated as a part of the United We DREAM Network, though because of the diffuse nature of DREAM networks, it was somewhat difficult to say. Both *DreamActivist.org* and *UnitedweDream.org* used to use the phrase "united we dream" and claim to speak on behalf of the network. As of this writing, *DreamActivist.org* clearly states it is not a part of United We DREAM or the National Immigrant Youth Alliance.

28. Brown, *Closet Space*; Chauncey, *Gay New York*; Gross, *Contested Closets*; Sedgwick, *Epistemology of the Closet*; Signorile, *Queer in America, Outing Yourself*. Brown cites Paul Beale, *A Concise Dictionary of American Slang* (London: Routledge, 1989), which suggests that "coming out of the closet" was used in the 1950s in Canada. This reference seems to be cited incorrectly, because the closest source I can find is Eric Partridge, *A Concise Dictionary of Slang and Unconventional English*, ed. Paul Beale (London: Routledge, 1989), so I cannot corroborate the veracity of this claim.

29. I want to thank an English professor in the audience at Drake University for highlighting this point. For the entire section on distinctions between the closet and the shadow, I am especially grateful to students and faculty at Drake University who gave me feedback on this analysis in April 2011.

30. Signorile, *Queer in America*, xvii. The practice of "outing"—or revealing the homosexuality or homosexual practice of public figures who stay in the closet in order to maintain their privilege, which Signorile became famous for doing—served to challenge this structure.

31. *Oxford English Dictionary Online*, s.v. "closet," http://www.oed.com:80/Entry/34625, accessed May 8, 2011.

32. Ross, "Beyond the Closet," 172.

33. M. Brown, *Closet Space*, 13.

34. Ibid., 11.

35. Ibid., 147.

36. Signorile, *Queer in America*, 84.

37. Human Rights Campaign, "History of the National Coming Out Day: 1987: In the Beginning, There Was a March," *Human Rights Campaign*, http://www.hrc.org/issues/3350.htm, accessed February 1, 2011 (URL is no longer active).

38. Human Rights Campaign, "History of National Coming Out Day: 1990: Combining Forces," *Human Rights Campaign*, http://www.hrc.org/issues/3351.htm, accessed February 1, 2011 (URL is no longer active).

39. Human Rights Campaign, "A Resource Guide to Coming Out," *Human Rights Campaign*, http://www.hrc.org/resources/entry/resource-guide-to-coming-out, accessed January 2, 2013.

40. Canaday, *Straight State*; D. Miller, *Freedom to Differ*.

41. M. Brown, *Closet Space*; Sedgwick, *Epistemology of the Closet*.

42. Perhaps it also includes British and Continental European manners of thinking about sexuality; certainly, the idea is western.

43. Decena, *Tacit Subjects*.

44. Too much overt stating of the subject is a phenomenon often displayed by Spanish speakers whose first language is English. Some Spanish speakers refer to the overuse of subjects as "yo-ismo."

45. Cantú, *Sexuality of Migration*; Decena, *Tacit Subjects*.

46. Gopinath, *Impossible Desires*, 79.

47. Das Gupta, *Unruly Immigrants*, 165. See also Manalansan, *Global Divas*.

48. Braidotti, *Nomadic Subjects*; Jay, *Downcast Eyes*.

49. M. Fraser, "Classing Queer." See also Hennessy, "Queer Visibility"; Walker, "How to Recognize a Lesbian."

50. Clare, *Exile and Pride*.

51. Binnie, *Globalization of Sexuality*.

52. The shadow metaphor is not exclusive to the migrant youth movement. Shadow metaphors have been used in a variety of contexts in the US public sphere to refer to marginalized laborers, organizations that supposedly control political parties, and other uses.

53. *Oxford English Dictionary Online*, s.v. "shadow," http://www.oed.com:80/Entry/177212, accessed May 8, 2011.

54. Cannon, "Struggling up the Ladder," A1; emphasis added.

55. Smith said, "We have neither the resources, the capability, nor the motivation to uproot and deport millions of illegal aliens, many of whom have become, in effect, members of the community. By granting limited legal status to the productive and law-abiding members of this shadow population, we will recognize reality and devote our enforcement resources to deterring future illegal arrivals." Joint Hearing before the Subcommittee on Immigration, Refugees, and International Law of the House Committee on the Judiciary and the Subcommittee on Immigration and Refugee Policy of the Senate Committee on the Judiciary, 97th Cong., 1st Sess., 9 (1981).

56. *Plyler, Superintendent, Tyler Independent School District, et al. v. Doe, Guardian, et al.*, 80–1538 (1982).

57. As cited in D. Anderson, *United Press International*, Washington News section, June 27, 1985.

58. Thornton, "Immigration Changes," A3.

59. For example, Brooks, "Workers in the Shadows"; Egan, "Irish Wait to Escape"; LeDuff, "Nation Challenged," "Out of the Shadows."

60. For example, Buff, *Immigrant Rights*; Chavez, *Shadowed Lives*; Hondagneu-Sotelo, *Doméstica*.

61. Galindo, "Repartitioning the National Community," 55.

62. Ibid., 58. See also Beltrán, "Going Public."

63. Stanley Renshon, "Department of Unhelpful Immigration Metaphors (2):

'Out of the Shadows,'" *Immigration Blog* (blog), October 3, 2010, http://www.cis.org/renshon/unhelpful-metaphors-2, accessed January 29, 2011. Conservative commentator George Will also wonders how migrants can be in the media and public about their status and still considered in the shadows. Will, "Out of What 'Shadows'?" 74.

64. Sedgwick, *Epistemology of the Closet.*

65. As my friend and colleague Christa Olson noted, coming out is not just visual but is also an aesthetic argument because one wants to be seen in a particular way.

66. On the politics of various kinds of queer visibility, see Brouwer, "Precarious Visibility Politics"; Morris and Sloop, "'What Lips These Lips Have Kissed.'"

67. Bitzer, "Rhetorical Situation."

68. Ahmed, *Strange Encounters.*

69. The artist, Salvador Jiménez Flores, originally created two images for the flyer announcing the event: one with a feminine figure and one with a masculine figure. The full flyer version that had this image included text that told people where to meet and march and said: "Join us in a march for the rights of hard working people who have lived in the shadows of a broken immigration system. Come and support the immigrant community and defend everyone's right to live in the spotlight of American Democracy."

70. *Oxford English Dictionary Online,* s.v. "sombre | somber," http://www.oed.com:80/Entry/184441, accessed May 8, 2011.

71. This is the quotation from Mohammad's blog post "National Coming out of the Shadows Week—March 15th to the 21st," *DreamActivist* (blog), March 5, 2010, http://www.dreamactivist.org/comeout, accessed January 25, 2011. This quotation draws upon several parts of Milk's speech and takes some liberties in editing it. For the full text of Milk's original speech, see Shilts, *Mayor of Castro Street.* Though Mohammad is presumably Mohammad Abdollahi, only his first name is used on the post, so I use that here.

72. IYJL, "Coming Out," *Immigrant Youth Justice League,* March 14, 2010, http://www.iyjl.org/?p=547, accessed February 2, 2011.

73. I think it is important to mention here, as Susan Stryker told me in a conversation in February 2013, that the problem of undocumentation has always been significant for trans people, even those who possess legal citizenship. I would maintain that an analogy cannot be made between trans and undocumented people and, further, that this problem would be exacerbated for undocumented trans people.

74. IYJL, "Coming Out."

75. "'Our Plaza,'" *Immigrant Youth Justice League,* March 14, 2010, http://www.iyjl.org/?p=547, accessed February 2, 2011.

76. Anguiano and Chávez, "DREAMers' Discourse."

77. Ross, "Beyond the Closet," 162. Many thanks to one of the reviewers for pointing me to this specific argument.

78. Mohammad, "National Coming Out."

79. "Coming Out, A How to Guide," New York State Youth Leadership Council and United We Dream Network, March 2010, http://www.dreamactivist.org/

wp-content/uploads/2010/03/Complete-Guide.doc, accessed June 1, 2010 (URL is no longer active; I retain a copy of the original document in my files). By 2011 a version of this guide was newly prepared by the National Immigrant Youth Alliance. In this document the descriptions of the levels were modified and the actions associated with each level were different, including preparing a rally at Level 4 and engaging in direct action or civil disobedience at Level 5. The names associated with the levels in the 2010 document are no longer a part of the 2011 document. They include the following: Level 1—The Dreamer; Level 2—Shout It Out or Going Public; Level 3—Loud and Proud; Level 4—Out of the Shadows and into the Streets; and Level 5—Undocumented, Unafraid, and Unapologetic. Strategies and approaches are always changing, and given the diffuse nature of the DREAM networks, this is not surprising. For the updated guide, see "A Guide to Coming Out for Undocumented Youth," National Immigrant Youth Alliance, 2011, http://action.dreamactivist.org/comeout, accessed January 5, 2013.

80. This quotation comes from Lorde's essay "Transformation of Silence into Language and Action."

81. Of course this is not even to mention the fact that, as some have argued, Lorde herself remains more prominent in feminist memory as compared to many other women of color since she addressed so much of her time and rhetoric to white people. This is the claim made by a participant in Janelle White's study on black women and violence. I encountered this argument in Smith, *Native Americans and the Christian Right*, xxvi. See also White, "Our Silence Will Not Protect Us."

82. This singular focus was especially true in the early days of this movement. Many DREAM activists have now extended their focus to other dimensions of immigration reform, as will be clear later in this chapter.

83. Jones, "Coming Out Illegal."

84. Since I am not doing a visual analysis of this video here, it is not entirely relevant to my argument, but I wanted to mention that one Drake University student commented that the pictures in the video looked eerily like mug shots. This is an interesting point and one worth considering in another venue.

85. It is also worth mentioning that many migrants from Latin American countries may consider using this strategy, not in the way Nair might suggest, but in the tradition of the *testimonio*, a mode of resistance and historical truth telling, often given in first-person narrative form. Since so many in the migrant youth movement are Latin@, this connection is worth mentioning, and I thank my friend Brittany Chávez for calling my attention to it. See Latina Feminist Group, *Telling to Live*.

86. United States Citizenship and Immigration Services, "Consideration of Deferred Action for Childhood Arrivals Process," August 15, 2012, updated September 14, 2012, http://tinyurl.com/7ksa6of, accessed January 4, 2013.

87. See Moratorium on Deportations Campaign, "Defer the Bullshit," August 13, 2012, http://moratoriumondeportations.org/2012/08/13/defer-the-bullshit, accessed August 15, 2012.

88. There are no clear numbers on how many DREAM-eligible youth have been deported, but it is widely acknowledged that Obama created the DACA process under pressure from migrant youth activists since many of them were being deported, and this announcement earned headlines in a host of liberal and progressive outlets, such as one from *Colorlines* declaring, "Obama Will Halt Deportations of DREAMers." Hing, "Breaking: Obama Will Halt Deportations." Moreover, anecdotally speaking, at least once a week I receive an email or a Facebook message from an immigration rights group somewhere in the United States asking me to sign a petition to help halt the deportation of a DREAMer or one of their family members.

89. Nevarez, "Undocubus."

90. Julio Salgado, "Being Undocumented Is Not Just a Heterosexual Issue," *I Exist!* (blog), 2011, http://juliosalgado83.tumblr.com/post/14555932541/dont-get-me -wrong-but-what-does-being-a-queer, accessed November 1, 2012.

91. Lorde, "Transformation of Silence," 41–42.

92. See Anguiano and Chávez, "DREAMers' Discourse."

93. At the time of this writing, none of the undocuqueers on Salgado's publicly available posters feature any activists with visible, physical disabilities.

94. Clare, *Exile and Pride*.

95. Ross, "Beyond the Closet."

96. 67 Sueños, "Mission Statement," American Friends Service Committee, http:// www.67suenos.org/mission, accessed December 30, 2012.

97. Pabón López and López, *Persistent Inequality*.

98. Batalova and McHugh, "DREAM vs. Reality."

99. Raúl Al-qaraz Ochoa, "Letter to the DREAM Movement: My Painful Withdrawal of Support for the DREAM Act," *Un pueblo sin fronteras* (blog), September 17, 2010, http://antifronteras.com/2010/09/18/letter-to-the-dream-movement-my-painful -withdrawal-of-support-for-the-dream-act, accessed November 1, 2012.

100. See *Moratorium on Deportations Campaign*, http://moratoriumondeportations .org, accessed January 3, 2013.

101. José Guadalupe Herrera Soto, "Forced out—José's Testimony," *Moratorium on Deportations Campaign* (blog), April 6, 2012, http://moratoriumondeportations .org/2012/04/06/forced-out-joses-testimony, accessed November 1, 2012. Many thanks to Chicago-based activist Rozalinda Borcilă, who I encountered through Yasmin Nair. Borcilă turned me toward Herrera Soto's testimony and provided the initial framing of the testimony as counter to DREAM activism.

102. El-Tayeb, *European Others*, xxxvi.

103. De Genova, "Queer Politics of Migration."

104. This was reported in a comment by Rozalinda Borcilă on the Facebook event "Immigration Hearing for José Herrera: Call for a Different Kind of Solidarity," November 2, 2012, https://www.facebook.com/events/343278149102009, accessed December 30, 2012.

105. Butler and Spivak, *Who Sings the Nation-State?*

Chapter 4. Coalitional Politics on the US-Mexico Border

1. Proposition 200 continues to be challenged in the courts. In October 2010, the 9th Circuit Court of Appeals struck down the provision that requires providing proof of citizenship in order to register to vote. The court reasoned that this provision is superseded by federal law as found in the National Voter Registration Act of 1993. Under that act, voters sign that they are citizens and risk perjury if they are lying. See Ye Hee Lee, "Appeals Court Strikes Down Voter ID Law."

2. Busha and Rodriguez, "Guest Commentary."

3. As mentioned in my introduction, there is much debate over the terms "coalition" and "alliance," with feminist scholars offering particular meanings for each. I use the term "coalition" to describe the relationship between the two organizations I worked with, Wingspan and CDH, because it is an emic term, one that the participants use themselves to describe their work. Importantly, the way participants in my study used the term "coalition" is more akin to what much of the literature would describe as "alliance." Yet, as also stated in my introduction, Lugones opens up usage of "coalition" beyond the strategic and temporary, and consistently with the rest of this book, I further use "coalition" in that sense here. On alliance, see Anzaldúa, "Bridge, Drawbridge"; Albrecht and Brewer, "Women's Multicultural Alliances."

4. Lorde, "Master's Tools."

5. Thanks to Alexis Mazón for alerting my attention to the study by Stephen et al. in 2007. As briefly mentioned in the introduction, Luibhéid and Khokha, Das Gupta, as well as numerous activists also call for bringing migration politics into conversation with queer politics. See Chávez, "Coalitional Politics"; Das Gupta, *Unruly Immigrants*; Luibhéid and Khokha, "Building Alliances"; Stephen, Lanier, Ramírez, and Westerling, "Building Alliances."

6. Stephen, Lanier, Ramírez, and Westerling, "Building Alliances." My use of "antigay" and "Latino" reflects the language used in the report.

7. The Bracero Program ran formally from 1942 through 1964 (though Braceros remained until 1967) in the United States. It was a guest worker program designed to benefit US agribusiness and provide legal channels for migrant Mexican farmworkers to come to the United States temporarily and return home. By most accounts of Braceros and their advocates, the program was largely exploitative of migrants and did not prevent undocumented crossings. For more, see Ngai, *Impossible Subjects*, ch. 4.

8. Stephen, Lanier, Ramírez, and Westerling, "Building Alliances," 23–24.

9. To engage in this research, I utilized an activist methodology. See Speed, "At the Crossroads"; Hale, "Activist Research."

10. Kvale, *Interviews*, 28.

11. Busha and Rodriguez, "Guest Commentary."

12. Kat, interview with author, May 10, 2007, Tucson, AZ.

13. Isabel, interview with author, March 20, 2007, Tucson, AZ.

14. Lorde, "Age, Race, Class, and Sex," 117.

15. Isabel, interview.

16. Department of Homeland Security, "Enforcement News," http://www.dhs.gov/enforcement-news, accessed January 3, 2013.

17. Kat, interview.

18. Alexis, interview with author, March 24, 2007, Tucson, AZ.

19. Deviant discourse was central during my research. With Lou Dobbs's nightly commentary on the war on the middle class apparently perpetuated by immigrants and an amnesty-loving Congress, and with the media frenzy over vigilante organizations and ICE raids on meatpacking plants, sensationalist rhetoric permeated the public sphere. A primary concern for CDH, however, involved the seemingly less-sensationalistic rhetoric that subtly supported the more overt rhetoric, such as in May 2007 when the *Arizona Daily Star*, one of the primary local newspapers in Tucson, reported misleading Border Patrol statistics about a decrease in bodies recovered in the Arizona desert. "Border Patrol Finds Body," B6. While there had been a decrease in bodies recovered in the Tucson sector from 2006 to 2007, according to the Pima County medical examiner, there was an increase in bodies recovered across the entire Sonora-Arizona border. See Kat Rodriguez, "84 Bodies Recovered." The *Star* did not report this fact, which offered tacit support for border militarization projects and bolstered the xenophobic border security positions of those such as Dobbs. Furthermore, Border Patrol's misleading methodology and the citation of the results in local media position those with an analysis of migrant rights in relation to human rights as off-base, fringe, and inaccurate.

20. Cathy, interview with author, April 26, 2007, Tucson, AZ.

21. Wingspan, "Wingspan Responds to Jennifer Waddell's Sensationalistic Journalism," February 2, 2007, http://www.wingspan.org/content/news_wingspan_details.php?story_id=371, accessed May 30, 2007 (URL is no longer active; I retain a copy in my files). The full text of the complaint can be found at http://kynn.livejournal.com/679239.html, accessed January 5, 2013.

22. Wingspan, "Wingspan Responds."

23. In response to this report, GLAAD joined Wingspan in calling on the queer and allied community to watch the segment and express outrage at this report. GLAAD's statement was located at http://www.glaad.org/media/release_detail.php?id=3964 (URL is no longer active). GLAAD's involvement in this event is mentioned in its 2007 summary of media advocacy, *Media Advocacy: Fighting Defamation. Changing Hearts and Minds.* Available at www.glaad.org/files/performancereport2007.pdf, accessed January 5, 2013.

24. Oscar, interview with author, March 27, 2007, Tucson, AZ. Oscar was later promoted to the director of programs at Wingspan, the position Cathy held during my research. Oscar no longer works for Wingspan.

25. Kat, interview.

26. M. Alexander, *New Jim Crow*; Amnesty International USA, "Stonewalled,"; Mogul, Ritchie, and Whitlock, *Queer (In)Justice*; Spade, *Normal Life*; Stanley and Smith, *Captive Genders*.

27. Field notes C, August 24, 2006.

28. Russ Dove has been identified by the Southern Poverty Law Center as a nativist who is "desperately concerned that illegal immigrants are sneaking into this country and skewing the American electoral process." See Buchanan and Kim, "Nativists."

29. Field notes C.

30. Ibid. The Associated Press corroborates part of this story, telling it as follows: "As one member of the group [Border Guardians] burned the second flag, a young woman hurled a water bottle at the flag-burners, who were separated from the larger rally by a ring of Tucson police and another of migrant supporters. As police escorted the woman from the park, hands behind her back, others demonstrators began jostling and tried to defend her. Police said six people, three of them teenagers, were arrested on either disorderly conduct charges or aggravated assault on a peace officer." See Rotstein, "Demonstration in Tucson." As often happens with such incidents, police and media reports differ from the reports given by people involved.

31. Field notes G, September 23, 2006.

32. Field notes O, November 30, 2006.

33. Lupe, interview with author, March 29, 2007, Tucson, AZ.

34. Field notes H, October 4, 2006.

35. Hsiao, "Gays, Jews Top Targets."

36. One needs think no further than Stonewall or the Compton Cafeteria Riots. See Stryker, "Transgender History, Homonormativity."

37. Cathy, interview.

38. Ibid.

39. For more on the problems with analogies, see Grillo and Wildman, "Obscuring the Importance of Race"; Reddy, *Freedom with Violence*.

40. Carrillo Rowe, *Power Lines*.

41. Cathy, interview.

42. Kat, interview.

43. Field notes X, January 29, 2007c.

44. Generally speaking, and in my experience, CDH's queer analysis primarily addressed questions of sexuality and not necessarily transgender/cisgender tensions and concerns.

45. Spivak, *Teaching Machine*.

46. Ray, "Ethical Encounters."

47. Lorde, "Age, Race, Class, and Sex," 122.

48. Lorde, "Master's Tools."

49. Collins, *Black Feminist Thought*, 245.

50. Yuval-Davis, *Gender and Nation*, 131.

51. For example, Anzaldúa, "Bridge, Drawbridge"; Bunch, "Making Common Cause"; Lorde, "Master's Tools," "Redefining Difference."

52. Kat, interview.

53. Ibid.

54. Alexis, interview.

55. Carrillo Rowe, *Power Lines*.

56. Wingspan and CDH Musser Foundation Grant Proposal, 2005.

57. Lichterman, "Talking Identity."

58. Smith, "Introduction."

59. Thank you to one of the reviewers for supplying this reading.

60. Anzaldúa, "Bridge, Drawbridge," 225.

61. Johnson Reagon, "Coalition Politics," 356.

62. Ibid., 359.

63. Collins, *Black Feminist Thought*, 246–47.

64. Lugones and Spelman, "Have We Got a Theory," 577.

65. Ibid., 581.

66. Carrillo Rowe, "Locating Feminism's Subject."

67. Cazden, "Musical Consonance and Dissonance," 5. See also "Definition of Consonance and Dissonance."

68. This is also akin to Gould's discussion about emotion being what compels the moving in movements. Gould, *Moving Politics*.

69. The Catholic Church has a significant influence on Latin@ communities in Southern Arizona and remains an important actor in the immigration debates. For example, in 2004 Arizona's Catholic bishops came out in strong opposition to Proposition 200, which sought to minimize the rights of migrants as well as, by implication, other Latin@s in the state. Innes, "Kicanas Joins Other Bishops." Though Proposition 200 has been continually subjected to legal challenges, Arizonans originally approved the measure, with 56 percent voting in favor of it. For more on the role of the Catholic Church's support of immigrant struggles, see Heredia, "From Prayer to Protest."

70. "Samaritans" refer to several local groups of mostly religious people who do humanitarian work in the Arizona desert, including providing water tanks with clean water at remote locations for migrant crossers.

71. Audre Lorde Project, "Community at a Crossroads."

72. Carrillo Rowe, *Power Lines*.

73. Allen, Broome, Jones, Chen, and Collier, "Intercultural Alliances."

74. Innes, "Gay-Marriage Ban Pits Church vs. Church," B1. Importantly, other religious groups opposed Protect Marriage Arizona.

75. "Arizona Catholic Conference Bishops Oppose Proposition 200," Roman Catholic Church of Phoenix, 2004, www.voiceofthepoor.org/News/ACConProp200.pdf, accessed June 10, 2007.

76. Pelotte, Kicanas, and Olmsted, "Why Is Marriage Important?" 1. Pelotte, Kicanas, and Olmsted are the three bishops representing each diocese of the ACCB.

77. Amelia, interview with author, April 7, 2007, Tucson, AZ.

78. Kat, interview.

79. Ibid.

80. Ibid.; Isabel, interview; Karen, interview with author, April 7, 2007, Tucson, AZ.

81. Michelle, interview with author, March 27, 2007, Tucson, AZ. Michelle stopped volunteering for CDH in March 2007. For more on the discourse of family values, see Cloud, "Rhetoric of Family Values"; Dingo, "Securing the Nation"; Jakobsen, "Can Homosexuals?"

82. Field notes I, October 7, 2006.

83. Kat, interview.

84. Sena-Rivera, "Extended Kinship," 123.

85. Ashcraft, "Organized Dissonance."

86. Karen, interview.

87. Anzaldúa, "Bridge, Drawbridge"; Carrillo Rowe, *Power Lines*; Houston, "When Black Women Talk."

88. Moraga and Anzaldúa, This *Bridge*, 23.

89. Combahee River Collective, "Black Feminist Statement," 212–13.

90. Interview with author, March 22, 2007, Tucson, AZ. At Geovanna's request, I did not audio-record this interview; I took detailed notes as she spoke. Consequently, the quotes attributed to her in this chapter are paraphrased, and not word-for-word transcriptions.

91. Field notes R, December 21, 2006.

92. Anzaldúa, "Bridge, Drawbridge."

93. Geovanna, interview.

94. Ibid.

95. Alexis, interview.

96. Anzaldúa, *Borderlands*.

97. Field notes P, November 30, 2006.

98. Kendra, personal communication to author, November 3, 2008.

99. Field notes N, November 9, 2006.

100. Field notes Q, December 21, 2006. "Theories of translation" is a vague way to represent this particular conflict, which raised issues of power, culture, and education. However, because most participants in my study asked to use their real names, and this particular instance would unnecessarily implicate parties on both sides, I made the ethical choice to represent the problem in this way.

101. Amelia, interview.

102. Ibid.

103. Karen, interview.

104. Kent, interview with author, March 27, 2007, Tucson, AZ.

105. Cathy, interview.

106. Holmes, "Monitoring Organisational Boundaries."

107. I continue to maintain relatively regular contact with several activists in CDH, most of whom are still volunteering with or working for the organization. I also maintain contact with Cathy from Wingspan even though she has moved out of state. I have casual contact with one other formal Wingspan activist, Oscar.

108. Stephen, Lanier, Ramírez, and Westerling, "Building Alliances," 37–38.

109. Japhy Grant, "LA Prop 8 Protesters Target Blacks," *Queerty* (blog), November 8, 2008, http://www.queerty.com/la-prop-8-protesters-target-blacks-20081110, accessed April 6, 2013.

110. Dan Savage, "Black Homophobia," *Slog* (blog), November 5, 2008, http://slog .thestranger.com/2008/11/black_homophobia, accessed April 6, 2013; emphasis in original.

Conclusion

1. Leitsinger, "US Immigration Chief."

2. Butler, *Undoing Gender,* 29.

3. Carrillo Rowe, "Moving Relations"; emphasis in original.

4. On questions of the particular audience, see Perelman and Olbrechts-Tyteca, *New Rhetoric*.

5. Lugones, *Pilgrimages/Peregrinajes.*

3

Bibliography

Ahmed, Sara. *The Cultural Politics of Emotion*. New York: Routledge, 2004.

———. *Queer Phenomenology: Orientations, Objects, Others*. Durham, NC: Duke University Press, 2006.

———. *Strange Encounters: Embodied Others in Post-Coloniality*. London: Routledge, 2000.

Aizura, Aren Z. "Transnational Transgender Rights and Immigration Law." In *Transfeminist Perspectives in and beyond Transgender and Gender Studies*, edited by Anne Enke, 133–52. Philadelphia: Temple University Press, 2012.

Albrecht, Lisa, and Rose M. Brewer. "Bridges of Power: Women's Multicultural Alliances for Social Change." In *Bridges of Power: Women's Multicultural Alliances*, 2–22. Philadelphia: New Society Publishers, 1990.

Alexander, M. Jacqui. "Not Just (Any) Body Can Be a Citizen: The Politics of Law, Sexuality, and Postcoloniality in Trinidad and Tobago and the Bahamas." *Feminist Review* 48 (1994): 5–23.

———. *Pedagogies of Crossing: Meditations on Feminism, Sexual Politics, Memory, and the Sacred*. Durham, NC: Duke University Press, 2005.

Alexander, Michelle. *The New Jim Crow: Mass Incarceration in the Age of Colorblindness*. New York: New Press, 2010.

Alinsky, Saul D. *Rules for Radicals: A Pragmatic Primer for Realistic Radicals*. 1971. New York: Vintage Books, 1989.

Allen, Brenda J., Benjamin J. Broome, Tricia S. Jones, Victoria Chen, and Mary Jane Collier. "Intercultural Alliances: A Cyberdialogue among Scholar-Practitioners." In *Intercultural Alliances: Critical Transformations (International and Intercultural Commu-*

nication Annual Volume XXV 2002), edited by Mary Jane Collier, 279–319. Thousand Oaks, CA: Sage, 2003.

Amnesty International USA. "Stonewalled: Police Abuse and Misconduct against Lesbian, Gay, Bisexual and Transgender People in the U.S." New York: Amnesty International USA, 2005.

Anderson, Benedict. *Imagined Communities: Reflections on the Origin and Spread of Nationalism*, 2nd ed. New York: Verso, 1991.

Anderson, David E. *United Press International*, Washington News section, June 27, 1985.

Anguiano, Claudia A., and Karma R. Chávez. "DREAMers' Discourse: Young Latino/a Immigrants and the Naturalization of the American Dream." In *Latina/o Discourse in Vernacular Spaces: Somos De Una Voz?* edited by Michelle A. Holling and Bernadette Marie Calafell, 81–100. Lanham, MD: Lexington Books, 2011.

Anker, Deborah E. "Woman Refugees: Forgotten No Longer." *San Diego Law Review* 32 (1995): 771–818.

Anzaldúa, Gloria. *Borderlands/La Frontera: The New Mestiza*. 2nd ed. San Francisco: Aunt Lute Books, 1999.

———. "Bridge, Drawbridge, Sandbar, or Island: Lesbians-of-Color *Hacienda Alianzas*." In Albrecht and Brewer, *Bridges of Power*, 216–33.

Archibold, Randal C. "Lawmakers Want Look at Sheriff in Arizona." *New York Times*, February 14, 2009, 12A.

Arendt, Hannah. *On Revolution*. 1963. New York: Penguin Books, 2006.

———. *The Origins of Totalitarianism*. San Diego: Harcourt, Brace, and Co., 1951.

Asencio, Marysol, and Katie Acosta. "Migration, Gender Conformity, and Social Mobility among Puerto Rican Sexual Minorities." *Sexuality Research and Social Policy* 6, no. 3 (2009): 34–43.

Ashcraft, Karen Lee. "Organized Dissonance: Feminist Bureaucracy as Hybrid Form." *Academy of Management Journal* 44, no. 6 (2001): 1301–22.

Audre Lorde Project. "Community at a Crossroads: U.S. Right Wing Policies and Lesbian, Gay, Bisexual, Two Spirit, and Transgender Immigrants of Color in New York City." New York: Audre Lorde Project, Inc., 2004.

———. "Statement: For All the Ways They Say We Are, No One Is Illegal." April 21, 2006. http://alp.org/whatwedo/statements/nooneisillegal. Accessed October 6, 2012.

Bacon, David. *Illegal People: How Globalization Creates Migration and Criminalizes Immigrants*. Boston: Beacon Press, 2008.

Bahrampour, Tara. "Students Raise the Stakes against Immigration's Status Quo." *Washington Post*, July 21, 2010, A03.

Baim, Tracy. Introduction to *Out and Proud in Chicago: An Overview of the City's Gay Community*, 6–7. Chicago: Surrey Books, 2008.

Bassichis, Morgan, Alexander Lee, and Dean Spade. "Building an Abolitionist Trans and Queer Movement with Everything We've Got." In *Captive Genders: Trans Embodiment and the Prison Industrial Complex*, edited by Eric A. Stanley and Nat Smith, 15–40. Oakland, CA: AK Press, 2011.

Batalova, Jeanne, and Margie McHugh. "DREAM vs. Reality: An Analysis of Potential DREAM Act Beneficiaries." Migration Policy Institute, *Insight*, July 2010. http://www.migrationpolicy.org/pubs/DREAM-Insight-July2010.pdf. Accessed September 10, 2011.

Batstone, David, and Eduardo Mendieta, eds. *The Good Citizen*. New York: Routledge 1999.

Battle, Juan, and Sandra L. Barnes, eds. *Black Sexualities: Probing Powers, Passions, Practices, and Policies*. New Brunswick, NJ: Rutgers University Press, 2009.

Bauman, Zygmunt. *Modernity and Ambivalence*. Ithaca, NY: Cornell University Press, 1991.

Beltrán, Cristina. "Going Public: Hannah Arendt, Immigrant Action, and the Space of Appearance." *Political Theory* 37, no. 5 (2009): 595–622.

Bennett, Susan, and Owen Ullman. "Clinton Reaffirms Intention to Lift Ban on Gays in Military." *Philadelphia Inquirer*, November 12, 1992, A15.

Berlant, Lauren. *Cruel Optimism*. Durham, NC: Duke University Press, 2011.

———. *The Queen of America Goes to Washington City: Essays on Sex and Citizenship*. Durham, NC: Duke University Press, 1997.

Bersani, Leo. *Homos*. Cambridge, MA: Harvard University Press, 1995.

Bhabha, Jacqueline. "Embodied Rights: Gender Persecution, State Sovereignty, and Refugees." *Public Culture* 9, no. 1 (1996): 3–32.

Billig, Michael. *Banal Nationalism*. Thousand Oaks, CA: Sage, 1995.

Binnie, Jon. *The Globalization of Sexuality*. London: Sage, 2004.

Bitzer, Lloyd F. "The Rhetorical Situation." *Philosophy and Rhetoric* 1, no. 1 (1968): 1–14.

Bondurant, Joan V. *Conquest of Violence: The Gandhian Philosophy of Conflict*. Princeton, NJ: Princeton University Press, 1958.

"Border Patrol Finds Body West of Sasabe." *Arizona Daily Star*, May 16, 2007, B6.

Bosniak, Linda. *The Citizen and the Alien: Dilemmas of Contemporary Membership*. Princeton, NJ: Princeton University Press, 2006.

Brady, Mary Pat. "The Homoerotics of Immigration Control." *Scholar and Feminist Online* 6, no. 3 (2008). http://sfonline.barnard.edu/immigration/brady_01.htm. Accessed January 3, 2013.

Braidotti, Rosi. *Nomadic Subjects: Embodiment and Sexual Difference in Contemporary Feminist Theory*. New York: Columbia University Press, 1994.

Brandzel, Amy L. "Haunted by Citizenship: Whitenormative Citizen-Subjects and the Uses of History in Women's Studies." *Feminist Studies* 37, no. 3 (2011): 503–33.

———. "Queering Citizenship? Same-Sex Marriage and the State." *GLQ* 11, no. 2 (2005): 171–204.

Brooks, David. "Workers in the Shadows." *New York Times*, January 10, 2004, 13.

Brouwer, Dan. "The Precarious Visibility Politics of Self-Stigmatization: The Case of HIV/AIDS Tattoos." *Text and Performance Quarterly* 18 (1998): 114–36.

Brown, Michael P. *Closet Space: Geographies of Metaphor from the Body to the Globe*. New York: Routledge, 2000.

Brown, Wendy. *Walled States, Waning Sovereignty*. Brooklyn, NY: Zone Books, 2010.

Buchanan, Susy, and Tom Kim. "The Nativists." Southern Poverty Law Center, *Intelligence Report* 120. Winter 2005. http://www.splcenter.org/get-informed/intelligence-report/browse-all-issues/2005/winter/the-nativists-0?page=0,7. Accessed December 23, 2012.

Buff, Rachel Ida, ed. *Immigrant Rights in the Shadows of Citizenship*. New York: New York University Press, 2008.

Bunch, Charlotte. "Making Common Cause: Diversity and Coalitions." In Albrecht and Brewer, *Bridges of Power*, 49–56.

Busha, Cathy, and Kat Rodriguez. "Guest Commentary: All Arizonans Should Be Concerned about Anti-Immigrant, Anti-LGBT Ballot Initiatives." *Tucson Weekly*, February 25, 2005. http://www.tucsonweekly.com/tucson/guest-commentary/Content?oid=1079319. Accessed January 3, 2013.

Butler, Judith. "Contingent Foundations: Feminism and the Question of 'Postmodernism.'" In *Feminist Contentions: A Philosophical Exchange*, edited by Seyla Benhabib, Judith Butler, Drucilla Cornell, and Nancy Fraser, 35–57. New York: Routledge, 1995.

———. *Precarious Life: The Powers of Mourning and Violence*. London: Verso Books, 2004.

———. *Undoing Gender*. New York: Routledge, 2004.

Butler, Judith, and Gayatri Chakravorty Spivak. *Who Sings the Nation-State? Language, Politics, Belonging*. New York: Seagull Books, 2007.

Bystydzienski, Jill M., and Steven P. Schacht, eds. *Forging Radical Alliances across Difference: Coalition Politics for the New Millennium*. Lanham, MD: Rowman and Littlefield, 2001.

Calhoun, Craig. *Nationalism*. Minneapolis: University of Minnesota Press, 1997.

Canaday, Margot. *The Straight State: Sexuality and Citizenship in Twentieth-Century America*. Princeton, NJ: Princeton University Press, 2009.

Cannon, Lou. "Struggling up the Ladder; 2 Hispanic Entities Flourish Side by Side: Hispanics Climb up Economic Ladder." *Washington Post*, March 27, 1978, A1.

Cantú Jr., Lionel. *The Sexuality of Migration: Border Crossings and Mexican Immigrant Men*. Edited by Nancy A. Naples and Salvador Vidal-Ortiz. New York: New York University Press, 2009.

Cantú Jr., Lionel, Eithne Luibhéid, and Alexandra Minna Stern. "Well-Founded Fear: Political Asylum and the Boundaries of Sexual Identity in the U.S.-Mexico Borderlands." In Luibhéid and Cantú, *Queer Migrations*, 61–74.

Capó Jr., Julio. "Queering Mariel: Mediating Cold War Foreign Policy and U.S. Citizenship among Cuba's Homosexual Exile Community, 1978–1994." *Journal of American Ethnic History* 29, no. 4 (2010): 78–106.

Carrillo, Héctor. "Imagining Modernity: Sexuality, Policy, and Social Change in Mexico." *Sexuality Research and Social Policy: Journal of NSCR* 4, no. 3 (2007): 74–91.

———. "Immigration and LGBT Rights in the USA: Ironies and Constraints in US Asylum Cases." In *Routledge Handbook of Sexuality, Health, and Rights*, edited by Peter Aggleton and Richard Parker, 444–52. London: Routledge, 2010.

———. "Leaving Loved Ones Behind: Mexican Gay Men's Migration to the USA." In *Mobility, Sexuality, and AIDS*, edited by Felicity Thomas, Mary Haour-Knipe, and Peter Aggleton, 24–39. London: Routledge, 2009.

———. "Sexual Culture, Structure, and Change: A Transnational Framework for Studies of Latino/a Migration and HIV." In *HIV Prevention with Latinos: Theory, Research, and Practice*, edited by Kurt C. Organista, 41–62. New York: Oxford University Press, 2012.

———. "Sexual Migration, Cross-Cultural Sexual Encounters, and Sexual Health." *Sexuality Research and Social Policy* 1, no. 3 (2004): 58–70.

Carrillo, Héctor, and Jorge Fontdevila. "Rethinking Sexual Initiation: Pathways to Identity Formation among Gay and Bisexual Mexican Male Youth." *Archives of Sexual Behavior* 40 (2011): 1241–54.

Carrillo, Héctor, Jorge Fontdevila, Jaweer Brown, and Walter Gómez. "Risk across Borders: Sexual Contexts and HIV Prevention Challenges among Mexican Gay and Bisexual Immigrant Men: Findings and Recommendations from the Trayectos Study." San Francisco: Center for Research on Gender and Sexuality and the Center for AIDS Prevention Studies, 2008.

Carrillo Rowe, Aimee. "Be Longing: Toward a Feminist Politics of Relation." *NWSA Journal* 17, no. 2 (2005): 15–46.

———. "Moving Relations: On the Limits of Belonging." *Liminalities: A Journal of Performance Studies* 5, no. 5 (2009): 1–10.

———. *Power Lines: On the Subject of Feminist Alliances*. Durham, NC: Duke University Press, 2008.

———. "Whose 'America'? The Politics of Rhetoric and Space in the Formation of U.S. Nationalism." *Radical History Review* 89 (2004): 115–34.

Carrillo Rowe, Aimee M. "Locating Feminism's Subject: The Paradox of White Femininity and the Struggle to Forge Feminist Alliances." *Communication Theory* 10, no. 1 (2000): 64–80.

Castoriadis, Cornelius. *The Imaginary Institution of Society*. Translated by Kathleen Blamey. Cambridge, MA: MIT Press, 1987.

Cattan, Nacha. "Black Eyed Peas Join Mexico in Protesting Arizona Immigration Law SB1070." *Christian Science Monitor*, July 29, 2010. http://www.csmonitor.com/World/Americas/2010/0729/Black-Eyed-Peas-join-Mexico-in-protesting-Arizona-immigration-law-SB1070-video. Accessed May 9, 2013.

Cazden, Norman. "The Definition of Consonance and Dissonance." *International Review of the Aesthetics and Sociology of Music* 11, no. 2 (1980): 123–68.

———. "Musical Consonance and Dissonance: A Cultural Criterion." *Journal of Aesthetics and Art Criticism* 4, no. 1 (1945): 3–11.

Chauncey, George. *Gay New York*. New York: Basic Books, 1994.

Chávez, Karma R. "Border (In)Securities: Normative and Differential Belonging in LGBTQ and Immigrant Rights Discourse." *Communication and Critical/Cultural Studies* 7, no. 2 (2010): 136–55.

———. "Coalitional Politics and Confronting the Constructions of Queers and Migrants in the State of Arizona." PhD diss., Arizona State University, 2007.

———. "Counter-Public Enclaves and Understanding the Function of Rhetoric in Social Movement Coalition Building." *Communication Quarterly* 59, no. 1 (2011): 1–18.

———. "Spatializing Gender Performativity: Ecstasy and Possibilities for Livable Life in the Tragic Case of Victoria Arellano." *Women's Studies in Communication* 33, no. 1 (2010): 1–15.

Chavez, Leo R. *Shadowed Lives: Undocumented Immigrants in American Society*. Fort Worth, TX: Harcourt, Brace, and Jovanovich, 1992.

Chesebro, James W. "Rhetorical Strategies of the Radical-Revolutionary." *Today's Speech* 20, no. 1 (1972): 37–48.

Christensen, Henrik Serup. "Political Activities on the Internet: Slacktivism or Political Participation by Other Means?" *First Monday* 16, no. 2, February 7, 2011. http://firstmonday.org/htbin/cgiwrap/bin/ojs/index.php/fm/article/viewArticle/3336/2767. Accessed December 23, 2012.

Clare, Eli. *Exile and Pride: Disability, Queerness, and Liberation*. 2nd ed. 1999. Boston: South End Press, 2009.

Clarke, Cheryl. "Lesbianism: An Act of Resistance." In *Words of Fire: An Anthology of African-American Feminist Thought*, edited by Beverly Guy-Sheftall, 242–51. New York: New Press, 1995.

Cloud, Dana L. "The Rhetoric of 'Family Values': Scapegoating, Utopia, and the Privatization of Social Responsibility." *Western Journal of Communication* 62, no. 4 (1998): 387–419.

Coalición de Derechos Humanos and Wingspan. "Joint Statement: Continued Stand against Racism and Homophobia." November 28, 2006. http://wingspan.org/content/news_wingspan_details.php?story_id=359. Accessed December 1, 2006.

———. "Joint Statement: Stand against Racism and Homophobia," October 24, 2006. http://wingspan.org/content/news_wingspan_details.php?story_id=353. Accessed December 1, 2006.

Cohen, Cathy J. "Punks, Bulldaggers, and Welfare Queens: The Real Radical Potential of Queer Politics?" *GLQ* 3, no. 4 (1997): 437–65.

Collins, Patricia Hill. *Black Feminist Thought: Knowledge, Consciousness, and the Politics of Empowerment*. 2nd ed. New York: Routledge, 2000.

Combahee River Collective. "A Black Feminist Statement." In Moraga and Anzaldúa, *This Bridge Called My Back*, 210–18.

Conrad, Ryan. "Against Equality, in Maine and Everywhere." In *Against Equality*, 43–50. Lewiston, ME: Against Equality Press, 2010.

———, ed. *Against Equality: Don't Ask to Fight Their Wars!* Lewiston, ME: Against Equality Press, 2011.

———, ed. *Against Equality: Prisons Will Not Protect You*. Lewiston, ME: Against Equality Press, 2012.

———, ed. *Against Equality: Queer Critiques of Gay Marriage*. Lewiston, ME: Against Equality Press, 2010.

Cormack, Patricia, ed. Introduction to *Manifestos and Declarations of the Twentieth Century*, 1–8. Toronto: Garamond, 1998.

Costanza-Chock, Sasha. "Digital Popular Communication: Lessons on Information and Communication Technologies for Social Change from the Immigrant Rights Movement." *National Civic Review* 100, no. 3 (2011): 29–35.

Cotten, Trystan, ed. *Transgender Migrations: The Bodies, Borders, and Politics of Transition.* New York: Routledge, 2012.

Cox, Robert, and Christina R. Foust. "Social Movement Rhetoric." In *The Sage Handbook of Rhetorical Studies*, edited by Andrea A. Lunsford, Kirt H. Wilson and Rosa A. Eberly, 605–27. Thousand Oaks, CA: Sage, 2009.

Crenshaw, Kimberle. "Mapping the Margins: Intersectionality, Identity Politics, and Violence against Women of Color." *Stanford Law Review* 43 (1991): 1241–99.

D'Emilio, John. "Homophobia and the Trajectory of Postwar American Radicalism: The Career of Bayard Rustin." *Radical History Review* 62 (1995): 80–103.

———. "The Homosexual Menace: The Politics of Sexuality in Cold War America." In *Passion and Power: Sexuality in History*, edited by Kathy Peiss and Christina Simmons, 226–40. Philadelphia: Temple University Press, 1989.

Darsey, James. *The Prophetic Tradition and Radical Rhetoric in America*. New York: New York University Press, 1997.

Das Gupta, Monisha. *Unruly Immigrants: Rights, Activism, and Transnational South Asian Politics in the United States*. Durham, NC: Duke University Press, 2006.

de Certeau, Michel. *The Practice of Everyday Life*. Translated by Stephen Rendall. Berkeley: University of California Press, 1984.

De Genova, Nicholas. "The Queer Politics of Migration: Reflections on 'Illegality' and Incorrigibility." *Studies in Social Justice* 4, no. 2 (2010): 101–26.

Decena, Carlos Ulises. *Tacit Subjects: Belonging and Same-Sex Desire among Dominican Immigrant Men*. Durham, NC: Duke University Press, 2011.

Defourny, Jacques. "From Third Sector to Social Enterprise." In *The Emergence of Social Enterprise*, edited by Carlo Borzaga and Jacques Defourny, 1–18. New York: Routledge, 2001.

Del Castillo, Adelaida R. "Illegal Status and Social Citizenship: Thoughts on Mexican Immigrants in a Postnational World." *Aztlán* 27, no. 2 (2002): 11–33.

DeLaure, Marilyn Bordwell. "Planting Seeds of Change: Ella Baker's Radical Rhetoric." *Women's Studies in Communication* 31, no. 1 (2008): 1–28.

Deleuze, Gilles, and Félix Guattari. *A Thousand Plateaus: Capitalism and Schizophrenia*. Translated by Brian Massumi. Minneapolis: University of Minnesota Press, 1987.

DeLuca, Kevin Michael. *Image Politics: The New Rhetoric of Environmental Activism*. New York: Guilford Press, 1999.

DeLuca, Kevin Michael, and Jennifer Peeples. "From Public Sphere to Public Screen: Democracy, Activism, and the 'Violence' of Seattle." *Critical Studies in Media Communication* 19, no. 2 (2002): 125–51.

Dettmer, Lisa. "Beyond Gay Marriage." *Race, Poverty and the Environment* 17, no. 2 (2010): 34–37.

Dickinson, Greg. "Selling Democracy: Consumer Culture and Citizenship in the Wake of September 11." *Southern Communication Journal* 70, no. 4 (2005): 271–84.

Dingo, Rebecca. "Securing the Nation: Neoliberalism's U.S. Family Values in a Transnational Gendered Economy." *Journal of Women's History* 16, no. 3 (2004): 173–86.

Driskill, Qwo-Li. "Doubleweaving Two-Spirit Critiques: Building Alliances between Native and Queer Studies." *GLQ* 16, no. 1–2 (2010): 69–92.

Duggan, Lisa. "The New Homonormativity: The Sexual Politics of Neoliberalism." In *Materializing Democracy: Toward a Revitalized Cultural Politics*, edited by Russ Castronovo and Dana D. Nelson, 175–94. Durham, NC: Duke University Press, 2002.

———. *The Twilight of Equality? Neoliberalism, Cultural Politics, and the Attack on Democracy.* Boston: Beacon Press, 2003.

Dwyer, Devin. "Illegal Immigrants Make 1,500-Mile March to Washington: Seeking Pathway to Citizenship, Students Shrug off Risk of Detention and Deportation." *ABC News*, January 26, 2010. http://abcnews.go.com/Politics/immigration-illegal-students-make-1500-mile-march-washington/story?id=9636199. Accessed January 25, 2011.

Edelman, Lee. *No Future: Queer Theory and the Death Drive.* Durham, NC: Duke University Press, 2004.

Egan, Timothy. "Irish Wait to Escape Emigre Shadow." *New York Times*, November 25, 1990, 36.

El-Tayeb, Fatima. *European Others: Queering Ethnicity in Postnational Europe.* Minneapolis: University of Minnesota Press, 2011.

Eng, David L. *The Feeling of Kinship: Queer Liberalism and the Racialization of Intimacy.* Durham, NC: Duke University Press, 2010.

Espín, Oliva. *Latina Realities: Essays on Healing, Migration, and Sexuality.* Boulder, CO: Westview Press, 1997.

Faux, Jeff. "How NAFTA Failed Mexico; Immigration Is Not a Development Policy." *American Prospect*, July/August 2003, 35.

Ferguson, Roderick A. *Aberrations in Black: Toward a Queer of Color Critique.* Minneapolis: University of Minnesota Press, 2004.

Floyd, Kevin. "The Importance of Being Childish: Queer Utopians and Historical Contradiction." *Cultural Logics* (2010): 1–19. http://clogic.eserver.org/2010/Floyd.pdf. Accessed December 23, 2012.

———. "Queer Principles of Hope." *Mediations: Journal of the Marxist Literary Group* 25, no. 1 (2010). http://www.mediationsjournal.org/articles/queer-principles-of-hope. Accessed June 29, 2012.

Foley, Elise. "Deportation Hits Another Record under Obama Administration." *Huffington Post*, December 21, 2012. http://www.huffingtonpost.com/2012/12/21/immigration-deportation_n_2348090.html. Accessed December 23, 2012.

Francoeur, Adam. "The Enemy Within: Constructions of U.S. Immigration Law and Policy and the Homoterrorist Threat." *Stanford Journal of Civil Rights and Civil Liberties* 3 (2007): 345–76.

Franke, Lindsay A. "Not Meeting the Standard: U.S. Asylum Law and Gender-Related Claims." *Arizona Journal of International and Comparative Law* 17 (2000): 605–27.

Fraser, Mariam. "Classing Queer: Politics in Competition." *Theory, Culture, and Society* 16, no. 2 (1999): 107–31.

Fraser, Nancy. "Rethinking the Public Sphere: A Contribution to the Critique of Actually Existing Democracy." In *Habermas and the Public Sphere*, edited by Craig Calhoun, 109–42. Cambridge: MIT Press, 1992.

Freeman, Elizabeth. *Time Binds: Queer Temporalities, Queer Histories*. Durham, NC: Duke University Press, 2010.

Freeman, Elizabeth, ed. "Queer Temporalities," Special Issue of *GLQ* 13, no. 2–3 (2007).

Fujiwara, Lynn. *Mothers without Citizenship: Asian Immigrant Families and the Consequences of Welfare Reform*. Minneapolis: University of Minnesota Press, 2008.

Galindo, René. "Repartitioning the National Community: Political Visibility and Voice for Undocumented Immigrants in the Spring 2006 Immigration Rights Marches." *Aztlán* 35, no. 2 (2010): 37–64.

Gaonkar, Dilip Parameshwar. "Toward New Imaginaries: An Introduction." *Public Culture* 14, no. 1 (2002): 1–19.

Gay Liberation Network. "Immigration/Marriage." Letter to the Editor. *Windy City Times*, June 18, 2008. http://www.windycitymediagroup.com/gay/lesbian/news/ARTICLE.php?AID=18679. Accessed January 3, 2013.

Gerken, Christina. "Immigrant Anxieties: 1990s Immigration Reform and the Neoliberal Consensus." PhD diss., Bowling Green State University, 2007.

———. "Neo-Liberalism and Family Values in 1990s Immigration Reform Discourse." *disClosure: A Journal of Social Theory* 17 (2008): 45–71.

Gilmore, Ruth Wilson. "In the Shadow of the Shadow State." In *The Revolution Will Not Be Funded: Beyond the Non-Profit Industrial Complex*, edited by INCITE! Women of Color Against Violence, 41–52. Cambridge, MA: South End Press, 2007.

Göle, Nilüfer "Islam in Public: New Visibilities and New Imaginaries." *Public Culture* 14, no. 1 (2002): 173–90.

Goodman, Amy. "New Violence Against Women Act Includes Historic Protections for Native American and LGBT Survivors." *Democracy Now*, March 8, 2013. http://www.democracynow.org/2013/3/8/new_violence_against_women_act_includes. Accessed April 16, 2013.

Gopinath, Gayatri. *Impossible Desires: Queer Diasporas and South Asian Public Cultures*. Durham, NC: Duke University Press, 2005.

Gould, Deborah B. *Moving Politics: Emotion and ACT UP's Fight against AIDS*. Chicago: University of Chicago Press, 2009.

Gray, Mary L. *Out in the Country: Youth, Media, and Queer Visibility in Rural America*. New York: New York University Press, 2009.

Greenhouse, Steven. "Visa Ban on H.I.V.-Infected to Be Waived for Gay Games." *New York Times*, February 25, 1994, B4.

Grewal, Inderpal. "'Women's Rights as Human Rights': Feminist Practices, Global Feminism, and Human Rights Regimes in Transnationality." *Citizenship Studies* 3, no. 3 (1999): 337–54.

Grillo, Trina, and Stephanie M. Wildman. "Obscuring the Importance of Race: The Implications of Making Comparisons between Racism and Sexism (or Other -Isms)." In *Critical Race Theory: The Cutting Edge*, edited by Richard Delgado and Jean Stefancic, 648–56. Philadelphia: Temple University Press, 2000.

Gross, Larry P. *Contested Closets: The Politics and Ethics of Outing.* Minneapolis: University of Minnesota Press, 1993.

Haiman, Franklyn S. "The Rhetoric of the Streets: Some Legal an Ethical Considerations." *Quarterly Journal of Speech* 53, no. 2 (1967): 99–114.

Halberstam, Judith. *In a Queer Time and Place: Transgender Bodies, Subcultural Lives.* New York: New York University Press, 2005.

———. *The Queer Art of Failure.* Durham, NC: Duke University Press, 2011.

Hale, Charles R. "Activist Research v. Cultural Critique: Indigenous Land Rights and the Contradictions of Politically Engaged Anthropology." *Cultural Anthropology* 21, no. 1 (2006): 96–120.

Hammerback, John C., and Richard J. Jensen. *The Rhetorical Career of César Chávez.* College Station: Texas A&M University Press, 1998.

———. "The Rhetorical Works of César Chávez and Reies Tijerina." *Western Journal of Speech Communication* 44 (1980): 166–76.

Haney-López, Ian. *White by Law: The Legal Construction of Race.* New York: New York University Press, 1996.

Haritaworn, Jin, Tamsila Tauqir, and Esra Erdem. "Gay Imperialism: Gender and Sexuality Discourse in the 'War on Terror.'" In *Out of Place: Interrogating Silences in Queerness/Raciality*, edited by Adi Kuntsman and Esperanza Miyake, 71–95. York, UK: Raw Nerve Books, 2008.

Harvey, David. *A Brief History of Neoliberalism.* Oxford, UK: Oxford University Press, 2006.

HAVOQ, "Undoing Borders: A Queer Manifesto," April 2011. https://undoingborders.wordpress.com/undoing-borders. Accessed January 4, 2013.

Hennessy, Rosemary. "Queer Visibility in Commodity Culture." *Cultural Critique* 29 (1994–1995): 31–76.

Heredia, Luisa. "From Prayer to Protest: The Immigrant Rights Movement and the Catholic Church." In *Rallying for Immigrant Rights: The Fight for Inclusion in 21st Century America*, edited by Kim Voss and Irene Bloemraad, 101–22. Berkeley: University of California Press, 2011.

Herring, Susan C. "Gender and Power in Online Communication." In *The Handbook of Language and Gender*, edited by Janet Holmes and Miriam Meyeroff, 202–28. Oxford, UK: Blackwell, 2003.

Herring, Susan C., and John C. Paolillo. "Gender and Genre Variation in Weblogs." *Journal of Sociolinguistics* 10, no. 4 (2006): 439–59.

Hing, Julianne. "Breaking: Obama Will Halt Deportations of DREAMers." *Colorlines:*

News for Action, June 15, 2012. http://colorlines.com/archives/2012/06/breaking_obama_will_halt_deportations_of_dreamers.html. Accessed December 23, 2012.

Hodgkinson, Virginia Ann, and Murray S. Weitzman. "Overview: The State of the Independent Sector." In *The Nature of the Nonprofit Sector*, edited by J. Steven Ott, 9–22. Boulder, CO: Westview Press, 2001.

Holmes, Janet. "Monitoring Organisational Boundaries: Diverse Discourse Strategies Used in Gatekeeping." *Journal of Pragmatics* 39 (2007): 1993–2016.

Holpuch, Amanda. "US House Votes Not to Reauthorise Domestic Violence Funding Bill." *Guardian*, January 2, 2013. http://www.guardian.co.uk/world/2013/jan/02/us-house-domestic-violence-programme. Accessed January 3, 2013.

Hondagneu-Sotelo, Pierrette. *Doméstica: Immigrant Workers Cleaning and Caring in the Shadows of Affluence*. 2nd ed. Berkeley: University of California Press, 2007.

———. *Gender and U.S. Immigration: Contemporary Trends*. Berkeley: University of California Press, 2003.

Houston, Marsha. "When Black Women Talk with White Women: Why Dialogues Are Difficult." In *Our Voices: Essays in Culture, Ethnicity, and Communication*, edited by Alberto González, Marsha Houston, and Victoria Chen, 98–104. Los Angeles: Roxbury, 2000.

Howard, Robert Glenn. "Electronic Hybridity: The Persistent Processes of the Vernacular Web." *Journal of American Folklore* 121, no. 480 (2008): 192–218.

———. "The Vernacular Web of Participatory Media." *Critical Studies in Media Communication* 25, no. 5 (2008): 490–513.

Hsiao, Irene. "Gays, Jews Top Targets of Hate Crimes Here." *Tucson Citizen*, February 23, 2004.

Hull, Kathleen E. "The Political Limits of the Rights Frame: The Case of Same-Sex Marriage in Hawaii." *Sociological Perspectives* 44 (2001): 207–32.

Innes, Stephanie. "Gay-Marriage Ban Pits Church vs. Church." *Arizona Daily Star*, October 13, 2006, B1.

———. "Kicanas Joins Other Bishops Who Oppose Curb on Migrants." *Arizona Daily Star*, September 16, 2004, A6.

———. "Security Fence May Split Tribes." *News From Indian Country: The Independent Native Journal* (2002). http://www.indiancountrynews.info/fullstory.cfm-ID=496.htm. Accessed March 15, 2013.

Jakobsen, Janet R. "Can Homosexuals End Western Civilization as We Know It? Family Values in a Global Economy." In *Queer Globalizations: Citizenship and the Afterlife of Colonialism*, edited by Arnaldo Cruz-Malavé and Martin F. Manalansan IV, 49–70. New York: New York University Press, 2002.

Jay, Martin. *Downcast Eyes: The Denigration of Vision in Twentieth-Century French Thought*. Berkeley: University of California Press, 1994.

Jensen, Richard J., and John C. Hammerback. "Working in 'Quiet Places': The Community Organizing Rhetoric of Robert Parris Moses." *Howard Journal of Communications* 11, no. 1 (2000): 1–18.

———. "'Your Tools Are Really the People': The Rhetoric of Robert Parris Moses." *Communication Monographs* 65, no. 2 (1998): 126–40.

Johnson, Kevin R. "Free Trade and Closed Borders: NAFTA and Mexican Immigration to the United States." *University of California Davis Law Review* 27 (1993–1994): 937–78.

Johnson Reagon, Bernice. "Coalition Politics: Turning the Century." In *Home Girls: A Black Feminist Anthology*, edited by Barbara Smith, 356–69. New York: Kitchen Table: Woman of Color Press, 1983.

Jones, Maggie. "Coming Out Illegal." *New York Times*, October 21, 2010. http://www.nytimes.com/2010/10/24/magazine/24DreamTeam-t.html. Accessed January 25, 2011.

Joseph, Miranda. *Against the Romance of Community*. Minneapolis: University of Minnesota Press, 2002.

Kahn, Richard, and Douglas Kellner. "New Media and Internet Activism: From the 'Battle of Seattle' to Blogging." *New Media and Society* 6, no. 1 (2004): 87–95.

Keating, Cricket. "Building Coalitional Consciousness." *NWSA Journal* 17, no. 2 (2005): 86–103.

Klumpp, James F. "Challenge of Radical Rhetoric: Radicalization at Columbia." *Western Speech* 37, no. 3 (1973): 146–56.

Kuntsman, Adi. "Between Gulags and Pride Parades: Sexuality, Nation, and Haunted Speech Acts." *GLQ* 14, no. 2–3 (2008): 263–88.

———. "Double Homecoming: Sexuality, Ethnicity, and Place in Immigration Stories of Russian Lesbians in Israel." *Women's Studies International Forum* 26, no. 4 (2003): 299–311.

———. *Figurations of Violence and Belonging: Queerness, Migranthood, and Nationalism in Cyberspace and Beyond*. Oxford, UK: Peter Lang, 2009.

———. "Hospitality in Flames: Queer Immigrants and Melancholic Be/Longing." In *Mobilizing Hospitality: The Ethics of Social Relations in a Mobile World*, edited by Jennie German Molz and Sarah Gibson, 145–58. Burlington, VT: Ashgate, 2007.

———. "Queerness as Europeanness: Immigration, Orientalist Visions, and Racialized Encounters in Israel/Palestine." *darkmatter* (2008). http://www.darkmatter101.org/site/2008/05/02/queerness-as-europeanness-immigration-orientialist-visions-and-racialized-encounters-in-israelpalestine. Accessed March 14, 2013.

Kuntsman, Adi, and Esperanza Miyake, eds. *Out of Place: Interrogating Silences in Queerness/Raciality*. York, UK: Raw Nerve Books, 2008.

Kvale, Steinar. *Interviews: An Introduction to Qualitative Research Interviewing*. Thousand Oaks, CA: Sage, 1996.

La Fountain-Stokes, Lawrence. "Cultures of the Puerto Rican Queer Diaspora." In *Passing Lines: Sexuality and Immigration*, edited by Brad Epps, Keja Valens, and Bill Johnson González, 275–309. Cambridge, MA: Harvard University Press, 2005.

———. *Queer Ricans: Cultures and Sexualities in the Diaspora*. Minneapolis: University of Minnesota Press, 2009.

Landau, Joseph. "'Soft Immutability' and 'Imputed Gay Identity': Recent Developments in Transgender and Sexual Orientation-Based Asylum Law." *Fordham University School of Law* 32 (2005): 237–63.

Latina Feminist Group. *Telling to Live: Latina Feminist Testimonios*. Durham, NC: Duke University Press, 2001.

LeDuff, Charlie. "A Nation Challenged: For Some, Lives in the Shadows Ended in Attack, Indiscernibly." *New York Times*, December 30, 2001, 1.

Leitsinger, Miranda. "US Immigration Chief: Same-Sex Ties Are Family Ties." *NBC News*, September 28, 2012. http://usnews.nbcnews.com/_news/2012/09/28/14140024 -us-immigration-chief-same-sex-ties-are-family-ties. Accessed October 2, 2012.

Lewis, Rachel. "Lesbians under Surveillance: Same-Sex Immigration Reform, Gay Rights, and the Problem of Queer Liberalism." *Social Justice* 37, no. 1 (2010–2011): 90–106.

Lichterman, Paul. "Talking Identity in the Public Sphere: Broad Visions and Small Spaces in Sexual Identity Politics." *Theory and Society* 28, no. 1 (1999): 101–41.

Lim, Merlyna. "Clicks, Cabs, and Coffee Houses: Social Media and Oppositional Movements in Egypt, 2004–2011." *Journal of Communication* 62 (2012): 231–48.

Long, Scott, Jessica Stern, and Adam Francoeur. "Family, Unvalued: Discrimination, Denial, and the Fate of Binational Same-Sex Couples under U.S. Law." New York: Human Rights Watch and Immigration Equality, 2006.

Lorde, Audre. "Age, Race, Class, and Sex: Women Redefining Difference." In *Sister Outsider: Essays and Speeches,* 114–23. Berkeley, CA: Crossing Press, 1984.

———. "The Master's Tools Will Never Dismantle the Master's House." In Moraga and Anzaldúa, *This Bridge Called My Back,* 98–101.

———. "The Transformation of Silence into Language and Action." In *Sister Outsider: Essays and Speeches*, 40–45. Berkeley, CA: Crossing Press, 1984.

Lugones, María. "Heterosexualism and the Colonial/Modern Gender System." *Hypatia* 22, no. 1 (2007): 186–209.

———. *Pilgrimages/Peregrinajes: Theorizing Coalition against Multiple Oppressions*. Latham, MD: Rowman and Littlefield, 2003.

———. "Toward a Decolonial Feminism." *Hypatia* 25, no. 4 (2010): 742–59.

Lugones, María C., and Elizabeth V. Spelman. "Have We Got a Theory for You! Feminist Theory, Cultural Imperialism, and the Demand for 'the Woman's Voice.'" *Women's Studies International Forum* 6, no. 6 (1983): 573–81.

Luibhéid, Eithne. *Entry Denied: Controlling Sexuality at the Border*. Minneapolis: University of Minnesota Press, 2002.

———. "Heteronormativity, Responsibility, and Neo-Liberal Governance in U.S. Immigration Control." In *Passing Lines: Sexuality and Immigration*, edited by Brad Epps, Keja Valens, and Bill Johnson González, 69–101. Cambridge, MA: Harvard University Press, 2005.

———. "Introduction: Queer Migration and Citizenship." In Luibhéid and Cantú, *Queer Migrations*, ix–xlvi.

———. "Sexuality, Migration, and the Shifting Line between Legal and Illegal Status." *GLQ* 14, no. 2–3 (2008): 289–316.

Luibhéid, Eithne, and Lionel Cantú Jr., eds. *Queer Migrations: Sexuality, U.S. Citizenship, and Border Crossings*, Minneapolis: University of Minnesota Press, 2005.

Luibhéid, Eithne, and Sasha Khokha. "Building Alliances between Immigrant Rights and Queer Movements." In *Forging Radical Alliances across Difference: Coalition Politics for the New Millennium*, edited by Jill M. Bystydzienski and Steven P. Schacht, 77–90. Lanham, MD: Rowman and Littlefield, 2001.

Lyon, Janet. *Manifestoes: Provocations of the Modern*. Ithaca, NY: Cornell University Press, 1999.

Madison, D. Soyini. *Acts of Activism: Human Rights as Radical Performance*. Cambridge, UK: Cambridge University Press, 2010.

Manalansan IV, Martin F. *Global Divas: Filipino Gay Men in the Diaspora*. Durham, NC: Duke University Press, 2003.

———. "Queer Intersections: Sexuality and Gender in Migration Studies." *International Migration Review* 40, no. 1 (2006): 224–49.

Mansbridge, Jane. "Using Power/Fighting Power: The Polity." In *Democracy and Difference: Contesting the Boundaries of the Political*, edited by Seyla Benhabib, 46–60. Princeton, NJ: Princeton University Press, 1996.

Marciniak, Katarzyna. *Alienhood: Citizenship, Exile, and the Logic of Difference*. Minneapolis: University of Minneapolis Press, 2006.

Mascaro, Lisa. "Border Security Bill Is on Its Way to Obama; The Measure Calls for 1,500 More Troops and Immigration Workers in the Southwest." *Los Angeles Times*, August 13, 2010, A8.

Massumi, Brian. *Parables for the Virtual: Movement, Affect, Sensation*. Durham, NC: Duke University Press, 2002.

McKerrow, Raymie E. "Critical Rhetoric: Theory and Praxis." *Communication Monographs* 56, no. 2 (1989): 91–111.

McKinnon, Sara L. "(In)Hospitable Publics: Theorizing the Conditions of Access to U.S. Publics." In *Public Modalities: Rhetoric, Culture, Media, and the Shape of Public Life*, edited by Daniel C. Brouwer and Robert Asen, 131–53. Tuscaloosa: University of Alabama Press, 2010.

Mendieta, Eduardo. "Becoming Citizens, Becoming Hispanics." In *The Good Citizen*, edited by David Batstone and Eduardo Mendieta, 113–32. New York: Routledge, 1999.

Miller, Diane Helene. *The Freedom to Differ: The Shaping of the Gay and Lesbian Struggle for Civil Rights*. New York: New York University Press, 1998.

Miller, Toby. *The Well-Tempered Self: Citizenship, Culture, and the Postmodern Subject*. Baltimore: Johns Hopkins University Press, 1993.

Minter, Shannon. "Sodomy and Public Morality Offenses under U.S. Immigration Law: Penalizing Lesbian and Gay Identity." *Immigration and Nationality Law Review* 15 (1993–1994): 428–74.

Mogul, Joey, Andrea Ritchie, and Kay Whitlock. *Queer (In)Justice: The Criminalization of LGBT People in the United States*. Boston: Beacon Press, 2011.

Mohanty, Chandra Talpade. *Feminism without Borders: Decolonizing Theory, Practicing Solidarity*. Durham, NC: Duke University Press, 2003.

Moraga, Cherríe, and Gloria Anzaldúa, eds. *This Bridge Called My Back: Writings by Radical Women of Color*. 2nd ed. New York: Kitchen Table: Women of Color Press, 1983.

Morgan, Deborah A. "Not Gay Enough for the Government: Racial and Sexual Stereotypes in Sexual Orientation Asylum Cases." *Law and Sexuality: A Review of Lesbian, Gay, Bisexual, and Transgender Legal Issues* 15 (2006): 135–62.

Morgan, Wayne. "Queering International Human Rights Law." In *Law and Sexuality: The Global Arena*, edited by Carl F. Stychin and Didi Herman, 208–25. Minneapolis: University of Minnesota Press, 2001.

Morgensen, Scott Lauria. *Spaces between Us: Queer Settler Colonialism and Indigenous Decolonization*. Minneapolis: University of Minnesota Press, 2011.

Morozov, Evgeny. "The Brave New World of Slacktivism." *Foreign Policy*, May 19, 2009. http://neteffect.foreignpolicy.com/posts/2009/05/19/the_brave_new_world_of_slacktivism. Accessed January 5, 2013.

Morris III, Charles E., and John M. Sloop. "'What Lips These Lips Have Kissed': Refiguring the Politics of Queer Public Kissing." *Communication and Critical/Cultural Studies* 3, no. 1 (2006): 1–26.

Morrissey, Megan. "A DREAM Disrupted: Undocumented Migrant Youth's Disidentifications from U.S. Citizenship." *Journal of International and Intercultural Communication* 6, no. 2 (2013): 145–62.

Muñoz, José Esteban. *Cruising Utopia: The Then and There of Queer Futurity*. New York: New York University Press, 2009.

———. *Disidentifications: Queers of Color and the Performance of Politics*. Minneapolis: University of Minnesota Press, 1999.

Nair, Yasmin. "Nair Views: Gay Immigration (and) Inequality." Commentary, *Windy City Times*, July 1, 2007. http://www.windycitymediagroup.com/gay/lesbian/news/ARTICLE.php?AID=15470. Accessed June 1, 2008.

———. "Viewpoints: Queer Immigration: Change the Paradigms." Commentary, *Windy City Times*, January 9, 2008. http://www.windycitymediagroup.com/gay/lesbian/news/ARTICLE.php?AID=17177. Accessed June 1, 2008.

———. "Views: Gay Marriage and Queer Immigration: Laboring over Love." Commentary, *Windy City Times*, May 28, 2008. http://www.windycitymediagroup.com/gay/lesbian/news/ARTICLE.php?AID=18447. Accessed June 1, 2008.

Nevarez, Griselda. "The Undocubus: DREAM Activists Arrive in Charlotte to Make Their Voices Heard at the Democratic National Convention." *Huffington Post*, September 3, 2012. http://www.huffingtonpost.com/2012/09/03/undocubus-dream-activists-democractic-convention_n_1852019.html. Accessed September 15, 2012.

Ngai, Mae M. *Impossible Subjects: Illegal Aliens and the Making of Modern America*. Princeton, NJ: Princeton University Press, 2004.

Ong, Aihwa. "Cultural Citizenship as Subject-Making: Immigrants Negotiate Racial and Cultural Boundaries in the United States." *Current Anthropology* 37, no. 5 (1996): 737–62.

Ono, Kent, and John Sloop. *Shifting Borders: Rhetoric, Immigration, and California's Proposition 187*. Philadelphia: Temple University, 2002.

Ordover, Nancy. *American Eugenics: Race, Queer Anatomy, and the Science of Nationalism*. Minneapolis: University of Minnesota Press, 2003.

Organista, Kurt C. "Towards a Structural-Environmental Model of Risk for HIV and Problem Drinking in Latino Labor Migrants: The Case of Day Laborers." *Journal of Ethnic and Cultural Diversity in Social Work* 16, no. 1/2 (2007): 95–125.

Organista, Kurt C., Héctor Carrillo, and George Ayala. "HIV Prevention with Mexican Migrants: Review, Critique, and Recommendations." *Journal of Acquired Immune Deficiency Syndrome* 37 (2004): S227–39.

Organista, Kurt C., and Samantha F. Ehrlich. "Predictors of Condom Use in Latino Migrant Day Laborers." *Hispanic Journal of Behavioral Sciences* 30, no. 3 (2008): 379–96.

Organista, Kurt C., Pamela B. Organista, Javier E. Garcia de Alba, Marco Antonio Castillo Morán, and Luz Elena Ureta Carrillo. "Survey of Condom-Related Beliefs, Behaviors, and Perceived Social Norms in Mexican Migrant Laborers." *Journal of Community Health* 22 (1997): 185–99.

Organista, Pamela Balls, and Kurt C. Organista. "Culture and Gender Sensitive AIDS Prevention with Mexican Migrant Laborers: A Primer for Counselors." *Journal of Multicultural Counseling and Development* 25, no. 2 (1997): 121–29.

"Out of the Shadows." *New York Times*, October 1, 2003, 26.

Pabón López, María, and Gerardo R. López. *Persistent Inequality: Contemporary Realities in the Education of Undocumented Latina/o Students*. New York: Routledge, 2010.

Pearce, Kimber Charles. "The Radical Feminist Manifesto as Generic Appropriation: Gender, Genre, and Second Wave Resistance." *Southern Communication Journal* 64, no. 4 (1999): 307–15.

Pelotte, Donald E., Gerald Kicanas, and Thomas Olmsted. "Why Is Marriage Important to the Catholic Church?" *Catholic Sun*, March 2, 2006, 1.

Peña, Susana. "'Obvious Gays' and the State Gaze: Cuban Gay Visibility and U.S. Immigration Policy during the 1980 Mariel Boatlift." *Journal of the History of Sexuality* 16, no. 3 (2008): 482–514.

Perelman, Chaim, and Lucie Olbrechts-Tyteca. *The New Rhetoric: A Treatise on Argumentation*. South Bend, IN: University of Notre Dame Press, 1991.

Pérez, Emma. "Queering the Borderlands: The Challenges of Excavating the Invisible and Unheard." *Frontiers* 24, no. 2–3 (2003): 122–31.

Perez, Jonathan, Jorge Guitierrez, Nancy Meza, and Neidi Dominguez Zamarano. "DREAM Movement: Challenges with the Social Justice Elite's Military Option Arguments and the Immigration Reform 'Leaders.'" Op-ed, *Truthout*, September 21, 2010. http://www.truth-out.org/dream-movement-challenges-with-social-justice-elites-military-option-arguments-and-immigration-refo. Accessed February 2, 2011.

Pharr, Suzanne. *Homophobia: A Weapon of Sexism*. Inverness, CA: Chardon Press, 1988.

Phelan, Shane. *Sexual Strangers: Gays, Lesbians, and Dilemmas of Citizenship*. Philadelphia: Temple University Press, 2001.

Poirot, Kristan. "(Un)Making Sex, Making Race: Nineteenth-Century Liberalism, Difference, and the Rhetoric of Elizabeth Cady Stanton." *Quarterly Journal of Speech* 96, no. 2 (2010): 185–208.

Preston, Julia. "Bill Proposes Immigration Rights for Gay Couples." *New York Times*, June 2 2009, A19.

———. "Illegal Immigrant Students Protest at McCain Office." *New York Times*, May 17, 2010. http://www.nytimes.com/2010/05/18/us/18dream.html. Accessed January 25, 2011.

Probyn, Elspeth. *Outside Belongings*. New York: Routledge, 1996.

Puar, Jasbir K. *Terrorist Assemblages: Homonationalism in Queer Times*. Durham, NC: Duke University Press, 2007.

Queers for Economic Justice. "Queers and Immigration: A Vision Statement." *Scholar and Feminist Online* 6, no. 3 (2008). http://sfonline.barnard.edu/immigration/qej_01.htm. Accessed January 4, 2013.

Ralls, Steve. "We Are Tearing Families Apart, When We Should Be Uniting Them." *Huffington Post*, April 15, 2009. http://www.huffingtonpost.com/steve-ralls/tearing-families-apart-wh_b_186630.html. Accessed December 29, 2012.

Rand, Erin J. "An Inflammatory Fag and a Queer Form: Larry Kramer, Polemics, and Rhetorical Agency." *Quarterly Journal of Speech* 94, no. 3 (2008): 297–319.

Randolph, Robert. "Plowed Under: As NAFTA Opens up Mexican Agriculture and a More Modern Industry Takes Root, a Way of Life Is Getting Left Behind." *Business Mexico*, March 1, 1999, 32–39.

Ray, Sangeeta. "Ethical Encounters: Spivak, Alexander, and Kincaid." *Cultural Studies* 17, no. 1 (2003): 42–55.

Reddy, Chandan. "Asian Diasporas, Neoliberalism, and Family: Reviewing the Case for Homosexual Asylum in the Context of Family Rights." *Social Text 84–85* 23, no. 3–4 (2005): 101–19.

———. *Freedom with Violence: Race, Sexuality, and the US State*. Durham, NC: Duke University Press, 2011.

Rich, Wilbur C., ed. *The Politics of Minority Coalitions: Race, Ethnicity, and Shared Uncertainties*. Westport, CT: Praeger, 1996.

Richardson, Diane. "Claiming Citizenship? Sexuality, Citizenship and Lesbian/Feminist Theory." *Sexualities* 3, no. 2 (2000): 255–72.

———. "Locating Sexualities: From Here to Normality." *Sexualities* 7, no. 4 (2004): 391–411.

Rodríguez, Dylan. "The Political Logic of the Non-Profit Industrial Complex." In *The Revolution Will Not Be Funded: Beyond the Non-Profit Industrial Complex*, edited by INCITE! Women of Color Against Violence, 21–40. Cambridge, MA: South End Press, 2007.

Rodríguez, Juana María. *Queer Latinidad: Identity Practices, Discursive Spaces*. New York: New York University Press, 2003.

Rodriguez, Kat. "84 Bodies Recovered on Arizona Border; Border Patrol Claim Decrease." Press release. Tucson, AZ: Coalición de Derechos Humanos, 2007.

Romero, Mary. *Maid in the U.S.A.* 2nd ed. New York: Routledge, 2002.

Rosaldo, Renato. "Cultural Citizenship and Educational Democracy." *Cultural Anthropology* 9, no. 3 (1994): 402–11.

———. "Cultural Citizenship, Inequality, and Multiculturalism." In *Latino Cultural Citi-*

zenship: Claiming Space, Identity, and Rights, edited by William V. Flores and Rina Benmayor, 27–38. Boston: Beacon Press, 1998.

Rosenberg, Jordana, and Amy Villarejo. "Introduction: Queerness, Norms, Utopia." *GLQ* 18, no. 1 (2012): 1–18.

Ross, Marlon B. "Beyond the Closet as Raceless Paradigm." In *Black Queer Studies: A Critical Anthology*, edited by E. Patrick Johnson and Mae G. Henderson, 161–89. Durham, NC: Duke University Press, 2005.

Rotstein, Arthur H. "Demonstration in Tucson Starts Peacefully, Ends in Tussle." *Associated Press State and Local Wire*, April 11, 2006.

Ruiz, Albor. "'No Papers' but Endless Courage." *New York Daily News*, August 12, 2010, 52.

Sandoval, Chela. *Methodology of the Oppressed*. Minneapolis: University of Minnesota, 2000.

Scott, Robert L. "The Conservative Voice in Radical Rhetoric: A Common Response to Division." *Speech Monographs* 40, no. 2 (1973): 123–35.

Scott, Robert L., and Donald K. Smith. "The Rhetoric of Confrontation." *Quarterly Journal of Speech* 55, no. 1 (1969): 1–8.

Sedgwick, Eve Kosofsky. *Epistemology of the Closet*. Berkeley: University of California Press, 1990.

Segrest, Mab. *Born to Belonging: Writings on Spirit and Justice*. New Brunswick, NJ: Rutgers University Press, 2002.

Seif, Hinda. "'Unapologetic and Unafraid': Immigrant Youth Come out from the Shadows." *New Directions for Child and Adolescent Development* 134 (2011): 59–75.

Sena-Rivera, Jaime. "Extended Kinship in the United States: Competing Models and the Case of *La Familia Chicana*." *Journal of Marriage and the Family* 41, no. 1 (1979): 121–29.

Shah, Nayan. *Contagious Divides: Epidemics and Race in San Francisco's Chinatown*. Berkeley: University of California Press, 2001.

———. *Stranger Intimacy: Contesting Race, Sexuality, and the Law in the North American West*. Berkeley: University of California Press, 2011.

Shilts, Randy. *The Mayor of Castro Street: The Life and Times of Harvey Milk*. New York: St. Martin's, 1982.

Shugart, Helene A. "Counterhegemonic Acts: Appropriation as a Feminist Rhetorical Strategy." *Quarterly Journal of Speech* 83, no. 2 (1997): 210–29.

Signorile, Michelangelo. *Outing Yourself: How to Come out as Lesbian or Gay to Your Family, Friends, and Coworkers*. New York: Fireside, 1996.

———. *Queer in America: Sex, the Media, and the Closets of Power*. 2nd ed. Madison: University of Wisconsin Press, 2003.

Simmons, Tracy. "Sexuality and Immigration: UK Family Reunion Policy and the Regulation of Sexual Citizens in the European Union." *Political Geography* 27, no. 2 (2008): 213–30.

Skinnell, Ryan. "Elizabeth Cady Stanton's 1854 'Address to the Legislature of New

York' and the Paradox of Social Reform Rhetoric." *Rhetoric Review* 29, no. 2 (2010): 129–44.

Slevin, Peter. "Deportation of Illegal Immigrants Increases under Obama Administration." *Washington Post*, July 26, 2010, A1.

Smith, Andrea. "Introduction: The Revolution Will Not Be Funded." In *The Revolution Will Not Be Funded: Beyond the Non-Profit Industrial Complex*, edited by INCITE! Women of Color Against Violence, 1–18. Cambridge, MA: South End Press, 2007.

———. *Native Americans and the Christian Right: The Gendered Politics of Unlikely Alliances.* Durham, NC: Duke University Press, 2008.

———. "Queer Theory and Native Studies: The Heteronormativity of Settler Colonialism." *GLQ* 16, no. 1/2 (2010): 41–68.

Solomon, Alisa. "Trans/Migrant: Christina Madrazo's All-American Story." In Luibhéid and Cantú, *Queer Migrations,* 3–29.

Somerville, Siobhan B. "Notes toward a Queer History of Naturalization." *American Quarterly* 57, no. 3 (2005): 659–75.

———. "Queer *Loving.*" *GLQ* 11, no. 3 (2005): 335–70.

———. *Queering the Color Line: Race and the Invention of Homosexuality in American Culture.* Durham, NC: Duke University Press, 2000.

———. "Sexual Aliens and the Racialized State: A Queer Reading of the 1952 U.S. Immigration and Nationality Act." In Luibhéid and Cantú, *Queer Migrations,* 75–91.

Soto, Sandra K. *Reading Chican@ Like a Queer: The De-Mastery of Desire.* Austin: University of Texas Press, 2011.

Spade, Dean. *Normal Life: Administrative Violence, Critical Trans Politics and the Limits of the Law.* Cambridge, MA: South End Press, 2011.

Speed, Shannon. "At the Crossroads of Human Rights and Anthropology: Toward a Critically Engaged Activist Research." *American Anthropologist* 108, no. 1 (2006): 66–76.

Spivak, Gayatri Chakravorty. *Outside in the Teaching Machine.* New York: Routledge, 1993.

Squires, Catherine R. "Rethinking the Black Public Sphere: An Alternative Vocabulary for Multiple Public Spheres." *Communication Theory* 12, no. 4 (2002): 446–68.

Stanley, Eric A., and Nat Smith, eds. *Captive Genders: Trans Embodiment and the Prison Industrial Complex.* Oakland, CA: AK Press, 2011.

Stein, Marc. "All the Immigrants Are Straight, All the Homosexuals Are Citizens, but Some of Us Are Queer Aliens: Genealogies of Legal Strategy in *Boutilier v. INS.*" *Journal of American Ethnic History* 29, no. 4 (2010): 45–77.

Stephen, Lynn, Jan Lanier, Ramón Ramírez, and Marcy Westerling. "Building Alliances: An Ethnography of Collaboration between Rural Organizing Project (ROP) and CAUSA in Oregon." New York: New York University and Leadership for a Changing World, 2005.

Stewart, Charles J. "The Internal Rhetoric of the Knights of Labor." *Communication Studies* 42, no. 1 (1991): 67–82.

Stryker, Susan. *Transgender History*. Berkeley, CA: Seal Press, 2008.

——. "Transgender History, Homonormativity, and Disciplinarity." *Radical History Review* 100 (2008): 145–57.

Stychin, Carl F. "Same-Sex Sexualities and the Globalization of Human Rights Discourse." *McGill Law Journal* 49 (2004): 951–69.

——. "'A Stranger to Its Laws': Sovereign Bodies, Global Sexualities, and Transnational Citizens." *Journal of Law and Society* 27, no. 4 (2000): 601–25.

Tang, Shirley S. "Diasporic Cultural Citizenship: How Cambodians Negotiate and Create Places and Identities in Their Refugee Migration and Deportation Experiences." *Trotter Review* 19, no. 4 (2010): 1–20.

Taylor, Charles. "Modern Social Imaginaries." *Public Culture* 14, no. 1 (2002): 91–124.

Terrill, Robert. "Protest, Prophecy, and Prudence in the Rhetoric of Malcolm X." *Rhetoric and Public Affairs* 4, no. 1 (2001): 25–53.

Thornton, Mary. "Immigration Changes Are Signed into Law; Reagan Invites Aliens 'into the Sunlight.'" *Washington Post*, November 7, 1986, A3.

Tinsley, Omise'eke Natasha. *Thiefing Sugar: Eroticism between Women in Caribbean Literature*. Durham, NC: Duke University Press, 2010.

Tongson, Karen. *Relocations: Queer Suburban Imaginaries*. New York: New York University Press, 2011.

Vaid, Urvashi. *Virtual Equality: The Mainstreaming of Lesbian and Gay Liberation*. New York: Anchor/Doubleday, 1995.

Vail, Mark. "The 'Integrative' Rhetoric of Martin Luther King Jr.'s 'I Have a Dream' Speech." *Rhetoric and Public Affairs* 9, no. 1 (2006): 51–78.

Van Dyke, Nella, and Holly J. McCammon, eds. *Strategic Alliances: Coalition Building and Social Movements*. Minneapolis: University of Minnesota Press, 2010.

Walker, Lisa. "How to Recognize a Lesbian: The Cultural Politics of Looking Like What You Are." *Signs: Journal of Women in Culture and Society* 18, no. 4 (1993): 866–91.

Warner, Michael. *The Trouble with Normal: Sex, Politics, and the Ethics of Queer Life*. New York: Free Press, 1999.

Warnick, Barbara. *Rhetoric Online: Persuasion and Politics on the World Wide Web*. New York: Peter Lang, 2007.

Weisman, Jonathan. "Women Figure Anew in Senate's Latest Battle." *New York Times*, March 14, 2012. http://www.nytimes.com/2012/03/15/us/politics/violence-against -women-act-divides-senate.html?_r=1. Accessed September 2, 2012.

Weston, Kath. *Families We Choose: Lesbians, Gays, Kinship*. New York: Columbia University Press, 1991.

——. "Get Thee to a Big City: Sexual Imaginary and the Great Migration." *GLQ* 2, no. 3 (1995): 253–77.

White, Janelle. "Our Silence Will Not Protect Us: Black Women Confronting Sexual and Domestic Violence." PhD diss., University of Michigan, 2004.

Will, George F. "Out of What 'Shadows'?" *Newsweek*, June 4, 2007, 74.

Wilson, Kirt H. "Interpreting the Discursive Field of the Montgomery Bus Boycott:

Martin Luther King Jr.'s Holt Street Address." *Rhetoric and Public Affairs* 8, no. 2 (2005): 299–326.

Winkiel, Laura. *Modernism, Race, and Manifestoes*. Cambridge, UK: Cambridge University Press, 2008.

Wolf, Sherry. *Sexuality and Socialism: History, Politics, and Theory of LGBT Liberation*. Chicago: Haymarket Books, 2009.

Worley, Sam. "Activists Disappointed with Immigration Bill." *Windy City Times*, December 23, 2009. http://www.windycitymediagroup.com/gay/lesbian/news/ARTICLE.php?AID=23903. Accessed February 5, 2011.

Xenos, Michael, and Patricia Moy. "Direct and Differential Effects of the Internet on Political and Civic Engagement." *Journal of Communication* 57 (2007): 704–18.

Ye Hee Lee, Michelle. "Appeals Court Strikes Down Voter ID Law: Arizona Statute Required Proof of Citizenship for Registration." *Arizona Republic*, October 27, 2010. http://www.azcentral.com/arizonarepublic/news/articles/2010/10/27/20101027voters1027.html. Accessed January 5, 2013.

Young, Iris Marion. "Activist Challenges to Deliberative Democracy." *Political Theory* 29, no. 5 (2001): 670–90.

Young, Susan. "A Gay Mom Faces Deportation." *People*, April 20, 2009, 90–92.

Yue, Audrey. "Queer Asian Mobility and Homonational Modernity: Marriage Equality, Indian Students in Australia, and Malaysian Transgender Refugees in the Media." *Global Media and Communication* 8, no. 3 (2012): 269–87.

———. "What's So Queer About *Happy Together*? A.K.A. Queer (N)Asian: Interface, Community, Belonging." *Inter-Asia Cultural Studies* 1, no. 2 (2000): 251–64.

Yuval-Davis, Nira. *Gender and Nation*. Thousand Oaks, CA: Sage, 1997.

Zinn, Howard. *Marx in Soho: A Play on History*. Cambridge, MA: South End Press, 1999.

Index

KARMA R. CHÁVEZ is an assistant professor of Communication Arts and Chican@ and Latin@ Studies at the University of Wisconsin–Madison. She is the cofounder of the Queer Migration Research Network and the coeditor of *Standing in the Intersection: Feminist Voices, Feminist Practices in Communication Studies*.

The University of Illinois Press
is a founding member of the
Association of American University Presses.

_____

Composed in 10.25/13 Marat Pro Regular
with Marat Pro display
by Celia Shapland
at the University of Illinois Press
Manufactured by Cushing-Malloy, Inc.

University of Illinois Press
1325 South Oak Street
Champaign, IL 61820-6903
www.press.uillinois.edu